LOVE IS
THE HEART
OF EVERYTHING

LOVE IS THE HEART OF EVERYTHING

CORRESPONDENCE BETWEEN
VLADIMIR MAYAKOVSKY AND LILI BRIK
1915–1930

Edited by BENGT JANGFELDT
Translated by JULIAN GRAFFY

GROVE PRESS, New York

Original title:

В. В. МАЯКОВСКИЙ И Л. Ю. БРИК:
ПЕРЕПИСКА 1915–1930

Published in 1982 by Almqvist & Wiksell Förlag AB, Stockholm.
English language edition first published in Great Britain in 1986 by
Polygon.

The Correspondence between Mayakovsky and Brik 1915–1930
© 1986 Bengt Jangfeldt.
Preface and annotations © Bengt Jangfeldt 1986.
English language translation © 1986 Julian Graffy.

Published by Grove Press, Inc.
920 Broadway
New York, N.Y. 10010

Library of Congress Cataloging-in-Publication Data

Mayakovsky, Vladimir, 1893–1930.
    Love is the heart of everything.

    Translation of: V. V. Maiakovskii i L.IU. Brik,
perepiska, 1915–1930.
    Includes index.
    1. Mayakovsky, Vladimir, 1893–1930—Correspondence.
2. Poets, Russian—20th century—Correspondence.
3. Mayakovsky, Vladimir, 1893–1930—Translations,
English. I. Brik, Lili IUr´evna. II. Jangfeldt,
Bengt, 1948-   . III. Title.
PG3476.M312A413 1987   891.71′42   86–33483
ISBN 0–394–55569–4

Manufactured in the United States of America
First Edition 1987

10 9 8 7 6 5 4 3 2 1

CONTENTS

TRANSLATOR'S NOTES

DATES

The change from the Julian to the Gregorian calendar was not made in Russia until after the Revolution, in February 1918. Before this, dates were twelve days behind the Gregorian calendar in the nineteenth century, and thirteen days behind in the twentieth. In the introduction and notes to this book, pre-revolutionary dates are given both "old" and "new" style.

NAMES

In Russia it is very common to use diminutive forms of names. Mayakovsky and the Briks indulged in this habit with great enthusiasm. I have reproduced the variety of their diminutive forms in their letters to each other, since these are often themselves meaningful: Mayakovsky calls Lili Lichika (little face), Luchik (sunray), Lisa (fox), Lisitsa (vixen) etc. She calls him Volosik (little hair). He signs himself Vol (ox), or makes play with the closeness of diminutive forms of the name Osip to the Russian word for a little donkey. On the animal imagery that runs through these letters, see Bengt Jangfeldt's introduction. I have kept the number of variations on the word Shchenok (puppy) which the correspondents invent as names for Mayakovsky. On occasion Mayakovsky even signs himself Ochen (very). With characters other than Mayakovsky and the Briks I have simplified the range of diminutive forms used.

TRANSLITERATION

I have used the *Slavonic and East European Review* transliteration system, but have omitted soft and hard signs, except in the bibliography. For certain names that are widely known in English I have retained the familiar form: Diaghilev, Eisenstein, Meyerhold, Nijinsky.

PUNCTUATION

Mayakovsky's punctuation is remarkable chiefly by its absence. While I have attempted to preserve the sense of energy that this gives to his letters, some punctuation has been added in the interests of clarity.

NOTES

The notes are substantially those of the original Russian edition of this book. Some new information and materials have come to light since the appearance of that edition and are included here for the first time. On occasion, notes have been expanded for the benefit of English readers.

London, June 1985.   Julian Graffy.

PREFACE

My conception of Mayakovsky as man and poet has emerged from my many conversations with his closest friends (their names often appear in the correspondence) over a period of years: Lili Brik, Lev Grinkrug, Roman Jakobson, Llewella Varshavskaya, Vasily Katanyan, Veronika Polonskaya and others. Their trust and generosity were invaluable during the work on this book. Tatyana Yakovleva, Mayakovsky's last great love, has provided me with information about the final period of his life.

In the compilation of the notes many people assisted me. In particular I wish to thank Lev Grinkrug, Llewella Varshavskaya, Mikhail Yampolsky, Yury Tsivyan, Lazar Fleishman, Nina Berberova, Rita Rayt, Aleksandr Parnis, Henryk Lenczyc, Ben Hellman and Bengt Samuelson.

I wish to express my profoundest gratitude to Lili Brik (1891-1978), without whom this correspondence would not have been published.

The Russian language edition of this book appeared in 1982: *V.V. Majakovskij i L. Ju. Brik: Perepiska 1915-1930* (Stockholm Studies in Russian Literature, 13). The English edition follows the Russian closely, but diverges from it in that Mayakovsky's grammar, which follows no accepted Russian rules, has been slightly standardised; the notes have been shortened; and the bibliography and other sources are not given in full. On the other hand, the present edition contains certain materials and information which came to my notice only after the publication of the Russian edition.

All Lili Brik's letters, postcards and telegrams are published in this book for the first time, as are the telegrams from Osip Brik, which are included in view of the personal closeness of the three correspondents. Of Mayakovsky's letters and telegrams, 129 (125 to Lili and four to Osip Brik) were published in the USSR in 1958 (*Literaturnoye nasledstvo*, No. 65), though some passages were deleted. Those that were printed in full are marked *, those printed with cuts †. Letters and telegrams without either mark are published for the first time.

1

Mayakovsky, Lili and Osip Brik often signed their letters with drawings of animals: Mayakovsky a puppy, Lili a little cat and Osip a tom cat. Mayakovsky's drawings are reproduced, with rare exceptions, from the originals. I have not had access to the drawings of Lili and Osip Brik, since most of their letters are taken from typewritten copies. I have therefore always used Lili's cat from letter 78 and Osip's tom cat from letter 14. In practice their drawings varied little throughout the correspondence.

In the course of my work on this book I have received constant and active support from Elena; it is dedicated to her.

BENGT JANGFELDT

INTRODUCTION

VLADIMIR MAYAKOVSKY AND LILI BRIK

PRELIMINARY REMARKS ON THE REWRITING OF HISTORY

Vladimir Mayakovsky and Lili Brik are one of the most remarkable pairs of lovers in the history of world literature, and their love has always attracted the attention both of serious scholars and of scandalmongers in almost equal measure. For some their relationship is a repellent example of decadent bourgeois morality, arousing indignation and an almost incomprehensible hostility towards Lili and Osip Brik — such is the official Soviet position since the late 1960s. Others see their love affair as a sort of experiment in living, a bold attempt to create a new type of love and friendship — in this interpretation their relationship at times acquires the status of an idealised myth. In this essay, I shall attempt to shed light on certain key questions concerning the relationship of Mayakovsky and the Briks between 1915 and 1930.

In the USSR the role of the Briks in Mayakovsky's life has been discussed in a series of biased articles and memoirs, the aim of which was "to destroy Lily Brik as the great love of Mayakovsky's life".[1] In the early 1970s the old Mayakovsky museum in *Gendrikov pereulok* (Gendrikov Lane), in the house where Mayakovsky and the Briks had lived from 1926 to 1930, was closed down, and a new museum opened in *Proyezd Serova* (Serov Passage, formerly *Lubyanskiy proyezd*, Lubyanskiy Passage), where Mayakovsky had his work room.

The attempts to distort Mayakovsky's biography are motivated by a variety of factors: Lili Brik gets in the way of the image of Mayakovsky the political poet, the Socialist Realist; by her very existence she reminds us that she, and love in general, played an exceptionally important part in Mayakovsky's life; her publication of 125 letters and telegrams from Mayakovsky in 1958 revealed the poet's psychological make-up in a light that was not in accordance with the narrowly ideological interpretation of his poetry.[2] In addition it was essential, if the reading of Mayakovsky's work as realist and non-Futurist was to prevail, to deny his links with the literary milieu of the 1910s and 1920s. Also, the fact that Mayakovsky and the Briks lived together smacks of "moral adventurism", and is a dubious model for those to whom the biography of the poet of the revolution should be an example.

The following conclusion is typical: ". . . the sources of Mayakovsky's originality lie not in Futurism, but in his link with the Communist Party and with the proletarian liberation movement in Russia. . . ."[3] Commentators of this sort ignore the fact that Mayakovsky really was a Futurist, but was never a member of the Communist Party. In all these attempts to rewrite Mayakovsky's biography, it is maintained that he was a great poet "in spite of" everything — "in spite of" Futurism, "in spite of" Burlyuk, "in spite of" Lili and Osip Brik; as one commentator put it, "in spite of the efforts of the poet's enemies and of his 'friends'".[4]

In his autobiography, Mayakovsky calls his meeting with Lili and Osip Brik "a most joyous date". This statement is commented upon in one of the editions of Mayakovsky's works in the following way:

> "Mayakovsky made the acquaintance of the Briks in the summer of 1915. It is no accident that soon after, in his long autobiographical poem *The Backbone-Flute*, Mayakovsky writes angrily about the abuse of his love. 'Now you've robbed my heart, deprived it of everything, tortured my soul to the limit of delirium' — this is how the poet addresses the object of his love in *The Flute*. And in the 1916 poem *Anathema* (later called *To Everything*) he writes:
>
> > Love!
> > You were only in my
> > Fevered
> > Brain!
> > Stop the course of this stupid comedy!
> > Look —
> > I'm tearing off my toy armour,
> > I
> > The greatest of Don Quixotes!"[5]

One thing that particularly irritates the "anti-Brik" faction in the USSR is the fact that the love of Mayakovsky and Lili Brik was insufficiently harmonious and simple, insufficiently "happy". Of the long poem *I Love* (1922), we read:

> "Perhaps at least for the short space of time when this poem was being written (from November 1921 to the beginning of February 1922), the poet was happy in his love? We do not know. But very soon afterwards, in his new long poem 'About This', the poet again appears before us disturbed, suffering, tormented by an unsatisfactory love."[6]

4

The relationship of Mayakovsky and Lili Brik was far from idyllic, but it was a fact that posterity cannot alter.

The Danish philosopher Søren Kierkegaard supplied an answer to such demands for family happiness as early as 1845 in his book *In vino veritas:*

"Have you ever heard of a man who became a poet through his wife?"

* * *

As a result of the attempts to eradicate the Briks from Mayakovsky's biography, many traces of their "territorial" cohabitation have been swept away; in addition to the closure of the museum one might mention the retouching of photographs.[7] I therefore consider it essential to present in my introduction as many facts as possible with regard both to the life of Lili and Osip Brik before they met Mayakovsky, and to their life with him after 1915. (In this respect the Russian-language edition of this book is even more detailed.)

It is evident from their correspondence that both Mayakovsky and Lili Brik had various amorous adventures. I do not consider it my duty to establish a "Don Juan's list" (or its feminine counterpart), limiting myself in the description of these peripheral love affairs to the information I consider essential to an understanding of the relationship between the correspondents.

"A MOST JOYOUS DATE"

Vladimir Vladimirovich Mayakovsky and Lili Yurevna Brik met for the first time in the summer of 1915, but knew of each other by hearsay long before that. Lili Yurevna saw Mayakovsky for the first time on the 7th of May 1913, at a gala evening in honour of the Symbolist poet Konstantin Balmont, who had just returned from several years abroad. Mayakovsky performed his usual 'outrageous Futurist' act, greeting the Symbolist poet "in the name of his enemies". A scandal broke out, and among those outraged by it were Lili and Osip Brik, who at that stage were unfamiliar with Mayakovsky's poetry. Lili Brik recalls: "Brik and I liked all this a great deal, but we continued to be outraged, I in particular, by the scandal-makers, who could not get through a single performance without the police being called and chairs being broken."[8]

In the autumn of that same year, at the house of mutual acquaintances, the Khvas family, Mayakovsky met Lili Brik's younger sister, Elsa, whom he saw often in the following years. Mayakovsky called on Elsa in her parental home, but in the autumn of 1914 Lili and Osip moved to Petrograd, and therefore he did not make their acquaintance.

5

In 1914, Lili's father developed cancer. Elsa and her parents spent the early summer of 1915 in a dacha at Malakhovka near Moscow. Lili Yurevna would come from Petrograd to visit her father, and on one of these visits she met Mayakovsky for the first time. A month later, in Petrograd, they met for the second time, but the day which the poet in his autobiography calls "a most joyous date", recording "I make the acquaintance of Lili Yurevna and Osip Maksimovich Brik", came only in July 1915. Lili Yurevna writes: "Father had died. I had returned from the funeral in Moscow. Elsa came to Petrograd, . . . Volodya arrived from Finland. We whispered beseechingly to Elsa: 'Don't ask him to read.' But Elsa paid no attention, and we heard *A Cloud in Trousers (Oblako v shtanakh)* for the first time."[9]

This reading in the Briks' flat was probably the first performance of the final version of the poem:

> "The door between the two rooms had been removed to economise on space. Mayakovsky stood leaning against the door-frame. He took a small notebook from the inside pocket of his jacket, looked at it and stuck it back in the same pocket. He became pensive. Then he surveyed the room as if it were an enormous auditorium, read the prologue, and asked — not in verse, in prose, in a quiet voice which I have never forgotten: 'Do you think that it's the ravings of malaria? It happened. It happened in Odessa.'
>
> We raised our heads, and gazed upon this unprecedented miracle until the very end.
>
> Mayakovsky did not change his pose once. He did not look at anyone. He complained, raged, mocked, demanded, became hysterical, pausing between the sections."[10]

Lili and Osip were enraptured by the poem: "It was what we had dreamed about for so long. What we were waiting for. Recently we'd been unable to find anything we wanted to read. All the poetry around seemed pointless — the wrong people were writing on the wrong subjects in the wrong way, and suddenly the right person was writing in the right way about the right subject."[11]

Since no one wanted to publish the poem, Osip Brik decided to print it at his own expense. It appeared in September 1915, in an edition of 1,050 copies, with a printed dedication "To you, Lilya" — this was the first use of the form Lilya (instead of Lili); Mayakovsky felt it was more "Russian". From then on not only Mayakovsky, but others too, started using this Russified form of Lili Brik's name (she had been named Lili after one of Goethe's beloveds, Lili Schönemann).

Mayakovsky fell so impetuously in love with Lili Brik that he did not return to Kuokkala, abandoning there "both his lady friend and his linen at the laundry, and in general all his possessions".[12] Instead he immediately took a room in the Palais Royal hotel on Pushkin Street in Petrograd. He lived there until the beginning of November, when he moved to 52, Nadezhdinskaya Street (renamed Mayakovsky Street in 1936), five minutes' walk from Zhukovsky Street, where Lili and Osip Brik lived.

This July day was "a most joyous date" not only for Mayakovsky, but also for the Briks, whose life changed radically from that day. Even before the war they had been friendly with the poets Konstantin Lipskerov and Sofiya Parnok, but until they met Mayakovsky "we had a passive interest in literature ... our main literary activity at the time was to read aloud to each other: ... *Crime and Punishment, The Brothers Karamazov, The Idiot, War and Peace, Anna Karenina, Zarathustra,* Kierkegaard's *In vino veritas, Kater Murr.* ...."[13] With the exception of Kierkegaard, this is a traditional enough reading list, and the distance between it and the poetry of Mayakovsky may seem vast; nevertheless, Lili and Osip Brik immediately recognised and valued the poet's distinctive talent.

LILI AND OSIP BRIK
Lili Yurevna Kagan was born in Moscow on the 30th of October (11th of November) 1891. Her father, Uriy (Yury) Aleksandrovich Kagan, who came from Libau, was a lawyer. He devoted most of his time to so-called Jewish questions, that is to say to problems connected with the right of Jews to live in Moscow. "Because of his Jewishness, father remained an assistant for twenty-five years, and his assistants, who had long since become barristers, spoke for him at the circuit court. Jewishness was a sore point with me right from the beginning."[14] He also worked as a legal adviser for the Austrian embassy, and "sometimes Austrian actors, acrobats, eccentrically dressed lady singers from the cafés chantants, Tyroleans with bare knees, people who had come to Russia on tour and had trouble with entrepreneurs, would turn to him for advice . . .".[15] Lili Brik's mother, Yelena Yulevna (née Berman), was from a Rigan Jewish family which spoke both German and Russian. She was very musical, and had attended the Moscow Conservatoire, but had not received her diploma, since she got married before the final examination. Yelena Yulevna was a fine pianist, and music was always to be heard in the Kagan household: musical evenings were arranged, at which Yelena Yulevna played, either alone or with other musicians. She was a great admirer of Wagner, and used to attend the Bayreuth festival. In addition she wrote poetry; she spoke Russian at home, but she wrote her poetry,

to which she composed her own music, in German. She also set a number of poems by Bryusov and other poets to music.

Lili grew up, therefore, in an intellectual and enlightened milieu. German was her second native language, and French her first foreign one (incidentally, she had the same French governess, Mademoiselle Dache, as her sister Elsa and her friend Roman Jakobson). Her father and mother were confirmed anti-zionists and supporters of Jewish assimilation. The family lived in the very centre of Moscow, in Petroverigskiy Lane; Lili attended the Valitskaya private secondary school.

In the autumn of 1905 Lili entered class five at the school. Revolutionary events were leaving their mark even on school life. "We gathered at home or at school, demanded autonomy for Poland, passed resolutions and organised a circle for the study of political economy. Osya Brik, the brother of a girl at our school, was elected leader of the circle. He was in class eight of secondary school number three, and had just been expelled for spreading revolutionary propaganda."[16]

Osip Maksimovich Brik was born in Moscow on the 4th (16th) of January 1888. His father, Maksim Pavlovich Brik, was a merchant of the first guild and proprietor of the firm of "Pavel Brik, Widow and Son", which traded mainly in corals. Maksim Brik often travelled to Italy (sometimes taking Osip along) to buy black coral, which he then sold mainly in Central Asia and Siberia. Osip's mother, Paulina Yurevna, was an educated woman, and (like his father) knew several languages; she was extremely fond of Herzen, whom, in the words of Lili Brik, she "knew by heart". Like the Kagans, the Brik family lived in the centre of Moscow.

When Lili Kagan was thirteen and Osip Brik seventeen, they fell in love. "Osya started telephoning me. I was at a New Year party at their house. Taking me home in a cab, Osya suddenly asked: 'Lilya, don't you think there's something more than friendship between us?' I didn't think so, I simply didn't think about it, but I was very pleased with the expression, and because it was unexpected I answered: 'Yes, I think so'."[17] Lili spent the summer of 1906 with her mother and Elsa at the resort of Friedrichroda in Thüringen. While she was there, Osip wrote her a letter in which he explained that he did not love her as strongly as he had thought. After Lili returned from Germany they continued to meet often, but their love affair was resumed only five years later.

Lili was extremely gifted at mathematics, and in 1908 she left the secondary school with the first-class mark of 5+. "When I left the secondary school, I hoped to join the mathematics faculty of Professor

Guerrier's Higher Women's Courses. I had passed mathematics so brilliantly in the final examination that the director of my school summoned father and begged him not to ruin my mathematical talent. Jewish girls were not allowed to attend Guerrier's classes without a school-leaving certificate. I began to study for it."[18] Having passed the school-leaving examination at the Lazarevskiy institute for boys, Lili Brik joined the Higher Women's Courses in 1909; she immersed herself in mathematics for a whole year, even having books sent to her from Germany.

Her enthusiasm for mathematics waned, however, and Lili entered the Moscow Architectural Institute (from which Elsa was to graduate in 1918), where the study of sculpture had just been instituted. There she studied painting and modelling, and in the late spring of 1911 she left for Munich, where until Christmas she studied sculpture in the Schwägerle studio, one of the best in the city.

On the day of her return from Munich, Lili and Osip met at the Moscow Arts Theatre. "The next day Osya telephoned me. We met in the street and went for a walk. . . . We went to a restaurant, to a private room, asked for a pot of coffee, and just like that Osya asked me to marry him. I agreed."[19] On the 19th of December, Osip Brik wrote to his parents: "I no longer have the strength to conceal from you what my heart is full of, I do not have the strength not to inform you of my boundless happiness; though I am aware that this news will cause you some concern, and therefore I have not written to you until now. . . . But I can no longer keep it from you. I am going to be married. My fiancée, as you must have guessed, is Lili Kagan. I love her madly; I have always loved her. And she loves me, it seems, as no woman in the world has ever loved. You cannot imagine, my dear Papa and Mama, how amazingly happy I am now. . . . I know that you love me and want my greatest happiness. Well let me tell you that that happiness has come to me. . . . I am now terribly agitated and cannot write any more. I shall merely inform you of a couple of essential points. On the 9th of January I am leaving for Siberia; Lili is staying in Moscow. The wedding will take place immediately after I return from Siberia." (Lili Brik archive.)

They were married on the 26th of February (11th of March) 1912, and moved into a four-roomed flat in the centre of Moscow which Lili's parents rented for them.

Osip had studied at the law faculty of Moscow University, but he never practised as a lawyer. Before the war he worked in his father's firm. He and Lili visited Turkestan a few times on business, once in the company

9

of the poet Konstantin Lipskerov — "even by then we were showing signs of being patrons of the arts", Lili later remarked.[20] They even wanted to settle in Turkestan for a few years, but these plans were frustrated by the war, which broke out in the summer of 1914.

"From the first day of the war we were passionate defeatists," writes Lili Brik. "We felt no patriotic uplift whatsoever, and the day before war was declared we got away on a Volga steamer, on which we sailed until the first companies of reinforcements were sent to the front. When we received a telegram from Moscow that it was all right to return, we came back. . . ."[21] Leonid Sobinov, the famous tenor, helped Osip to get into a motor brigade in Petrograd, and the Briks moved to the capital. In consequence, Osip stopped working in his father's firm; their parents sent them money to live on. They moved first to 23, Zagorodnyy Avenue, and then into a two-roomed furnished flat at 7, Zhukovsky Street, where they lived for three years. In the autumn of 1917 they moved to a six-roomed flat lower down in the same house.

"LILICHKA!"

The time immediately after the July reading was spent under the sign of general enthusiasm and feverish publishing activity. They read the proofs of A Cloud, and at the same time prepared for publication the almanac Took (Vzyal), which came out in December; during the autumn Mayakovsky wrote the poem The Backbone-Flute (Fleyta-pozvonochnik), which appeared in February 1916. All three books were issued under the O.M.B. imprint. On the 8th of October, Mayakovsky was also called up, and he managed to get into the same motor brigade in which Osip Brik was serving. The lives of Mayakovsky and the Briks began to interconnect both in literature and in daily routine.

Mayakovsky began to introduce Lili and Osip to his friends. Vasily Kamensky, David Burlyuk, Velimir Khlebnikov, Nikolay Aseyev, Boris Pasternak, and other poets often visited the flat in Zhukovsky Street. But the Futurists were not the only visitors — among the frequent guests was the poet Mikhail Kuzmin, who performed his own songs on the Briks' grand piano. At the end of 1915 Lili began to study ballet. She set up a barre in one of the rooms and began taking lessons from the ballerina Aleksandra Dorinskaya ("Pasya"), who had danced in the Diaghilev company before the war. Another of her friends was the famous dancer Yekaterina Geltser. Mayakovsky and the Briks were also acquainted with people outside the artistic world. The closest of their friends, Lev Grinkrug, came up almost every Sunday from Moscow, where he worked in a bank. Among other visitors to the Briks' flat were people with links in the business world (see the correspondence for 1917-18).

Apart from literary matters and conversation, a favourite pastime was playing cards. They played almost every evening: vint, poker, "auntie", chemin de fer. The keenest players were Mayakovsky, the Briks and Lev Grinkrug. On Gorky's rare visits he also played cards.[22] These games were usually reckless and compulsive, and on such occasions a notice was hung on the door with the words: "The Briks are not receiving visitors today" (see No. 30, note 3).[23]

The natural centre of the Brik "salon" was Lili, whose charm left no one indifferent. Nikolay Aseyev writes of his first impressions of her: "And so I was taken (by Mayakovsky) to a flat that was unlike any other, florid with hand-painted material, resonant with verses which had only just been written or only just been read aloud; the bright burning eyes of the hostess could persuade you or perplex you with an opinion you had never heard before, one of her own, not one she'd picked up in the street, not one she'd borrowed from people who knew. We — Shklovsky and I, and, I think, Kamensky — were taken captive by those eyes, those statements, which by the way were never pressed upon us. They were offered seemingly in passing, but they were absolutely to the point, absolutely germane to what was being discussed."[24]

If Lili was the soul of the "salon", then Osip was its intellectual stimulus. Immediately after he met Mayakovsky, he was overwhelmed by a passionate interest in contemporary poetry, which he began to study scientifically. "At that time we loved only poetry. We were like drunks. I knew all Volodya's poems by heart, but Osya got absolutely riveted by them. That was the start of the so-called 'gnats' . . . the little signs with which he filled up whole notebooks. He later elaborated his theory of sound repetitions from them."[25] Soon philologists took to visiting the Brik flat: Roman Jakobson, Boris Kushner, Lev Jakubinsky, Viktor Skhlovsky and others. In the autumn of 1916, Brik published the first *Sbornik po teorii poeticheskogo yazyka* (Collection on the theory of poetic language), and the OPOYAZ, the Society for the Study of Poetic Language, was founded in February 1917.

Love for Lili Brik changed Mayakovsky's life. Before he had lived a Bohemian life without a proper home. He was not a family man in the traditional sense of the word, he shunned routine (*byt*), but with Lili and Osip Brik he formed a close and warm relationship. Through them he entered a new social and cultural sphere. Like many of the other Futurists, Mayakovsky came from a provincial family of modest means;

11

he never received a proper education, either at school or at home. Lili and Osip grew up in well-off Muscovite households, in an intellectual environment, were educated, had travelled abroad several times and mixed with others like them. The correspondence gives ample evidence of the difference in their educations: Lili Brik's letters are orthographically correct, whereas Mayakovsky's are full of spelling and other mistakes.

The Briks began to live for Mayakovsky's writings and to meet his friends, but at the same time Mayakovsky began to adopt the habits of their circle, cutting his long hair, definitively abandoning his yellow jacket and frock-coat, putting on an ordinary coat and even acquiring a cane. Lili helped him to have new teeth put in (Mayakovsky himself alludes to the bad state of his teeth in *The Backbone-Flute*: "I bare my rotten teeth"). This external metamorphosis is visible in the first photograph of Mayakovsky and Lili Brik together, which dates from September 1915.

Lili became the new and only heroine of both Mayakovsky's life and his work. *A Cloud in Trousers* carried a printed dedication to her, although other women had been the inspiration of the poem. The first long poem written after their meeting was *The Backbone-Flute*, which Mayakovsky worked on in the autumn of 1915. "*The Flute* was written slowly, every section was accompanied by a solemn reading aloud. A poem would be read first to me, then to Osya and me, and finally to everyone else. It was always like that, with everything that Volodya wrote. I promised Volodya to listen to each section of *The Flute* in his house. For tea there was a hyperbolic quantity of everything I love. There were flowers on the table, and Volodya had put on his most beautiful tie."[26] This attention towards a creative talent was one of Lili Brik's most remarkable qualities; her exceptional poetic discernment, her desire and capacity to listen to others, the keenness of her literary judgement were respected by many, especially Mayakovsky, who was outwardly noisy and brash, but inwardly lacking in self-confidence and in constant need of encouragement. From *A Cloud* onwards he dedicated all his long poems in print to Lili Brik.[27] When the first volume of his collected works appeared in 1928, the dedication read *L.Yu.B.*: by this he dedicated to her everything he had written both before and after their meeting.

Both in *The Backbone-Flute* and in other poems of 1915-16, Mayakovsky ecstatically glorifies his new love, without which he has neither sea nor sun, and whose name resounds more joyously than any other. He "sings" her, "painted, red-haired", ready to place his "cheek, burning like the Sahara" beneath her feet in the desert; he gives her a crown, "and

12

in the crown are my words like a convulsive rainbow"; he speaks her
name, and demands that the people chisel it out on their coinage:

> If I am called to be Tsar —
> On the sunlit gold of my coinage
> I shall order my people
> To mint
> Your face!
> And there,
> Where the earth is bleached by tundra,
> Where the river bargains with the northern wind,
> I shall scratch the name of Lili on my chains
> And kiss them over and over in the darkness of penal servitude.
>
> *(The Backbone-Flute)*

Mayakovsky's love for Lili Brik was enormous, and he lived through
the joys and griefs of love in his customary intense manner. In the first
years their love affair was "unofficial"; they apparently met even without
Osip's knowledge. But although Lili loved and valued Mayakovsky very
greatly as a poet, their personal relationship was more complicated.
Evidence of this is provided by the autobiographical note "How things
were", in which she throws light on her relationships with Mayakovsky
and Osip Brik: "Volodya didn't simply fall in love with me. He attacked
me, I was under attack. For two and a half years I didn't have a single
minute's peace — quite literally."

The poetry of these two and a half years bears the imprint of the poet's
love, but it is just as clear that this love is not fully reciprocated. The lyric
embodiment of despair, as always with Mayakovsky, is biographically
specific:

> God thinks:
> "Hold on, Vladimir!"
> He's the one, he's the one,
> To stop me guessing who you are,
> Who thought of giving you a real husband . . .
> . . .
> The doors
> Banged.
> He came in,
> Sprayed by the streets' gaiety.
> I
> Split in two in a wail.
> Shouted to him:
> "All right!

I'll leave!
All right!
She'll remain yours.
Dress her up in finery,
Let her timid wings grow fat in silks.
Watch she doesn't float away.
Round her neck like a stone
Hang your wife pearl necklaces!"
. . .
Now you've robbed my heart,
Deprived it of everything,
Tortured my soul to the limit of delirium,
Accept this gift, my dear one,
Perhaps I'll never think of anything else.

(The Backbone-Flute)

Once Lili told Mayakovsky how before her wedding night her mother
put sweetmeats, fruit and champagne on the bedside table in their new
flat. This biographical detail also found a place in Mayakovsky's poetry,
accompanied by an inference typical of a man who "wanted to exaggerate
everything":[28]

You didn't soil your hands in grubby murder.
You
Only let slip:
"In a soft bed
He,
Fruit,
Wine in the palm of the night table."
Love!
You were only in my
Fevered
Brain!

(To Everything, 1916)

Thus the first two or three years of their relationship were very difficult
for both of them. In his poetry Mayakovsky "crowned" Lili, but she felt
irritation, exhausted by his love. After the poem "Lilichka!" (written in
May 1916, but published only in 1934), Mayakovsky wrote a new long
poem "Don Juan": "I didn't know it was being written. Volodya recited it
to me unexpectedly as we were walking along the street — the whole
thing, by heart. I got angry because it was about love again — as if I wasn't
fed up with it! Volodya tore the manuscript from his pocket, shredded it
into tiny pieces and let the wind blow it away along Zhukovsky Street."[29]

14

The first long parting between Mayakovsky and Lili was in the winter of 1917-18, when Mayakovsky left for Moscow. The main reason for this sudden move was apparently his rejection of the Bolshevik cultural programme in the shape in which it was formulated by the People's Commissar of Enlightenment, Anatoly Vasilevich Lunacharsky (see No. 3, note 1). This parting lasted about six months. In spring 1918 Mayakovsky made three films. The last of them was *Fettered by Film*, the screenplay of which he wrote especially for Lili Brik. In a letter of April 1918, Lili writes: "Try to arrange for shooting to begin in a week or two. Then I'll come to Moscow specially" (see No. 13).

Lili came to Moscow, and the film was shot in May and June, with her and Mayakovsky in the leading roles: she played a ballerina, he a painter. After shooting they went back to Petrograd together, and on the 26th of June Mayakovsky registered as living in the house on Zhukovsky Street where the Briks lived. After that, all three of them left for Levashovo, outside Petrograd, where they rented three rooms with board. It was at that time that Mayakovsky and Lili began to live together.

"It was only in 1918 that I could speak to Osip with confidence about our love. Since 1915 my relationship with Osip had become one of pure friendship, and this love could not cloud either my friendship with him, or his friendship with Mayakovsky. Over the last three years they had become essential to each other — they were travelling the same path both in art and in politics, in fact in everything. We all decided never to part, and we lived our lives as close friends."[30] These are the words Lili Brik herself uses to describe the change in the relationship between the three of them. Although her relationship with Mayakovsky entered a new stage, the love of Lili and Osip Brik did not diminish. In another note she elaborates the premises of this friendship: "Osya and I were never again physically intimate, so all the tittle-tattle about a 'triangle', about love 'à trois' and so on bears absolutely no relation to reality. I loved, love and will continue to love Osya more than a brother, more than a husband, more than a son. I have not read about a love like this in any poetry, in any novel. . . . This love was no hindrance to my love for Volodya. On the contrary, it is possible that if it were not for Osya I should not have loved Volodya so strongly. It was impossible for me not to love Volodya if Osya loved him so much. Osya said that for him Volodya was not a person but an event. Volodya altered the way Osya thought about many things . . . and I do not know of friends and comrades who were truer to each other or loved each other more" (*How Things Were*).

The change in Lili's personal life was agonising for her mother. On the 4th of July 1918 Elsa, accompanied by her mother, set off for Paris to marry André Triolet, a French officer. "For mother such a change in Lili's life, for which she was totally unprepared, was a heavy blow. She did not want to see Mayakovsky, and was ready to leave without saying goodbye to Lili."[31] Lili came to Petrograd from Levashovo without Mayakovsky to say goodbye to her mother and sister.

After the summer in Levashovo, Mayakovsky and the Briks returned to Petrograd. Mayakovsky rented a small flat on the same staircase as the Briks. They lived in Petrograd until the beginning of March 1919, and then they moved to Moscow. In the autumn and winter of 1918-19 Mayakovsky and Osip Brik took a very active part in the work of the Artistic Section of the Commissariat of Enlightenment (*Izo Narkomprosa*), publishing the newspaper *Iskusstvo kommuny* (*Art of the Commune*), and battled for Futurism to be recognised as "the art of the proletariat". But as early as the spring of 1918 the capital had been transferred to Moscow, and the battle over culture was now being waged there. The move to Moscow turned out to be absolutely essential for Mayakovsky and Osip Brik to continue the struggle for their ideas.[32]

"DAYS AND NIGHTS IN ROSTA"

When they first moved to Moscow Mayakovsky and the Briks lived at 5, Poluektov Lane, sharing a flat with the artist and Commissar of the Artistic Section of the Commissariat of Enlightenment, David Shterenberg, and his wife. The flat is described in the poem *Good!*:

> Twelve
> square yards of living space.
> Four of us
> in the room —
> Lilya,
> Osya,
> I,
> And the dog
> Shchenik.

The years 1919 and 1920 were cold and hungry. In her little book *Shchen*, Lili describes life in Poluektov Lane: "There were a number of rooms in the flat, but it was difficult to heat them at that time.

"To keep warm we all huddled together in the smallest room. We covered the walls and floor with carpets to make sure there were no draughts.

16

"In the corner there were a stove and a fireplace. We lit the stove rarely, but we lit the fire morning, noon and night, using old newspapers, broken boxes, anything we could get hold of."

In addition to this flat, Mayakovsky had a study in Lubyanskiy Passage, which had been arranged for him by Roman Jakobson, who lived in the same house. Mayakovsky retained this room for the whole of his life (it was there that he committed suicide).

In the autumn of 1919 Mayakovsky began to make posters for ROSTA, the Russian Telegraph Agency. This activity occupied him fully for over two years. Lili Brik also took an active part in work on the posters. Working in a state institution gave them both money and food. Without detracting from the ideological aspect of the work, it should be pointed out that an important stimulus for their taking on this work was precisely that it brought material advantages. That is obvious from the correspondence of the autumn of 1921 (see especially No. 44).

The summer of 1919 was spent in Pushkino, outside Moscow. In this first Pushkino summer Mayakovsky found a dog under a fence which they gave the name of Shchen (Pup); after their return to town, Shchen lived with them in Poluektov Lane (see the quotation from *Good!* above). As early as 1918 Lili called Mayakovsky "little puppy" (see No. 7), and now, after the appearance of Shchen, Mayakovsky began to identify himself, and to be identified by others, with this dog. "They were very alike. Both had big paws and big heads. Both rushed around with their tails cocked. Both whined plaintively when they were asking for something, and hung at your heels until they got what they wanted. Sometimes they would bark at the first person to come along for no reason at all, just for effect.

"We started calling Vladimir Vladimirovich Shchen."[33]

From then on Mayakovsky signed his letters and telegrams with this name or with a drawing of a puppy.

Animal symbolism occupies a significant place in Mayakovsky's work. He often identifies himself with little dogs, horses, bears and other animals, which, like the poet, are alienated, isolated from the world of people, from the crowd. Worthy of note are the poet's words that he "loves animals because they are not people, yet they are living creatures".[34] The mythico-religious and psychological links between Mayakovsky and the world of animals have been subtly analysed by Lawrence Stahlberger,[35] and I shall not consider them in detail here. Animals and animal symbolism also played an important role in the relationship of Mayakovsky and the Briks, as is clear from the

17

correspondence. "Volodya taught me to love animals," writes Lili Brik. "In our life together animals were a constant subject of conversation. When I came home from somewhere, Volodya always asked whether I had seen 'any interesting dags or cots'."[36]

Mayakovsky and the Briks filled their "family" life systematically with animal symbolism: Mayakovsky was a puppy (Shchen, Shchenik, Shchenyatka and so on). Lili was a little cat (Kisa, Kisik, Kisit and so on) and Osip was a tom cat (Kis, Kislit, Kes, Keslit and so on). Just like Mayakovsky, Lili and Osip signed their letters with drawings (later Lili even made a special cat seal).

In September 1920, after their second summer in Pushkino, Mayakovsky and the Briks moved to 3, Vodopyanyy Lane, on the corner of Myasnitskaya Street, next to the main post office and the Vkhutemas (Higher State Artistic and Technical Workshops). They received two rooms in a communal flat: "A long corridor. The entrance to the Briks' was directly to the right. A small room, three windows, small, old Moscow windows. Right by the entrance on the left was a grand piano, and on the piano a telephone. . . . Beyond Lili's room was Osip's: a studio couch, upholstered in multi-coloured velvet, a broken-down desk with a single lion head, books."[37] Mayakovsky was also registered as living in the flat.

"I LOVE"

In 1921 Mayakovsky and the Briks again spent the summer in Pushkino. In October Lili left for Riga. She wanted to see her mother, who was working in the Soviet trade delegation, ARKOS, in London. Her sister Elsa had also been there for a time; she had separated from her husband and was now working for a London architect. Diplomatic relations had not yet been established between the Soviet Union and Great Britain, but it was apparently possible to obtain an English visa in Latvia.

There was, however, another, no less important, reason for this trip abroad, the first in eight years. During these years Mayakovsky was experiencing great difficulties in his relations with Gosizdat (the State Publishing House), which kept postponing and making difficulties over the publication of the long poem *150,000,000* and the third edition of the play *Mystery-Bouffe*; he was even forced to take the matter to court in August and September 1921. He had influential opponents in literary and publishing circles, men who were irritated by his uncompromising behaviour, like the critic Sosnovsky, who in connection with the trial gave currency to the term "Mayakovshchina" (see No. 17, note 2). One of Lili Brik's main concerns in Riga, therefore, was to find a foreign publisher who would print Mayakovsky's works in Latvia for export to Russia. At that time such an enterprise was neither a criminal offence nor a rare occurrence.

Lili's efforts to get books by Mayakovsky and the other Futurists published in Riga are evident from the correspondence. She seeks out contacts with Latvian and Jewish poets, and soon makes the acquaintance of "a certain *very important* capitalist", who is ready to publish the Futurists' books if at the same time he can make some money by publishing editions of Russian physics and mathematics textbooks (see No. 44). Mayakovsky and Osip Brik obtained permission in Moscow for the import of books published in Riga, and the Rigan publisher even sent them advances, but nothing came of this publishing project. Why the plans did not come to fruition is not clear: perhaps the Latvian publisher changed his mind, perhaps difficulties arose over the import and export of books. Lili, at any rate, did everything she could to propagandise Mayakovsky's poetry in Riga, even publishing an article about him in the *Novyy put* (*New Path*) newspaper, published by the Russian Legation.

Lili Brik spent four months in Riga. She did not manage to obtain an English visa, despite her connections in the Commissariat for Foreign Affairs, but she did arrange an invitation for Mayakovsky to go to Latvia to read his poetry. She returned to Moscow in February 1922, and by April had again left for Riga, apparently to prepare for Mayakovsky's visit. In early May they spent nine days together in the Bellevue Hotel in Riga. Mayakovsky's public appearances, however, were not without their problems, since the Latvian police did not harbour particularly warm feelings towards the poet's political convictions. The police confiscated almost the whole of the second edition of the poem *I Love* (first published in Moscow in March of that year), printed by the Rigan Jewish workers' organisation *Arbeiterheim* to coincide with Mayakovsky's visit.

The poem *Lyublyu* (*I Love*) was written during Lili's first visit to Riga, and was completed ready for her return home in February 1922. It reflects the state of the relationship between Mayakovsky and Lili Brik at that time, just as *The Backbone-Flute* and other poems give us an impression of their relationship during the war years. In general *I Love* is the lightest of Mayakovsky's long poems, full of love and *joie de vivre*, free from gloom and suicidal impulses.

> But I am exultant.
> It doesn't exist —
> The yoke!
> Oblivious with joy
> I jumped,

I leapt like a Red Indian brave at his wedding —
I felt so merry,
I felt so light.
. . .
When I come to you,
Am I not
Coming home?!
Earth's bosom accepts earthly men.
We return to our final destination.
So I
Am drawn inexorably back
To you,
As soon as we part,
Or pass out of sight.
. . .
Solemnly raising aloft my line-fingered verse,
I swear —
I love
Unchangingly and truly!

"ABOUT THIS"

On their return from Riga, Mayakovsky and Lili (along with Osip) again rented a dacha in Pushkino, where they spent the summer together. In August Lili left for Berlin (diplomatic relations had been re-established in April), and from there went to London. At the beginning of October Mayakovsky and Osip went to Berlin, where Lili and Elsa were waiting for them after travelling from London. Elsa recalls that on this meeting Mayakovsky irritated her by constantly playing cards.[38] Lili was also unhappy that he spent all his time at this activity, leaving his hotel room only to take part in literary evenings.

On the 18th of November, at Diaghilev's invitation, Mayakovsky went to Paris, where he met French writers and painters, among them Picasso, Léger and Delaunay. After a week in the French capital, he went back to Berlin, and from there, on the 13th of December, he returned to Moscow.

In the autumn of 1922, relations between Mayakovsky and Lili Brik underwent a crisis, their first serious trial since the "legalisation" of their love affair in 1918. The crisis was building up during their stay in Berlin, and it came to a head at the end of December: Lili and Mayakovsky took a decision to spend two months apart, he in his room in Lubyanskiy Passage, she in the flat in Vodopyanyy Lane. Lili has summarised the motivation for this decision: ". . . we were living well; we had grown used to each other, to the fact that we were shod, dressed and living in the

20

warm, eating regular tasty meals, drinking a lot of tea with jam. 'Little old routine' (*byt*) had been established.

"Suddenly we took fright at this and decided on the forcible destruction of 'shameful prudence'."[39]

The decisive impetus for such an important step was not, however, provided by theoretical discussions. A week after his return to Moscow Mayakovsky gave a lecture in the Polytechnic Museum called "What is Berlin up to?". Lili was present at the lecture, and to her amazement she heard Mayakovsky recounting things which he had not experienced himself but had heard from others, in particular from Osip. She lost her temper and left the hall. Then Mayakovsky suggested to her that he should cancel his next lecture, "What is Paris up to?" She replied that this was for him to decide. Mayakovsky gave his lecture about Paris on the 27th of December, this time without borrowing impressions from others. Lili was not present; she was lying in bed at home, in a state of depression after their first quarrel. On the next day, the 28th of December, their two-month-long separation began; the initiative belonged to Lili, as is clear from letter No. 113: "you did not want to prolong relations". Rita Rayt, who called in on them on the day of their parting, recalls that they were both crying.[40]

The separation was to last exactly two months, until the 28th of February 1923. During this time Mayakovsky did not visit Lili once. He went up to her house, hid on the staircase, crept up to the doors of her flat, wrote letters and notes, which were handed to her by the servants or by mutual friends; he sent her flowers, books and other presents, such as caged birds, which were intended to remind her of him. Lili sent short notes in reply. A few times they met by chance in the street or in editorial offices.

Mayakovsky found their separation very much more of a torment than Lili, who, unlike him, lived a normal life during these two months. His constant oscillations between joy and hope, on the one hand, and doubt and despair, on the other, are registered in the correspondence with exceptional clarity (Nos. 81-113). These letters and notes also shed new light on the long poem *Pro eto* (*About This*), with its dedication "To her and to me", written during their separation; certain parts of the correspondence went almost word for word into the text of the poem (see No. 98).

During their separation Mayakovsky kept a sort of diary, in which he wrote down his feelings and thoughts. This diary is important not only as a key document with regard to the period of separation, but also as an expression of Mayakovsky's attitude to love and poetry in general (No. 113). Found only after the poet's death, it is a substantial addendum to Mayakovsky's long existential poems *Man* and *About This*, underlining yet again the "extraordinary unity of the symbolism" in his work noted by Roman Jakobson.[41]

As is clear from the correspondence, both Lili and Mayakovsky were supposed to reappraise their attitudes to routine, to love and jealousy, to the inertia of their relationship, to "tea-drinking" and so on. It is clear that Mayakovsky at least attempted to do so; but these two months of putting themselves to the test did not lead to great changes in their life, and indeed this was not important to Mayakovsky just as long as they could go on being together: "What sort of life can we have, what sort will I agree to as a result of all this? Any sort. I'll agree to any sort. I miss you terribly and I terribly want to see you" (No. 113).

At three o'clock in the afternoon of the 28th of February Mayakovsky's "sentence of incarceration" was over. At eight in the evening he met Lili at the station, in order to go with her to Petrograd for a few days. He got into the carriage, read her *About This* and burst into tears.

Whatever the motivations were for their two-month separation, "ideological" or personal and emotional, this radical step is evidence that a change had taken place in the relations between Mayakovsky and Lili Brik.

"NOW I'M FREE OF LOVE . . ."

On the 3rd of July 1923 Mayakovsky and the Briks travelled by air for the first time, from Moscow to Königsberg. They spent their first three weeks in Germany at Flinsberg, near Göttingen, where they were visited by Roman Jakobson, who was then living in Prague. Then they went via Berlin to the island of Norderney, off the German North Sea coast, where they spent the whole of August in the company of Lili's mother, who had come over from London, and Viktor Shklovsky. In early September Mayakovsky and the Briks left for Berlin. On the 15th of September Mayakovsky returned home, but the Briks stayed on in Berlin for a little longer.

In the winter and spring of 1924, Mayakovsky and Lili travelled abroad separately a great deal. Lili spent three months, from February till May, in Paris, London and Berlin, where Mayakovsky arrived in the middle of April. They met in Berlin and returned to Moscow together on the 9th of May. Since Mayakovsky had spent a week in January giving recitals in the

22

Ukraine, they spent only three weeks out of the first three and a half months of 1924 together.

The year 1924 was a turning-point in the relationship between Mayakovsky and Lili Brik. We find a hint of this in the poem *Jubilee Year* (*Yubileynoye*), written to mark the 125th anniversary of the birth of Pushkin on the 6th of June 1924:

> Now
>   I'm
>   free
>   of love
>   and of posters.
> The clawed bear
>   of jealousy
>   lies skinned.

(This last sentence contains an allusion to the bear metaphor in *About This*.)

A little note from Lili to Mayakovsky has survived in which she announces that she no longer feels as she did about him, adding: "It seems to me that you too love me a lot less and that you won't feel a great deal of torment." This note should be dated to the spring of 1924; the poem *Jubilee Year* makes it possible to put a date to the change in their relationship.

One of the reasons for this change is obvious. In a letter of the 23rd of February 1924, Lili asks: "How is A.M.?" (No. 122). Aleksandr Mikhailovich Krasnoshchokov, former president and minister of foreign affairs in the government of the Far Eastern Republic, returned to Moscow in 1921, and in 1922 became president of the Industrial Bank and deputy Commissar for Financial Affairs. Lili met him in the summer of 1922. She began an affair with him, which Mayakovsky knew about. In September 1923, however, Krasnoshchokov was arrested, on a completely unfounded charge of misuse of power, and sentenced to a term of imprisonment (see No. 78, note 2 and No. 122, note 4).

Mayakovsky spent the summer of 1924 partly in Pushkino and partly in Moscow. On the 24th of October he went abroad. On the 2nd of November he arrived in Paris, where he stayed at the Hôtel Istria in Montparnasse. Elsa was living in the same hotel, and she recalls that on this visit the poet was "particularly gloomy". After he had been in Paris for a week, Mayakovsky wrote to Lili: ". . . I cannot write, and as for who and what you are, I still have absolutely, absolutely no idea. Because there really is no way to console myself; you are dear to me and I love you,

23

but all the same you are in Moscow and you are either someone else's or not mine" (No. 135). Lili replied: "What can be done about it? I cannot give up A.M. while he is in prison. It would be shameful! More shameful than anything in my entire life" (No. 139). Mayakovsky: "You write about *shame*. Are you really trying to tell me that that is *all* that binds you to him and *the only thing* that prevents you from being with me? I don't believe you! . . . Do what you like, *nothing will ever change my love for you in any way*" (No. 143).

At the beginning of October 1924, before Mayakovsky's trip to Paris, he and the Briks moved from Vodopyanyy Lane to Sokolniki. Moscow Council, on the pretext that Mayakovsky had a work room in Lubyanskiy Passage, took away his room in Vodopyanyy Lane. Mayakovsky and the Briks took the matter to court, but they were unable to hold on to the room; all they were left with was one room in a communal flat. They always had a lot of visitors (among other things the Vodopyanyy flat served as "headquarters" for Lef, the "Left Front of the Arts"), and therefore they were forced to look for somewhere else to live. They moved to a winter dacha in Sokolniki in which they were to live for a year and a half. They held on to the one remaining room in Vodopyanyy Lane to spend the night when they were in town (the cook, Annushka, continued to live there, but went out to Sokolniki to feed them every day). There was now a fourth member of the family, Krasnoshchokov's daughter Llewella, who was being brought up by Mayakovsky and the Briks while her father was in prison.

Mayakovsky did not live in Sokolniki for very long. He spent the whole of the autumn of 1924 in Paris, and then returned to France in May 1925, going on to Mexico and the United States. This trip was the longest and furthest of his life: he spent exactly six months abroad, returning in November 1925.

In New York Mayakovsky met an American woman of Russian extraction, Elly Jones, who in the summer of 1926 gave birth to a daughter whom Mayakovsky acknowledged as his (see No. 363, note 1). At the end of October, Lili went on a cure to the resort of Salsomaggiore in northern Italy, and Mayakovsky was supposed to join her there on his way home. He had difficulty in obtaining an Italian visa, however, and they met in Berlin, going on from there to Moscow together.

After his return from America, Mayakovsky's relations with Lili Brik definitively entered a new phase: "the character of our relationship changed," writes Lili.[43] The link between Mayakovsky and Lili Brik was never simple; in the preceding two or three years their love had been

24

subjected to particularly severe trials. Now, as their intimate life came to an end, they had already been living together for seven years.

"THREE CABIN-ROOMS"

After the first Sokolniki winter, the search for a new flat began. "Sokolniki was too far out, living there was difficult, there were no conveniences, and Volodya began to 'petition' for a flat in Moscow."[44] In July 1925 Lili informed Mayakovsky in Mexico that "nothing will come of a flat in town — there's no money. I'm looking for something a bit better here or in Serebryanyy bor" (No. 169). In December of the same year Mayakovsky recieved a "warrant" for a flat at 15, Gendrikov Lane, in the Taganka area of Moscow, and he and the Briks moved in during April 1926, after necessary repairs had been completed.

It was in this flat that the "Vladimir Mayakovsky Library-Museum" was opened in 1937. In 1972 the museum was transferred to Serov Passage, where Mayakovsky had a work room, and where he killed himself. It is therefore extremely difficult to form an impression of how Mayakovsky and the Briks lived in the years from 1926 to 1930. For a correct appraisal of their life in these years it is, however, essential to try to imagine their "collective" domicile. In her memoirs, Lili has left a good description of how the flat looked before it was turned into a museum: "At that time . . . there was a dining-room and three identical cabin-rooms. The only difference was that in mine the writing-desk was smaller and the wardrobe was bigger, and all the books were in Osip's room. There was a bath, which we had been deprived of for so long, and which we loved as if it were a living creature. It was so small that it's amazing that Vladimir Vladimirovich could get into it. We had 'our own kitchen', which was tiny but full of life. The staircase is now a 'museum staircase' and nobody goes up it. But then on the cold landing outside the door of the neighbouring flat there were clumsily knocked together cupboards, with padlocks, crammed with the books that didn't fit in the flat. There was no pretty garden with a fence round it. Instead there were trees and sheds for the inhabitants' firewood. The pitiful little houses that were around it have been demolished. . . . It was interesting to buy everything for the new flat and to order furniture. The first thing Volodya did was to order a copper plate for the entrance door — 'like people have'. He thought up one plate for all of us, like this:

"We bought a dining-room table and chairs in the Moscow Woodstore, but we had to order cupboards — the ones that were on sale wouldn't fit in our small rooms. The grand piano, a wonderful studio Steinway, was sold for a song — there was nowhere to put it. . . . The principle according to which the flat was decorated was the same one that had been used for the printing of the first edition of *A Cloud* — nothing superfluous. No beautiful objects — no mahogany, no pictures, no decorations. Everything was new, even the knives and forks, everything was essential. Bare walls. Only over Vladimir Vladimirovich's and Osip Maksimovich's ottomans, cloths brought back from Mexico, and over mine an old rug embroidered with a hunting-scene with wool and beads! Vladimir Vladimirovich had brought me it as a present from Moscow, when we were still living in Petrograd. On the floor there were flowered Ukrainian carpets for warmth, and Vladimir Vladimirovich had two photographs of me hanging in his room, which I had given him on his birthday in Petrograd the year we met."[45]

The flat in Gendrikov Lane became the "headquarters-flat" for New Lef. Every week the so-called Lef Tuesdays took place, with the participation of members of Lef and others: Nikolay Aseyev, Sergey Tretyakov, Aleksandr Rodchenko, Semyon Kirsanov, Viktor Shklovsky, Boris Pasternak, Vesevolod Meyerhold, Sergey Eisenstein, Lev Kuleshov and others; Anatoly Lunacharsky also visited the flat; new works by Mayakovsky and others were read here for the first time, including *Good!*, *The Bedbug* and *The Bath-House*.

It is paradoxical that Mayakovsky and Lili moved into a single flat only now that their "marital" life was over. In fact this is merely a further proof of the profound friendship that linked these people; it might be suggested that the new, less emotionally tense relations between Mayakovsky and Lili were a *prerequisite* of such an experiment in living.

By this time a change had also taken place in Osip Brik's life. In 1925 he had met Yevgeniya Zhemchuzhnaya (née Sokolova; at the time she was married to the film director Vitaly Zhemchuzhny), and his relationship with her was to last twenty years, right up to his premature death in 1945. Despite this, Osip continued to live in the same flat as Mayakovsky and Lili. Lili Brik told me that all three of them tried to arrange their lives in such a way that they could always spend the night at home, irrespective of their other relationships; the morning and the evening belonged to them, whatever might have happened during the day. Lili Brik's unpublished diary confirms that this was not just theory, that they really did live that way.

After his first visit to Riga in the spring of 1922, Mayakovsky made frequent trips across the borders of Soviet Russia; by 1930 he had made nine journeys abroad. He went abroad at least once a year, with the exception of 1926, during which he did not leave Russia. In the period from 1922 to 1929 he spent more than fifteen months abroad. Starting in 1924 Mayakovsky made frequent lecture tours around the Soviet Union; in all he spent about a year and a half on these tours, so that out of eight years he was away from Moscow for almost three. "I absolutely must travel," the poet declared. "For me, contact with living things is almost a substitute for reading books" (VII, 265). One must assume that these constant wanderings after 1925 were partly linked with the change in the nature of his relationship with Lili. But for all his thirst for new impressions, Mayakovsky always longed to be back, very soon informing Lili that he was "terribly homesick", "missed" her badly and so on. This sense of alienation abroad can of course be attributed in part to his inadequate knowledge of foreign languages, but it is absolutely clear also that he found it very difficult to bear long absences from his "family".

In 1926 Mayakovsky spent over five months travelling around the Soviet Union. In the summer he lectured in the Crimea, where in late July Lili was working as an assistant to Abram Roóm on the shooting of the film *Jews on the Land* (see No. 239, note 8). Mayakovsky and Lili spent the first half of August together in the Crimea, and then returned to Moscow. Their time in the Crimea was the first holiday they had had together since the summer of 1923.

In May 1926 Mayakovsky met Natalya Bryukhanenko, who worked in the library at the State Publishing House. They began seeing each other, and in August and September 1927 spent a month together in the Crimea. At the same time Lili had an affair with the film director Lev Kuleshov. The relationship between Mayakovsky and Natalya Bryukhanenko was serious enough for Lili to consider it necessary, albeit in jocular manner, to warn him: "Please don't get seriously married, because *everyone* is assuring me that you're terribly in love and will definitely get married!" (No. 302). To this Mayakovsky replied that he had "only Kitty Osya family" (No. 303). This relationship was the first threat to the existence of the Mayakovsky-Brik family; Mayakovsky continued to see Natalya Bryukhanenko, but they did not get married.

Despite their affairs and the other sources of tension between them, Mayakovsky and Lili planned a trip to Berlin together in the spring of 1928. Mayakovsky, however, was laid low by a severe attack of influenza, and therefore Lili set off in April alone. She visited Berlin on business: she was supposed to buy up pieces of foreign films for the film *The Glass Eye*, which she was making at the time with the director Vitaly Zhemchuzhny (see No. 332). In addition she had business regarding the publishing plans of Mayakovsky and Osip Brik.

In 1928, as in the previous summer, Mayakovsky and the Briks rented a dacha in Pushkino. In early October Mayakovsky left for Paris, where he stayed until the very beginning of December. Besides purely literary matters (and the purchase of a Renault!), there was a special reason for this visit. On the 20th of October he left Paris for Nice, where his American friend Elly Jones was on holiday with her little daughter. This was the first meeting Mayakovsky had had with Elly Jones since 1925, and the first meeting ever with a child of whom he was evidently the father. But Mayakovsky was not very fond of small children, and according to Lili Brik the meeting in Nice was not a success: by the 25th of October he had left for Paris.[46]

On the evening of the same day Mayakovsky met Tatyana Yakovleva, a young Russian woman who had arrived in Paris in 1925. Elsa Triolet says that it was she who introduced them;[47] certainly it was not a chance meeting. On the 24th of December Tatyana Yakovleva wrote to her mother in Penza: ". . . I was specially invited to a certain house to be introduced to him."[48] Mayakovsky and Tatyana Yakovleva immediately fell in love. It was only three weeks after meeting her that Mayakovsky wrote Lili a letter. On the 12th of November he answered her question "Why don't you write?" (No. 368) vaguely and evasively: "My life is rather strange, with no events but many details which are not material for a letter and can only be talked about" (No. 370). These "many details" referred to his new love.

"At that time Mayakovsky needed love," Elsa Triolet says emphatically,[49] and Roman Jakobson remembers the poet's words that "now only a big, good love can save me".[50] Now, for the first time since 1915, he had met a woman who was, as he wrote in the poem "A letter to Tatyana Yakovleva", his "equal in height". For five weeks they met every day. In November Mayakovsky wrote two poems dedicated to her: "A letter to comrade Kostrov from Paris on the nature of love" and "A letter to Tatyana Yakovleva". These were his first poetic love letters since 1915 not to be dedicated to Lili Brik. "Again/the stalled motor/of the heart/is set to work", he announces, in lines that are among the best of all his lyric poetry:

Loving
           means
                   running
Into the depths of the yard
                        and till rook-black night
With shining axe
                   chopping wood
Playing
        with one's
                   strength.
Loving is
        jumping
                from sheets
Rent by insomnia
                jealous of Copernicus,
Considering him,
                and not Marya Ivanna's husband
To be
     your
          rival.

The object of this love is also described:

Imagine
        a beauty
                enters the hall.
Set in furs
        and beads.
                ("A letter to comrade Kostrov . . .")

In fact the poems to Tatyana Yakovleva were the first light and
optimistic love lyrics since *I Love* (1922). There is no doubt that his love for
her was "big" enough to fill the emotional void which the poet had felt in
recent years. It is also quite obvious that the involvement with Tatyana
Yakovleva had a far stronger effect on the relationship between
Mayakovsky and Lili Brik than the love affair with Natalya
Bryukhanenko: if we compare the correspondence of Mayakovsky and
Lili with the letters and telegrams to Tatyana Yakovleva in 1928 and 1929,
it becomes clear that in many respects Tatyana Yakovleva had replaced
Lili Brik in the role of the poet's *confidente*.

Mayakovsky left Paris at the very beginning of December, and returned
there in February 1929; on that trip he stayed for over two months. He
asked Tatyana Yakovleva to marry him and go off with him to the USSR,
a proposal which she "greeted evasively".[51] But their love affair

continued, and Mayakovsky made plans to return to Paris in October of the same year.

The October visit did not take place; by all accounts, Mayakovsky was refused an exit visa. The circumstances surrounding this abortive visit are extremely hazy, a fact that has given rise to all sorts of hints and rumours. Did Mayakovsky in fact apply for a visa? If he did apply, who took the decision, or who influenced the decision not to let him have one? In whose interest was it that Mayakovsky should not marry Tatyana Yakovleva? Did he think of remaining in Paris if Tatyana Yakovleva was not prepared to go to Moscow with him?[52]

In two Soviet articles, by a process of "guilt by association", the blame for Mayakovsky's being refused a visa is laid at the door of the Briks, who would have nothing to gain from Mayakovsky's marrying Tatyana Yakovleva.[53] These hints are given without proof, but since the Briks themselves went abroad five months later, it is considered self-evident that they had the means to exert influence over the granting of visas.

It goes without saying that Lili and Osip did not "want" Mayakovsky to marry Tatyana Yakovleva. Their relationship was based upon the fact that they lived together. Love affairs and other temporary involvements, and even the permanent relationship that existed between Osip Brik and Yevgeniya Zhemchuzhnaya, were treated with tolerance. But Mayakovsky's marriage to Tatyana Yakovleva would have meant an end to their life together; had she returned to the Soviet Union, she would hardly have agreed to "share" Mayakovsky with Lili and Osip. Nor should one underestimate the role of Mayakovsky as "bread-winner". But to draw or to hint at the conclusion from this that the Briks actively prevented Mayakovsky from making his trip to Paris is incautious if nothing more. In the absence of proof of such intervention on their part, we must look for other explanations of why the visit did not take place.

Lili and Osip did indeed leave for Germany and England in February 1930. According to Lili's *Diary*, however, they had applied for a visa as early as the autumn of 1929, but had been refused. The refusal arrived on the 10th of October, at exactly the time when Mayakovsky was due to leave for Paris. Lili and Osip received their passports only on the 6th of February 1930, after Mayakovsky had "put in a word" for them to Kaganovich, and had written a newspaper article in defence of their trip which had been sharply criticised in *Komsomolskaya pravda*, the newspaper of the Young Communist League (see No. 393, note 1). One asks oneself why, if the Briks had sufficient power to frustrate Mayakovsky's trip, they could not arrange foreign passports for themselves. And how it came about that Mayakovsky, who had recently been refused a visa, suddenly turned out to be influential enough to be able to help Lili and Osip.

Rumours about various intrigues in connection with Mayakovsky's trip to Paris stem partly from the fact that among the acquaintances of Mayakovsky and the Briks at the time was the important member of the *Cheka* (Security Police), Yakov Agranov. At one time after the revolution Osip Brik had worked as a legal expert in the Cheka, but this had ceased by 1924 (see No. 37, note 7). It was Mayakovsky who brought Agranov to the "family". Agranov was interested in literature, and from 1928 to 1930 he spent a lot of time with Mayakovsky and the Briks. The possibility that this was a special work assignment cannot be ruled out. Thus Mayakovsky and the Briks had a highly placed protector in the person of Agranov, but he too learnt a great deal through knowing them; of course he also knew about the love affair with Tatyana Yakovleva.

1929 saw a turning-point in the USSR in both the political and the cultural sense. In February Lev Trotsky was expelled from the country, and in November Nikolay Bukharin had to leave the Politburo. In April the first Five Year Plan was decided upon, and during the year there were purges both in the party and in a number of cultural institutions: the Academy of Sciences, the Pushkin House literary institute in Leningrad, the Moscow Arts Theatre and the State Academy of Artistic Studies. In the late summer and autumn a savage press campaign was waged against Boris Pilnyak and Yevgeny Zamyatin, who had published their work abroad. "In the entire history of Russian culture this was the first widely organised campaign not against individual writers but against literature as a whole," and it was "thought out and set in motion by the state."[54] The campaign against the two writers coincided with an important change in the Council of People's Commissars: on the 12th of September, Anatoly Lunacharsky, who had been People's Commissar of Enlightenment since 1917, was forced to resign his post. Lunacharsky was always well disposed towards Mayakovsky and the Briks, he visited their house, he helped them in all sorts of ways. In conversation with me, Lili Brik more than once emphasised the extraordinary importance of this connection for them — it is worthy of note that the visa difficulties arose immediately after Lunacharsky's resignation.

In addition to these changes in the spheres of culture and politics, an incident took place in September 1929 which considerably complicated the situation for Soviet citizens wishing to travel abroad: a counsellor at the Soviet Embassy in Paris, the Old Bolshevik, Besedovsky, defected, and this led to the adoption of a law about non-returnees, the so-called "Lex Besedovsky". Taking into consideration all the events of the autumn of 1929, the refusal of a visa to Mayakovsky seems to be anything but an arbitrary event. "But who could have prevented the trip to Paris, a trip that was so important to him?" is the rhetorical question posed by the Soviet journal *Ogonyok*.[55] I surmise that the Soviet *authorities* were concerned lest Mayakovsky, famous poet and representative of the Soviet Union, should marry an émigrée and, who knows, remain in France.

On the 11th of October 1929 Mayakovsky learnt that Tatyana Yakovleva was to marry a Frenchman, the Vicomte du Plessix. He took this news extremely badly, for his love for Tatyana Yakovleva was "big" and "good". The end of his love affair with her was also the beginning of the last period in Mayakovsky's life. The search for the kind of love that might "save" him continued. As early as the summer of 1929, long before he heard the news from Paris, he had begun to pay court to the actress Veronika Polonskaya, and this involvement continued.

Mayakovsky saw Lili and Osip Brik for the last time on the 18th of February 1930, when they left for their trip to Berlin and London. When Mayakovsky shot himself they were on their way home. Their last postcard was sent from Amsterdam on the 14th of April 1930, the day of his suicide.

"If I had been home at the time," writes Lili Brik, "maybe once again death would have been put off for a while."[56] There are many reasons for Mayakovsky's suicide. In addition to the external factors which prompted him to take such a step — political and cultural developments, the failure of *The Bath-House*, the boycott of his "Twenty Years of Work" exhibition, quarrels with his friends, his entry into RAPP, the Russian Association of Proletarian Writers, the end of his love affair with Tatyana Yakovleva — another profounder and stronger impulse lay behind this decision: his instinctual attraction to suicide. It is this instinct that Lili Brik has in mind when she tentatively suggests that "maybe" she might have been able to help him to put off suicide "for a while".

Lili remembers Mayakovsky's "incessant conversations" about suicide, and Elsa Triolet writes that she was "always . . . afraid that Volodya would kill himself".[57] Roman Jakobson told Lili in 1919 that he could not "imagine Volodya old", to which she replied: "Volodya old? Never! He's already tried to shoot himself twice, leaving a single bullet in the revolver. Eventually the bullet will find its target."[58] The two attempted suicides mentioned by Lili Brik took place in 1916 and, probably, 1917 — see the entries in Mayakovsky's *Notebook* No. 1 for 1917: "18 July, 8.45, suddenly somehow there was absolutely no reason to live. 11 October 4.[30]15, The End". It is precisely in this attraction towards suicide and in the means to effecting it that one should seek for the key to Mayakovsky, man and poet.

Suicide and the suicide are one of the main motifs of Mayakovsky's creative work (where natural death is as unusual as it is in Dostoevsky) — see for example *Vladimir Mayakovsky, a Tragedy*, the short poem "Going cheap", the long poems *Man* and *About This*, the film scenario *How are you?*, the projected *A Comedy with Suicides, The Bedbug*, the film *Not born for money*. The thought of suicide was never far from his mind. Love, women, art, revolution, to Mayakovsky all of them were games in which he staked his life. He played as a compulsive gambler, seriously and without compromise; he knew that if he lost, all that was left to him was despair. Living life to such an extreme left only one way out. In this context Mayakovsky's games of Russian roulette seem utterly true to type.

The refusal of a visa, and the Briks' trip abroad, along with other factors, were significant in the timing of Mayakovsky's suicide. The decisive influence, however, lay far deeper.

"LOVE IS THE HEART OF EVERYTHING"
The love of Mayakovsky for Lili Brik was boundless. He could not imagine life without her. He loved her with an extraordinary emotional charge, sincerely, unreservedly, although he knew that her love for him was different. His need for love and tenderness was so strong that it bordered on the infantile. In his diary, written during their two-month separation in 1923, there is a heading "Do I love you?", under which Mayakovsky analyses his love for Lili: "I love you, I love you, despite everything and because of everything, I have loved you, I love you and I will love you, whether you're foul to me or affectionate, whether you belong to me or to someone else. All the same I love you. Amen. . . . Love is life, love is the main thing. My poetry, my actions, everything else stems from it. Love is the heart of everything. If it stops working, all the rest withers, becomes superfluous, unnecessary. But if the heart is working, its influence cannot but be apparent in all the rest. Without you (not without you because you've 'gone away', without you inwardly) I cease to exist. That was always the case, it is so now." (No. 113)

Mayakovsky's attachment to Lili Brik was such that it intruded into his relationships with other women, even after "the character of their relationship changed" in 1925. He evidently spoke constantly to his Russian-American girlfriend Elly Jones about his feelings for Lili, which forced her (in a letter of the 28th of November 1928) to exclaim: "Ask 'the person you love' to forbid you to burn the candle at both ends." Natalya Bryukhanenko remembers Mayakovsky's words: "I love only Lilya. Towards all others I can only be well disposed or VERY well disposed, but I can love them only in second place."[59] Veronika Polonskaya was "distressed" by Mayakovsky's love for Lili, until she realised that "in a certain sense she (that is, Lili) was and would remain first for him".[60] Even with Tatyana Yakovleva, whom Mayakovsky fell in love with in earnest, he spoke about Lili all the time. Tatyana Yakovleva told me that they bought Lili presents together, chose the Renault and the upholstery and so on. It can hardly have been easy for the poet's beloveds to hear endless tales about "the person I love"!

In the same diary there is also a heading "Do you love me?", under which Mayakovsky explains how he understands Lili's love for him: "It's probably a strange question for you — of course you love me. But do you love *me*? . . . No . . . You don't feel love towards me, you feel love towards everything. I too occupy my place in it (perhaps even a large place) but if I come to an end I'll be removed, like a stone from a stream, and your love will go on washing over all the rest. Is this bad? No, for you it's good, I'd like to love in that way" (No. 113). Here Mayakovsky is alluding to an important difference in their attitude towards love. For him Lili was everything, but for her the love she felt for Mayakovsky was not a unique experience in her life. They knew about each other's love affairs, but unlike Lili Mayakovsky suffered from this knowledge; even if he had wanted to, he was incapable of loving in the same way as she did.

Mayakovsky was extremely demanding in love, as he was in life in general, and in his relationships with those close to him. "Countless numbers of people were devoted to him, loved him," writes Lili, "but they were all a drop in the ocean for a man who had 'an insatiable thief in his soul', who needed the people who didn't read him to read him, the person who hadn't come to come, the one who he felt didn't love him to love him."[61]

Relations between Lili and Osip were less dramatic. According to people who were close to both of them, Osip was relatively indifferent to the erotic aspect of love, and therefore similar conflicts in the family did not arise between him and Lili. Although (as Lili told me) they "ceased to live as man and wife" as early as 1914, they never felt any urge to be divorced, and were still formally married when Osip died. Lili always loved Osip, she had loved him since her childhood; just as she exulted in Mayakovsky's poetry, so she always valued Osip for his intelligence and erudition. For her Mayakovsky and Osip complemented each other: one was emotional and creative, the other analytical and sober-minded. And loving Osip was easier for Lili than loving Mayakovsky, because Osip never made any demands on her.

Relations between Mayakovsky and Osip Brik were very warm, even tender. They not only complemented each other in the eyes of Lili, but they themselves also needed each other. It was Mayakovsky who in 1915 aroused Osip's interest in poetry, thus changing the course of his life; Osip's brilliant intellectual qualities, trained until then on the study of law and trading in corals, were redirected towards literary and cultural-political questions. Brik was one of the most subtle and penetrating of the Formalist critics, and later one of the most influential ideologists of culture. Often the material and source of inspiration for his theoretical models was the work of Mayakovsky.

At the same time as Mayakovsky "reformed Osya's thinking", Osip was playing a decisive role in the development of Mayakovsky as man and poet. Mayakovsky was not a great reader, but Brik went round the secondhand bookstalls every day, and had a large library of his own. He often read aloud to Mayakovsky from books and journals (see No. 42: "I draw, and he reads me Chekhov"). Mayakovsky had complete trust in Osip's literary taste; Osip edited his first collected works, corrected the proofs of individual volumes and wrote the *Literary Commentaries to Volume One* (Moscow 1928). It was no accident that in his suicide letter Mayakovsky left his unfinished poems to the Briks — "they will sort them out". Osip was very influential in the formation of Mayakovsky's political and aesthetic views, especially in the 1920s. Mayakovsky consulted him about his poems, sometimes rewriting them on Osip's advice: "The only adviser . . . whom he trusted more than himself, was Osip Brik."[62] The influence of Osip on Mayakovsky can be appraised in various ways, but it is impossible to deny the fact that Mayakovsky himself chose as his main adviser precisely Osip Brik, the person "who after Burlyuk stood closer than anyone to Mayakovsky's work".[63]

Mayakovsky, Lili and Osip had many amorous adventures during the fifteen years in which they knew each other and lived in the most intimate friendship; Osip even had a permanent relationship with another woman over several years. Of course this gave rise to conflicts in their relationship, especially between Mayakovsky and Lili, and it would be incorrect to portray their life together as a cloudless idyll. According to Lili, the model for their experiment in living was Chernyshevsky's novel *What is to be done?* Like Chernyshevsky's "new people", they really tried to struggle against jealousy and other manifestations of "the old routine"; a prerequisite of real love and friendship was respect for the freedom and independence of each of them. There is no reason to doubt the sincerity with which these ideas were held, but it is also clear that a high price had to be paid for this freedom in the jealousy which the "new people" so abominated, and in other spiritual torments. Mayakovsky paid dearest of all, but he was not alone in suffering from an inability to control his feelings in accordance with the rigorous schema of the Man of the Sixties. "We were all young," writes Rita Rayt, "we were all thirsty for life, we were all busy with all sorts of different things, both personal and public, which now came together, now drifted apart. . . . We quarrelled, and we made things up, we got hurt, and we were happy — in a word, "there was everything — there was standing under the window. . . ."[64]

Despite all the difficulties and crises in their relationship, all three of them stayed together for fifteen years, meeting almost every day. They were united by closeness of a very unusual kind, the distinguishing qualities of which were profound friendship, devotion, mutual trust, common interests — "the love of three people, which bound them more strongly than marriages and love affairs".[65] There is no cause to idealise their life, but there is still less cause to belittle the role of Lili and Osip Brik in the life of Mayakovsky, and the love of Mayakovsky for Lili, as is done in the poet's own country; such disparagement of those who were closest to Mayakovsky is nothing other than a blow stuck against the poet himself.

* * *

With the professionalisation of literary activity in the nineteenth century, the posthumous publication of writers' letters became a relatively common phenomenon. This, in its turn, had an influence on attitudes to the writing of letters, which were no longer seen just as a means of communication. Writers became aware that at some point their correspondence might be collected and published; and that they had to express themselves in a way that would not ruin their posthumous reputations. The writing of letters gradually developed into an art *per se*, into a particular genre. The Russian Symbolists quite consciously treated the epistolary genre as a part of the general search after truth carried out in their poetry and in their aesthetico-philosophical treatises. In 1922

Andrey Bely characterised his correspondence with Blok in the following way: "Part of it, I think, might appear in print quite soon, the personal element is the least important thing about it, its content is rather literature, philosophy, mysticism and the 'aspirations' of the young Symbolists at that time. It is a brilliant intimate literary diary of an epoch. That is the nature of this correspondence. It is brilliant. Thought jets out here."[66] What is of interest here is not so much the high opinion Bely has of his own correspondence as his desire to see it published. Even while Blok was still alive, in 1912, Bely wanted to publish extracts from Blok's letters in the journal *Trudy i dni* (*Works and Days*), an idea which Blok himself supported. Such a self-conscious approach to their own correspondence leads one to suppose that the possibility of eventual publication must have influenced their way of expressing themselves.

The correspondence between Mayakovsky and Lili Brik is of a completely different character; it is not an example of great epistolary art. Unlike the Symbolists, Mayakovsky (and the other Futurists) did not consider the writing of letters to be a particular literary genre, though this stance was not a conscious polemic with the previous generation; letters had no role to play in Mayakovsky's poetics (in the wider sense of the term), which was directed in the main towards problems of poetic language, and not towards philosophical questions. It is possible that Mayakovsky's social origin also played a part here. At any rate, he had no clearly defined position with regard to letters as a literary genre; for him this question simply did not occur. (Compare Blok's words in a letter to his wife: ". . . I know how to write letters".)

Of course it would not be appropriate to compare the philosophical correspondence of Blok and his fellow-writers with the letters between Mayakovsky and Lili; it goes without saying that Blok's letters to his wife are different from those he addressed to Bely, Rozanov and others. Mayakovsky wrote almost exclusively to Lili, but his surviving letters to other people are (with rare exceptions) of the same type as his letters to her: day-to-day letters, down-to-business letters, with no literary ambitions. Just as in his poetry, Mayakovsky rarely uses punctuation, and where he does it is difficult to see any signs of consistency. His syntax is so free from established norms that any attempt to correct it would only complicate reading and break up the rhythm. His orthography is both incorrect and inconsistent. All this gives his letters their particular spontaneity, their very specific, quickly pulsating rhythm which wonderfully conveys the temperament and emotions of the correspondent. Mayakovsky's letters contrast with those of Lili, which, though they also make no pretence to literariness, and are temperamental and capricious, conform to all the rules of orthography, and bear the marks of the good education she had received.

It is clear that the correspondence between Mayakovsky and Lili was conducted without regard for future biographers, which makes it a particularly interesting and reliable document. The value of this correspondence consists, among other things, in its absence of literariness, and in the exceptional intensity with which it was written. We learn a relatively meagre amount about the correspondents' ideas, but on the other hand we get a very clear picture of the relationship between Mayakovsky and Lili, and of the role of Osip Brik in the "family". Given all the rumours that have been aroused by these three people's living together, this is an extremely important point. I have therefore considered it essential to present in this volume all the letters, postcards and telegrams that were at my disposal. Many of them, in particular the telegrams, are not of any special interest in themselves, but taken together they become significant; the correspondence between Mayakovsky and Lili Brik is an extremely eloquent proof of the adage that the whole is always something more than the sum of its parts.

BENGT JANGFELDT

NOTES

Non-Russian sources are given in full, for Russian sources only the author and year are given; the reader may refer to the bibliography at the end of the book, in which Russian sources are given in full.

1 Edward J. Brown, *Mayakovsky. A Poet in the Revolution*, Princeton 1973, p. 346.
2 *Literaturnoye nasledstvo*, Vol. 65, Moscow 1958.
3 Mayakovsky 1973, p. 450.
4 Cheryomin 1975, p. 201. The level of works such as Vorontsov/Koloskov 1968, Koloskov 1968, Lavinskaya 1968, Cheryomin 1975 and the commentaries to the latest Collected Works of Mayakovsky (1973 and 1978), precludes the possibility of serious discussion. To this list should be added the book by Ann and Samuel Charters, *I Love: The Story of Vladimir Mayakovsky and Lili Brik*, New York 1979, which, it is true, contains some new factual material, but even more factual errors; it has to be assumed that their complete ignorance of the Russian language and of Russian literature can have been of little assistance to the authors in the compilation of their book. I have considered Vahan D. Barooshian's *Brik and Mayakovsky*, The Hague 1978, in another context (see Jangfeldt 1980).
5 Mayakovsky 1973, p. 456.
6 Vorontsov/Koloskov 1968, p. 10.
7 In the book by L. Rakhmanova and V. Valerianov, *Shest' adresov Vladimira Mayakovskogo* (Moscow 1964), there is a reproduction of a photograph taken during the shooting of *Fettered by Film* (1918): Mayakovsky stands leaning against a tree (p. 39). In the original, unretouched photograph, Lili Brik is standing next to him in front of this tree — all that remains in the book is a part of her heel (see illustrations Nos. 50 and 51 to this volume). This wretched photograph also got into the book by L. Volkov-Lannit, *Vizhu Mayakovskogo* (Moscow 1981), where it is reproduced not only without Lili Brik, but without even the tree, and with the inscription "Vladimir Mayakovsky in Mexico, 1925" (p. 17). In this illustrated biography of Mayakovsky, Lili Brik does appear in one photograph; in the inscription she is referred to by the words "and others" (p. 110). See also the recent book by V. D. Korkin, *Mayakovsky na Krasnoy Presne* (Moscow 1983), where there is an illustration of Mayakovsky's Renault, without Lili Brik, who in the unretouched photograph is holding the petrol-hose (see illustration No. 44 to this volume).
8 Lili Brik 1934, p. 60.
9 *Ibid*, p. 62.
10 Lili Brik 1956.
11 *Ibid*.
12 Lili Brik 1934, p. 62.
13 *Ibid*, pp. 62-63.
14 Lili Brik 1929.
15 Elsa Triolet 1975, p. 27.
16 Lili Brik 1929.
17 *Ibid*.
18 *Ibid*.
19 *Ibid*.
20 Lili Brik 1934, p. 63.
21 Lili Brik 1929.
22 On the complex relationship with Gorky, especially after 1918, see No. 97, note 1. Roman Jakobson told me that in 1927 in Prague Mayakovsky spoke of Gorky with irritation and even contempt. Lili Brik's memoirs are worthy of note: "Relations between Gorky and Mayakovsky were never as sickly-idyllic as present-day writers would have us believe.

It is quite wrong to portray them as those of a biblical prophet and his disciple. Their relationship was never close, Mayakovsky was never a member of his circle . . . Mayakovsky did not move from Futurism to Gorky, as many suppose, but from Gorky to Futurism" (1956). On the enmity between Gorky and Mayakovsky, see D. S. Babkin, 'Vstrechi s Mayakovskim', in *V. Mayakovsky v sovremennom mire* (Leningrad 1984), pp. 306-09.

23 References to the correspondence are given by number of letter and footnote.

24 Aseyev 1963, p. 412. Lili Brik's eyes especially captivated people. I quote the American writer Theodore Dreiser, who visited the USSR in 1927: "She had the broad, white brow which is the charm of so many Russian women; clear, sensitive, comprehending eyes, and a dazzling smile. At a tea table she shone and proved a center . . ." (*Dreiser looks at Russia*, New York 1928, p. 201).

25 Lili Brik 1934, p. 78.

26 *Ibid*, p. 72.

27 When the long poem 150,000,000 appeared, without indication of its author, and Mayakovsky was unable to dedicate it in print to Lili, he asked the printers to print three copies — for Lili, Osip and himself — with his name and a dedication. First off the press, however, were not these three copies but the basic print-run, and then Mayakovsky "forced the head of the printing-works to write an explanation, certified by the printing-works' stamp, stuck it into the first copy he received and presented it to me. On the fly-leaf he wrote No. 1 and added the inscription: 'To dear Lilyonok this book and all of me dedicate ourselves'." (Lili Brik 1956).

The explanation by the head of the printing-works:
"To comrade L. Yu. Brik,
The author's copy of 150,000,000 with the note LYuB should be printed first, but since a special type-setting is needed, and there have been delays, it will be printed after the general print-run has been completed.

State Publishing House Instructor
18/iv 1921   N. Koretsky."

28 Lili Brik 1975, p. 21.

29 Lili Brik 1934, p. 76.

30 Lili Brik 1956.

31 Elsa Triolet 1975, p. 38.

32 Cf. Bengt Jangfeldt, *Mayakovskij and Futurism 1917-1921*, Stockholm 1976, and 'Russian Futurism 1917-1919', in *Art, Society, Revolution: Russia 1917-1921*, Stockholm 1979.

33 Lili Brik 1942, p. 4.

34 Lili Brik 1934, p. 74.

35 Lawrence Stahlberger, *The Symbolic System of Majakovskij*, The Hague/Paris 1964.

36 Lili Brik 1934, p. 72.

37 Viktor Shklovsky 1974, p. 118. English translation: Viktor Shklovsky, *Mayakovsky and his Circle*, New York 1972, London 1974.

38 Elsa Triolet 1975, pp. 39-40.

39 Lili Brik 1941, p. 231.

40 Rita Rayt 1967, p. 121.

41 Roman Jakobson 1931, p. 11. English translation: 'On a Generation that Squandered its Poets', in Edward J. Brown (ed.), *Major Soviet Writers — Essays in Criticism*, London, New York 1973.

42 Whether the meeting between Lili Brik and Aleksandr Krasnoshchokov in the summer of 1922 was a factor in causing the two-month separation between Mayakovsky and Lili is difficult to establish. It is, however, worthy of note that the long poem *About This*, written during this separation, was conceived by Mayakovsky as early as the summer of 1922. In his autobiography, *I Myself*, under the heading "1922", we read: "I'm planning something: about love. An enormous poem. I'll finish it next year." The autobiography

was published in October 1922 in the Berlin journal *Novaya russkaya kniga* (*New Russian Book*), but it was written as early as July. In the 1928 version of the autobiography, the words about the planned poem are replaced by the following sentences (under the heading "1923"): "I wrote *About This*. Through personal motifs about life (*byt*) in general."

43 Lili Brik 1956.
44 *Ibid.*
45 *Ibid.*
46 On Mayakovsky's complex relationship with children, see Jakobson 1931 and Stahlberger 1964.
47 Elsa Triolet 1975, p. 64.
48 Vorontsov/Koloskov 1968, p. 11.
49 Elsa Triolet 1975, p. 65.
50 Roman Jakobson 1956, p. 184.
51 *Ibid*, pp. 178, 187.
52 Compare Lili's diary entries: "At home a conversation with Volodya about how someone had been substituted for him in Paris" (29.viii.1929); "Volodya touched me: he doesn't want to go abroad this year. He wants to spend three months travelling around the Soviet Union" (8.ix.1929); "Volodya . . . has now stopped talking about three months in the Soviet Union, and is planning to go to Brazil (which is to say Paris) in the spring" (19.ix.1929).
53 Vorontsov/Koloskov 1968 and Koloskov 1968.
54 Lazar Fleishman 1980, pp. 124, 126.
55 Vorontsov/Koloskov 1968, p. 13.
56 Lili Brik 1975, p. 21.
57 Elsa Triolet 1975, p. 33.
58 Roman Jakobson 1956. p. 191.
59 Natalya Bryukhanenko 1940-52.
60 Veronika Polonskaya 1938. While I have been working on this book, Polonskaya's memoirs have been published in the journal *Kontinent*, Paris, Nos. 29 and 30, 1981, and as a book: Semyon Chertok, *Poslednyaya lyubov' Mayakovskogo* [*Mayakovsky's Last Love]*), Ann Arbor, Michigan, 1983.
61 Lili Brik 1975, p. 20.
62 Lili Brik 1941, p. 228.
63 Pyotr Neznamov 1963, p. 377.
64 Rita Rayt 1967, p. 120.
65 *Ibid.*
66 Andrey Bely 1980, p. 215.

THE CORRESPONDENCE
1915-1930

We'll come on Saturday.

Lilya.

Dear Lichika,
dear Oska!

I kiss you at the very beginning of the letter and not at the end as I ought to: I can't wait! What news with you? People fortunate enough to have been in the fairy-tale land called "with you" limit themselves, the scoundrels, to the classic phrase "Lilya doesn't change!".

Yesterday I gave a reading.[2] The house was full, but unfortunately not with paying customers but with close friends. I could easily have started my lecture not with a cold "citizens" but with a tender "dear Abram Vasilevich,[3] Elsa[4] and Lyova!".[5]

I'm living on the Presnya.[6] They feed me and they walk about on tiptoe.

The former is good, the latter worse. I'm the family genius. A little bit like Averchenko.[7]

Whether I'll be able to dream up something that involves a trip to the country I don't know.

My closest friend here is Nika.[8]

Dear children, write to me!

I kiss you

Your Volodya, putting on weight

$$\frac{25}{IX}$$

(On the back)

To everyone! To everyone! To everyone!
HALLO

A poster would be nice.[9] How's "War and the World"?[10]

Dear, dear Lilik!
Sweet, sweet Osik!

"Where are you, my heart's desire,
Where, answer me!"[2]

45

Having put all the anguish of my young soul into the epigraph, I turn to facts.

Moscow, as they say, is a juicy ripe fruit which Dodya,[3] Kamensky[4] and I are plucking with zeal. The main plucking place is the "Poets' Café".[5]

For the time being the café is a very nice and jolly establishment. (As jolly as the "Dog"[6] was at first!) It gets absolutely crowded. Sawdust on the floor. Us on the stage (now "me", Dodya and Vasya have gone away till Christmas. Worser.) We tell the public to go to hell. We share out the money at midnight. That's all.

Futurism is in great favour.

We make loads of appearances. At Christmas there'll be a "Futurist Christmas tree".[7] Then the "Election of Poetry's Triumphant Trio".[8] I'm having talks about a reading of "Man"[9] at the Polytechnic.

Everything's started spinning.

Masses of amusing things, which will unfortunately have to be mimed owing to the wordlessness of the characters. Imagine Vysotsky, Marants and Shatilov[10] for example (after all the banks were shut!) listening with the utmost attention to Dodya's "He was terribly fond of flies with plump backsides".[11]

A million new people. Dense crowds and dense heads. Encircled by Lyova's maternal solicitousness, the Southern fund grows calmly and serenely. It's still difficult to go south.[12]

How are Lilichka's room,[13] Asis,[14] the Academy[15] and the other extremely important things? I read Oska's letter with its breath of nobility in "Novaya zhizn". I should like to receive one like it.[16]

I live at:

Moscow, Petrovka, Saltykov Alley, "San Remo", flat No. 2, V.V. Mayakovsky.

I'm going to go out often beyond the outskirts, and sorrowfully blocking out the slanting rays of the setting sun with my wasted palm, I'm going to gaze into the distance to see whether the familiar figure of the postman might not emerge in clouds of dust. Do not lead me to this step!

I kiss Lilinka.

I kiss Oska.

Your Volodya.

Give Pasya[17] and Shura[18] my ovations.

Greetings to Polya and Nyusha.[19]

Dear Volodenka, we're about to come to Moscow. I'm glad you're well. Give our regards to Dodya and Kamensky.

I've got a sore knee and I haven't danced for over a week.

Osya has a permanent job at "Novaya zhizn".[1] They've taken him on! (200 roubles).

We went to see Altman[2] and the Yasnys.[3] Probably nothing will come of it!! It's very warm here but terribly slippery.

Shura's gone to Archangel to buy a steamship.[4]

Oska just can't decide when we're going to leave for Moscow; as soon as there's any definite news I'll send Lyova a telegram.

They say no one goes out in Moscow after ten o'clock at night. That's awful.

I've put on three pounds and I'm in despair. I want to lose weight, but for some reason I feel hungry from morning till night and I can't restrain myself.

My room is nice, only not very; it lacks a lot of things (wallpaper, curtains, lamps). Osya has taken the Academy in hand.

Kushner is taking charge of Asis.[5]

What's up with Bobrov? What's he done with your poem.[6]

There's something about Oska every day in some paper or other, because of his letter in "Novaya zhizn": they abuse him from right and left.[7]

They say, and it was in the papers too, that on the seventeenth workers were singing in the street: . . . chew your hazel-grouse! Your last day is coming, bourgeois (I don't remember the start).[8]

I kiss you, Volodenka.

Oska kisses you too.

Lilya.

My dear Volodenka, I'm terribly happy when you write.

My nerves are completely on edge. We're leaving for Japan. I'll bring you back a dressing-gown.

My legs hurt, but I'm already dancing.

I'm fed up of Petersburg, more than I've ever been of anything. Oska will write to you himself with his news.

Shura's proposed to Pasya on condition that she takes him to Japan at her expense.

I've been terribly depressed all this time. Now I feel more cheerful since we've finally decided to leave.

Have you written anything new?

I don't go out at all. I don't even go to the ballet on my season ticket, — you should see the snowdrifts!

Shura asks me to give you his parental blessing.

"The Halt" is opening today. They're doing a vaudeville by Kuzmin.[1] I shan't go.

Kuzmin's got some very nice new poems to music by Lurye[2] They're jolly.

Write to me soon. I embrace you heartily and I kiss you.

Your Lilya.

I fainted yesterday!!!!!!!!!

We've just decided that in about ten days, before we leave for Japan, we'll come to Moscow.[3]

†6. Mayakovsky to Lili and Osip.
Letter from Moscow to Petrograd, first half of January 1918.

Dear, dear, dear Lilik,

Sweet, sweet, sweet Osyukha

I waited for you till the seventh (at least I was clever enough not to go to the station). That means you won't be coming. Lyova got a miserable letter from you. What's up, my dears? Please write! Because I'm a human being too.

Nothing changes with me. I live like a gypsy romance: I lie around all day, and caress my ear by night. I'm sick to death of the café. It's a petty little bedbug-hatchery. Erenburg and Vera Inber still vaguely resemble poets, but Koyransky[1] was right to remark even of their activity that

Erenburg howls wildly
Inber approves his drivel
Neither Moscow nor Petersburg
Can replace Berdichev for them.

I've done a great deal of performing. There was the Futurist Christmas tree at the Polytechnic.[2] There were as many people as at a Soviet demonstration. By the time the performance was due to begin, it was clear that of the four names announced on the poster, Burlyuk and Kamensky wouldn't turn up, and Goltsshmidt[3] was refusing to go on. I had to carry the whole evening myself. The very memory of it scares me out of my wits. I read at the circus. That was weird. They hissed at Khenkin[4] with his anecdotes, but they listened to me, and how! At the end of January I'm reading "Man" at the Polytechnic.[5]

I'm doing a brisk trade in books. A Cloud in Trousers 10 roubles, The Flute[6] 5 roubles. War and the World sold at auction 140 roubles. Bearing in mind the price of wine, it won't pay my hotel bill.

All the women love me. All the men respect me. All the women are sticky and boring. All the men are scoundrels. Lyova of course is neither a man nor a woman.

To the sou-ou-ou-outh!

Write!

How's Lichika's knee?

I kiss you all a hundred times

Your Volodya

P.S. Will a steemer (sic) suit Shura?

I'm in a great hurry to publish "Man" and the fuller version of "A Cloud". I think they'll come out.[7]

I got your letter on the fourth of January.

7. Lili to Mayakovsky.
Letter from Petrograd to Moscow, beginning of March 1918.[1]

My dear, dear little puppy! I kiss you for the books.[2] I already know "Man" by heart. Oska also reads it from morning till night.

I dreamt about you all night: that you're living with some woman, that she's terribly jealous, and you're afraid to tell her about me. Aren't you ashamed, Volodenka?

I'm ill all the time, I've got a fever; I even want to call the doctor.

How's your health? Why don't you write to me? Write and give it to Lyova — he'll send it through the work association.

The books have been printed amazingly well.

Osya spends the whole day at "Vechernyaya zvezda".[3] The paper's doing brilliantly.

I've been in a wretched mood all the time. The German planes have cheered me up these last two days.[4]

I miss you very badly. Don't forget me.

Lilya.

Dear, beloved, brutally sweet Lilik!

From now on nobody will be able to reproach me with not doing much reading, I read your letter all the time.

I don't know if it will make me educated, but I'm already cheerful.

If I am to be considered your little puppy,[1] then I'll tell you straight — I don't envy you, I'm not much of one: my ribs are sticking out, it goes without saying that my coat's coming out in lumps, and my long mangy ear hangs down specially by my bloodshot eye to wipe away the tears.

Naturalists maintain that puppies always turn out like that if they're given away into the loveless arms of strangers.

I'm getting better disgustingly slowly.

I don't go anywhere.

I always sit three or four places away from women in case they breathe something noxious over me.

Publishing comes to my rescue. I'm at the printer's by nine. Now we're publishing the "Futurist Newspaper".[2]

Thanks for the little book.[3] By the way: I went halves with Dodya for the landscape you took, so consider it a present from me.[4]

I wrote two poems in your notebook straightaway.

I'm sending you the big one (which you liked), "Our March",[5] in the newspaper, but here's the little one:

"Spring.
The town has taken off its winter clothes.
The snows' mouths are watering.
Spring has come again
Stupid and garrulous as a cadet."
V. Mayakovsky.

Of course I'm getting carried away.

More than anything else in the world I want to come to you. If you go off somewhere without seeing me you'll be bad.

Write, my child.

Be healthy my sweet Luchik!

I kiss you, your dear good kind
Volodya.

I'm not kissing anyone else or sending my regards to anyone in this letter — it's one of the "to you, Lilya" cycle. How happy I was to write on "Man" "to you, Lilya"![6]

50

Dear and sweet
Lilik
Study the attached drawing:
Graph of letters received from Lilya:

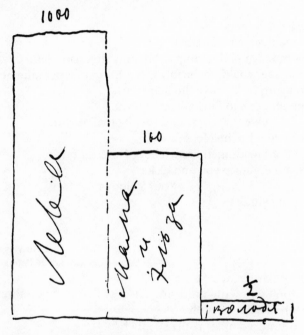

[Words in the drawing: Lyova, Mama and Elsa, Volodya]

Is that clear?[1]

From all this:
Schematic depiction of Lyova's face

51

Schematic depiction of Volodya's face

So write, Lilyonok!
I feel relatively abominable.
I'm bored. I'm ill. I'm angry. My only diversion (and even that I wish you could see, you'd be terribly merry). I'm playing kinemo. I wrote the screenplay myself. I have the main part.
I've given parts to Burlyuk and Lyova.[2]
   I want to come and see the two of you.
I can't write, I'm in a foul mood.
I've started reading in French out of affectation.
I kiss and embrace you and Oska.
       Your Volodya.
Write, my child!

†10 Mayakovsky to Lili.
Letter from Moscow to Petrograd, April 1918.

Dear but hardly sweet to me Lilik!
Why don't you write me a single word? I've sent you three letters and I haven't had a line in reply.
Is four hundred miles really so much?
You shouldn't do this, my child. It doesn't suit you!
Please write, I get up every day with the melancholy thought: "What's up with Lilya?".
Don't forget that besides you I don't need anything and nothing interests me.
I love you.
I escape in the kinemo.[1] I've put an awful lot of effort into it.
My eyes ache, the scum.
Next Monday I'm going in for an operation. They're going to cut my nose and throat.[2] When (if!) you see me, I'll be all neat and clean and newly repaired. A steam-engine straight out of the shed!
The cinematograph people say my acting skill is unprecedented. They tempt me with speeches, glory and money.

If you don't write again it'll be clear that as far as you're concerned I've croaked, and I'll start getting myself kitted out with a little grave and some worms. So write!

I kiss you

　　　　　your Volodya

I kiss Osya!

Regards to Shura and Jacques.[3]

11. Lili to Mayakovsky.
Letter from Petrograd to Moscow, April 1918.

Dear little puppy, I haven't forgotten you.

I miss you terribly and I want to see you.

I'm ill: every day I have a temperature of 38; my lungs are ruined.

The weather's very good and I go out a lot.

I'm envious of you with your filming — Yakov Lvovich[1] promised to get me into the cinematograph too.

I've got some very pretty new things. I've papered my room with black and gold wallpaper; I've put a red damask curtain on the door. This all sounds luxurious, and it really is rather pretty.

I'm in a dreadful mood because of my health. To cheer myself up I've bought some red stockings, and I put them on when no one can see — very jolly!!

After the operation, if you feel all right and if you want to — come and visit. You can stay with us.

I terribly love getting your letters, and I terribly love you. I never take your ring[2] off, and I've hung up your photograph in a frame.

Write to me and come and visit, only don't put your operation off in order to do so.

I embrace you, Volodenka, my child, and I kiss you.

　　　　　　Lilya.

*12. Mayakovsky to Lili.
Letter from Moscow to Petrograd, April 1918.[1]

Dear and extraordinary Lilyonok!

Don't be ill, for the sake of Christ! If Oska isn't going to look after you and carry your lungs (at this point I had to stop and dive into your letter to see how it's spelt: I wanted to put "lugns") wherever they have to go, then I'll bring a forest of conifers into your flat and I'll have a sea set up in Oska's study according to my own instructions. And if your thermometer climbs any higher than thirty six degrees, I'll break all his paws off.

53

By the way you can put down my fantasies about coming to you to my general state of dreaminess. If my affairs, nerves and health go on like this your little puppy will fall down in the gutter belly upwards, jerk his little legs weakly and give up his gentle soul to God.

But if a *miracle* happens, I'll be with you in about two weeks!

I'm finishing the kinemo picture.[2] I'm off now to the studio to try on Frelikh's trousers.[3] In the last act I'm a dandy.

I'm not writing any poetry, though I'd really like to write something full of emotion about a horse.[4]

By the summer I'd like to make a film with you.[5] I'd write a screenplay for you.

I'll develop this plan when I arrive. For some reason I'm convinced you'll agree. Don't be ill. Write. I love you my dear little warm sun.

I kiss Oska.

I embrace you till your bones crunch

your Volodya

[Word in the drawing: Me]

P.S. (pretty, isn't it?) Forgive me for writing on such elegant paper. It's from the Pittoresk[6] and they absolutely can't survive without elegance.

It's just as well they haven't gone in for cubism in the toilet yet, or I'd really be in torment.

13. Lili to Mayakovsky.
Letter from Petrograd to Moscow, April 1918.

Dear Volodenka,

Please, my child, write a screenplay for the two of us, and try to make it possible for us to shoot it in a week or two. Then I'll come to Moscow specially.

Let me know whether it's possible, and send your answer with Miklashevsky.[1]

I terribly want to be in a film with you.

I feel terribly sorry that you're ill. I'm feeling better now — I've put on five pounds.

I want to see you.

I kiss you

your Lilya.

If you don't catch Miklashevsky, send an answer with Liberman,[2] who's leaving on Friday.

†14. Mayakovsky and Osip to Lili.
Note, Petrograd October 1918.

You dear swine Lilyonochek!

(the swine is from Osya because you're late)

Oska's off to the Soviet and I'm off to the theatre. *You absolutely must come.* I think the rehearsal starts at 9. It's absolute bedlam in the theatre, they haven't done a f.... thing.[1]

We kiss you

your

your

P.S. Oska and I won't spoil before the holiday, because thanks to the corned beef we're salted right through.

V.M.

*15. Mayakovsky to Lili.
Letter from Petrograd to Moscow, March-April 1919.[1]

Beloved Lilyonok!

I miss you dazzlingly. I'm putting all my efforts into trying to get away no later than Sunday. Getting a ticket from here is a terribly long drawn out affair.

I love and I kiss you

your
fussing
like a dog
Puppy

Dear Lilik,

I telephoned you at 2 and at 3 and I called in, but alas. Unfortunately I can't wait any longer. I've got to be drawing[1] at half past four. I'm off to get something to eat. I'll phone from the Adelgeyms.[2] I kiss you

Shchen

Ask Lyova as soon as he arrives to phone me without fail. I very much ask him to do it first thing tomorrow.[3]

Vol.

Lichika I'm going for tickets and to Central Press[1] about the books; just in case (going to court),[2] I'm leaving a Kerenka.[3] I'll phone between 12.00 and 1.00, but I don't know how I'll get on about the tickets.

I kiss you, yours as far as the tail.

Puppy

Thursday

I went to see Vera Vasilevna[2] — she almost burst into tears of joy when she saw me. She lives and dreams of being back in Moscow.

Make sure the butter isn't spoilt, it's salted but not clarified.

Levidov[3] has just spoken to Aleksandri[4] — he promised to do everything necessary. It really would be great to get to London!!

Now I'm off to look for braces and books.

My dear puppies and cats!

I'm sending some books — I don't know if they're any good.

A dozen razor-blades.

There aren't any other braces in the whole of Riga. This is the only sort of Havana cigars they have; they say they're very good.

Rubber mugs in three sizes. Any left over you can give to the poor.

I met Aleksandri's wife in the street, I'm going to see her this evening.

How I envy everyone who will see you on Saturday![5]

Do you miss me?

I kiss you, I kiss you.

Lilya

Osik, Volodik, don't show anyone my letters. You can read extracts aloud to anyone who's interested.

19. Lili to Mayakovsky.
Letter from Riga to Moscow, 15 October 1921.

I kiss you, Puppy, obviously nothing's going to come of my attempts to go on further and I'll be in Moscow in about two weeks.

Vera Geltser's Fifi[1] has given birth to two puppies — they're tiny, black with white patches. They play together all day long. I kiss them on their little tummies and their little noses. Yesterday I saw three identical fat yellow dachshunds on leads. As you see I haven't forgotten you. I got your little letter today — it's unsatisfactory in every respect: it doesn't go into enough detail and you don't kiss me much. If you're going to send letters by post, address them to: Hotel Bellevue, room No. 32, or Hirschberg, 1, Alexander Street.[2] In my name.

I've been given a little room, on the sunny side. I've made friends with the floorman and the maid, so my room's nice and hot.

My sweet, my little one!

I go to the cinematograph and the cafés.

What news is there in Moscow? How are you getting on with the laureate?[3] There aren't any rubber basins here.[4]

I kiss you.

Your faithful Kitty Lilya

*20 Mayakovsky to Lili.
Letter from Moscow to Riga, 17 October 1921.

Dear, sweet and remarkable Kitty

Thank you for the letter and the presents. But if you're going to send so much you'll be left without a bean yourself. We therefore categorically forbid you to do so.

My life is monotonous and boring. On Thursday I went to Lyova's, on Friday I heard Menshoy[1] (it went off well), and on Saturday and Sunday I sat at home since we had Vinokur,[2] Levidov, Krichevsky[3] and Menshoy over. They all had dinner with us on Sunday. I'm really glad you liked Moscow.[4]

Write.

I kiss you terribly

your Shchen

17/X

21. Lili to Mayakovsky.
Letter from Riga to Moscow, 18-20 October 1921.[1]

18.X.21

Volosik, my sweet, try to arrange a trip to London for me through Anatoly Vasilevich.[2] Here they don't have the right to give me one: it has to come from Moscow. It turns out that I went about the whole thing the wrong way.

I'm sending this letter simple, registered and by courier, to make sure it gets through.

I kiss you, my puppy

your

(On the back:)

20.X.21

I'm sending you ten boxes of sprats, three boxes of oatmeal, four pounds of tea, two pounds of coffee, one pound of cocoa, five pounds of chocolate, two pounds of sweets. Don't forget to collect the parcel, and make sure it's got everything in it. The oatmeal is boiled in milk: 2½ glasses of milk to a glass of oatmeal. My parcels are very uninteresting, but there isn't any interesting food here, and luxury objects are unbearably expensive.

The courier has just arrived from Moscow. I'm shaken that there was no letter for me!! In the whole of my time here I've received one lousy little letter from you in total, Volodya! All right! So much the better!

58

Dear, dear, dear

Lisik

You went away a terribly long time ago, and you write terribly little, and I miss you terribly. I have no news, not even the tiniest! Starting on Sunday I spent three days lying around, I had the tiniest little dose of influenza, but today and yesterday my temperature is 36.2 and I'm taking up activity again. Lying around was very pleasant: Osya fattened me up, Lyova came round and worried, my sisters sped over like storm-clouds and dispersed in half an hour, but I didn't care a cat's whisker (although I've now grown not only whiskers but even a beard!) and read Shchepkina-Kupernik.[1]

The most interesting event is that on 6 November a dog show is opening in the zoological gardens. I'm going to move there. Oska is already talking about getting a little setter. But I really don't know how we can go and look at puppies without you!?

Today I hope to receive your beloved and sweet letter.

Don't forget your puppy please. Write!

20/X 21.

[Words in the drawing: Yours with paws (I tripped over my own paws) V. Shchen.]

My dear, my sweet and remarkable Lilyok!

I was expecting a letter as early as Saturday and today's already Monday — no letter. Write and send it through the diplomatic courier too: to Gay[1] for me. I live so without events, so without details that it's even disgusting. My business with the laureate was going well, but now it's going so lamentably that words fail me. I'm drawing a lot and conscientiously.[2] Yesterday I went to Press House to watch Foregger[3] — Lyova had sung his praises and so had our foreigners.[4] Lunacharsky was there, and the Flaxes.[5] It was boring rubbish. From Press House Gay, Levidov, Vinokur, Krichevsky, German[6] and I went to the Stall.[7] I

59

couldn't stand it and to my shame I ran away after five minutes. There you have it, my independent relaxation!

Every day I miss you very, very much. I've started writing. I'm making some sort of headway with the prologue.[8] I think Vinokur is leaving today, and Krichevsky intends to leave on Thursday. They'll give you "eye-witness impressions". Only God forbid that they should "lie like eye-witnesses".

Write soon, and if you don't go to England, come back soon. What is there there? A grey cat came round on Saturday and scratched us all.

Your Shchen from head to tail and back again. I kiss you 32 million times a minute.

Kitten, I kiss you; but there's nothing to write about. I'm very eager to get your letters, but there aren't any. Arvatov[9] and I are appearing and fighting for Futurism. Our mugs are bloodied, but our side is winning.

Kitty, I kiss you once again

Your Osya.

† 24. Mayakovsky to Lili.
Letter from Moscow to Riga, 26-27 October 1921.

My dear, my sweet, my beloved, my adored Lisik!

If you give letters to the couriers, you have to leave them unsealed, and it's terribly unpleasant to think of outsiders reading something tender. I'm taking the Vinokurian opportunity[1] to write you a real letter. I miss you, I pine for you — and how — I fret (today especially!) and I think only of you. I don't go anywhere, I loiter from corner to corner, I look into your empty cupboard — I kiss your photographs and your kitten signatures. I howl often, I'm howling now. I so, so much want you not to forget me! Nothing can be more melancholy than life without you. Don't forget me for the sake of Christ, I love you a million times more than all the others together do. I'm not interested in seeing anyone, I don't want to talk to anyone except you. The most joyful day of my life will be the day you return. Love me, my child. Take care of yourself, child, rest — write and tell me if you need anything. I kiss you, kiss you, kiss you, kiss you, kiss you, kiss you, kiss you, kiss you, kiss you, kiss you, kiss you, kiss you, kiss you, kiss you, kiss you and kiss you.

Your

26/X 21.

If you don't write anything about yourself, I'll go mad.

Don't forget me.
Love me.

Today I've just received your "trip" letter, I'll do everything a loving Shchen can do. I'll write how things work out in detail on a separate sheet.[2] For the time being I have little hope. Now it's 27/X. Lilyok, do you receive my letters?

I write to you with every train, addressed to Legation of the Russian Soviet Federal Socialist Republic, to Vinokur, for you. When Vinokur was here I just wrote Legation of R.S.F.S.R., official Brik — if you haven't got them, find them. Now I'll add Bellevue 32.

Your Shchen

I'm sending you a bit of money for perfume.

Kitty send some of your things here (some perfume or something), I want to look at the things every day and think that you'll come.

I kiss you, I kiss you

Your

Write a lot and in detail

Your Shchenit.

25. Mayakovsky to Lili.
Letter from Moscow to Riga, 26-27 October 1921.[1]

Dear and sweet Lilyatik!

Here is a detailed account of the situation as regards a trip on official business.

1) I have just (25^2) telephoned Anatoly Vasilevich. He couldn't see me as he was leaving for Petrograd for three or four days. And I don't think he would have done anything for me anyway. Besides, arranging official

business through him would have meant more fuss going on for weeks, and it's extremely unlikely that anything would have come of it.

2) I went off to Rabis[3] and explained the nature of your trip; and I received from them the following request: to comrade Leonidov, People's Commissariat for External Trade. The Moscow Regional section of the Union of Art Workers requests that the artist, L.Yu. Brik, at present working at the trade delegation of the R.S.F.S.R. in Riga, be sent on official business to London. The Moscow Regional section of the Union of Art Workers, taking advantage of comrade Brik's trip abroad, has entrusted her with the task of familiarising herself with the organisation of and inspecting the crafts exhibition, and clarifying the question of the nature and possibility of the exchange of works of artistic production in connection with the organisation by the economic section of associations for artistic production (No. 9387). Chairman, M.Yu.

If you go to London, you'll have to make enquiries about these questions. Of course this isn't an official trip, just a request. Rabis can't arrange an official trip.

3) The People's Commissariat for External Trade handed me two telegrams in sealed packets, the first: "London. Soviet Government Delegation. Krasin.[4] Telegraph agreement transfer worker Riga office artist Brik London stop No. 3104/10367." If Krasin telegraphs his agreement (and after all he promised you), then they'll transfer you. So that the telegram reaches Krasin himself, so that they insist on an affirmative answer, I'm handing this packet to Levidov, who's leaving tomorrow, the 27th, for London (unfortunately not through Riga!) and has given me his solemn vow to do everything he can.

The second telegram: "Riga External Trade Representative Yuzbashev.[5] Communicate Krasin agreement transfer Brik London 3105/10366." I'm sending this telegram to you with Vinokur. Decide yourself whether to send it straight on to London or to wait for Levidov's arrival there (he should be about ten days getting there). If you decide to send this telegram earlier, then write first to Krasin requesting that he confirm the trip, and secondly write to your mother and get her to check whether Krasin has got your letter and to get Shvets[6] to mention you. Just in case, Vinokur is bringing you another letter from Gay to Yuzbashev; read it, check through it, and if it's of any use (and I think it will be), then hand it to him.

That, Lilyatik, is all that a man can do. I think it's "something". If you need something else, write in detail.

I kiss you, my child, your Shchen.

If nothing comes of this, then remember every second that I'm standing paws spread on the station waiting for you, as soon as you arrive I'll take you in my paws and carry you around for two weeks without putting you down.

I kiss you and kiss you. All yours Shchen — I kissed your signature because I don't have a photograph.

27/X

I'm writing at Vinokur's. Oska's looking for Krichevsky, he's got to give him a letter.

Shchen

26. Lili to Mayakovsky and Osip.
Letter from Riga to Moscow, 27 October 1921.

I write to you with every courier. I kiss you! My dears! My beloved ones! My own ones! Lights of my life! My little suns! My little kittens! My little puppies! Love me! Don't betray me! If you do I'll tear off all your paws!!

Your kitty Lilya

27. Lili to Mayakovsky.
Letter from Riga to Moscow, end of October 1921.

Dear Volodenka, unfortunately I can't send you anything, since the couriers don't take things. They're even refusing to take letters — I'll have to send them by post.

One part of my programme I fulfil conscientiously: I go to the cinematograph every day. As for the other part . . . I don't think I'll go anywhere!!

Find out whether Grzhebin[1] has left, and if he has, where for, and will he be in Riga?

I want to print "The Flute"[2] here. Send me permission for the importation of five thousand copies.

Did you get my parcels? Were the cigars good?

Tell Oska that if he doesn't write, then I shan't either.

Don't forget me, Shchenik, and remember what I asked you about. Wait for me please!

I love you, I embrace you, I kiss you,

Your Lilya

My beloved Shchenik! Don't cry because of me! I love you terribly strongly and forever! I'll come without fail! I'd come now if I wasn't ashamed to. Wait for me!

Don't betray me!!!

I'm terribly afraid of that. I am faithful to you absolutely. I now know lots of people here. I even have some admirers, but there's not one of them I like to even the slightest degree. By comparison with you all of them are fools and freaks! After all, you're my beloved Shchen, so how could I like them? Every evening I kiss the bridge of your nose! I don't drink at all! I don't want to. In a word, you'd be satisfied with me.

My nerves have had a good rest. When I arrive I'll be in a good mood.

Thank you, my own one, for all the trouble you went to — it's possible it may be of use to me, though I now think that it'll all be arranged anyway. I'll stay on here another month. If I don't go in a month — take me back again.

Send me registered letters at my aunt's address: 1, Alexander Street, flat 8, Hirschberg, for me.

I yearn for you constantly.

Write some poetry for me.

I can't send any of my things, since I have bought absolutely nothing — it's all very dear. Thank you for the money for perfume. You silly! Why didn't you buy some in Moscow! Here it's absolutely impossible to get foreign ones! And if you can they're incredibly expensive.

Did you get the rubber tooth-mugs? And are the cigars good? Write by post. Not everything gets through with the couriers.

I wrote with every courier.

I got a telegram from Misha[1] that money had been sent to me. I wonder how much. I'll write to Lyova separately at his own address.

I kiss you from head to paws. Are you shaving your head?

Your, your, your

Lilya

No. 1   30/X

My dear and sweet Lilyatik!

All these days I've been terribly worried about you. There have been no letters. I expected one with Monday's train. No. Finally Gay brought one today. A letter in which you write about a parcel and say that it's not allowed to send anything. A letter without a date. On account of which I don't understand a thing. Let's agree in the first place to write the date on each letter, and then to write a number so that we can tell whether anything's got lost.

In addition to that I'm very dissatisfied with you: you write with terribly little detail. What are you doing? Where do you go? Write more, kitten.

Write whether you got my last letter about the trip, and whether Vinokur told you everything about us and from us.

I'll find out about Grzhebin tomorrow.

I live in exactly the same way. Today is Sunday, it's 8 o'clock in the evening, and I've spent the whole time drawing; later I'll go to Lunacharsky's lecture.[1] And that's all.

Write, my child.

I kiss you, I kiss you,

I kiss you. And I'm waiting.

All yours

Dear kitten!

You're a little swine. I've written you a whole 3 letters, and you haven't
$\equiv$
written me a single one! and you even threaten to stop writing to me altogether. I don't understand any of it. And I'm not going to write anything until you write to me.

Nevertheless I kiss you

Osya

Volodik and Lyovochka, go halves and send me through Gay a million roubles' worth of Soviet postage stamps. There's a dealer-collector here, who will pay a very great deal for them. Buy stamps in all the denominations that exist, in identical quantities of each denomination — so that there are full sets.[2] Do this as quickly as possible. If you're in funds, send them to a greater value, if you're hard up, then less.[3]

I kiss you warmly.

Lilya

Let this be your birthday present to me.

No. 2

My dear and sweet little Lichik!

I'm still grieving — there are no letters from you. Today I'll go and see Menshoy — maybe some have come. I'd terribly like to appear before you suddenly and see how you live. But alas. I get a little consolation out of assuring myself that maybe you haven't forgotten me and it's just that your letters don't get through. So write, Lilyonok!

The sculptor, Zhukov,[1] has arrived from Vladivostok and brought a collection of articles by Chuzhak[2] (mainly old ones) and a newspaper, the Far Eastern Telegraph, in which there's a big article by Chuzhak about Sosnovsky.[3] Chuzhak sent me a fee for the materials I sent him.[4] Zhukov is having dinner with us today.

I seem to have a tiny bit of news. Yesterday the man Rita[5] was talking about turned up (from the Kharkov Regional Political Enlightenment Section), and he wants to take me to Kharkov for three evenings.[6] The terms are good. If he doesn't change his mind today (he's also supposed to be coming to dinner), then next week on Thursday or Friday (so that I manage to get your dear letter) I'll leave for Kharkov for about 8 or 10 days. I'll have a rest and do some writing. I have a fantastic amount of work at the moment and it's very difficult.

Needless to say I'll make sure Oska gets fed, and I'll leave him Lyova and Annushka[7] as nannies. Write, my little sun.

I love you. I'm waiting

and I kiss you and kiss you

your

2/XI 21.

I still can't find anything out about Grzhebin! There's no one in at his place.

Of course I'll write to you from every station if I go away. You write too. I'll arrange to get them sent on.

I kiss you, I kiss you, I kiss you, I kiss you.

32. Lili to Mayakovsky and Osip.
Letter from Riga to Moscow, 2 November 1921.

2.XI.21

You mangy little beasts! Puppies and kittens! I'm writing! I'm writing! I'm writing! And you, you devils, don't receive anything?!

I write with every courier and almost every day by post! I'm in despair that nothing gets through! I sent you a parcel through the delegation. Did you get it? Make some enquiries!

Tomorrow I'm sending some tinned food, some chocolate biscuits, cocoa, coffee, tea.

Comrade Yastrebov will also bring you some chocolate, and if he'll take it a bottle of orange vodka.

Tell Lyova that I've written to him several times.

I wrote you very detailed and tender letters. I could weep that they didn't get through.

Send me official permission for the importation of books into Russia. I wrote to you about that. Write whether you got that letter or not, if you didn't I'll write the whole thing again.

I thanked you and kissed you for the flowers. I bought myself some perfume.

Write by post!! At this address: Riga, 1, Alexander Street, flat 8, Hirschberg, for me. And use the couriers as well.

Misha sent me ten English pounds. Nika is in Berlin.[1] I've already written about all this in detail.

I love you and I pine without you and I miss you terribly.

It's not so boring here now, as I know a lot of people; and I wrote about that as well!

Write whether you got even one detailed letter. I shall now write in detail only when someone can take it for me, but by post and with the couriers I'll write a few words just in case.

I am behaving irreproachably!

Love me!

Don't forget me!

Don't betray me! Write to me about everything!

Terribly yours till death Kitty-Lilya

I kiss all your little paws, your coats, the bridges of your noses, your little tails, your fur, your skulls!

33. Lili to Mayakovsky and Osip.
Letter from Riga to Moscow, beginning of November 1921.

My dears, my own, my sweet ones! At last I've received real, affectionate letters from you! I thought you'd already completely stopped loving me!

Volosik! You were ill?! It's terrible that I wasn't there! Did Osik buy you grapes? Are you completely fit yet? Wear your fur coat when you go out!!!

Give my regards to all the puppies at the dog show.[1]

Why didn't you get a letter on Saturday? I send one with every courier.

I live well; I'm losing weight; I'm in a better mood now, since I can see that I love you horribly terribly, and that you love me; I don't do anything — I go to the cinema, the people I know aren't too bad: I'm in great demand, but no one's proposed to me; Mrs Vinokur has taught me how to play chess and I get mated every minute.

Did you receive my parcel with the oatmeal etc? And the letter about the postage-stamps? And the letter about Osya Volk?[2] Phone him on 2-03-03, and tell him that his sisters absolutely insist their parents come to Riga!

I didn't get a letter with the last courier! Is this an accident or a swinish trick?

I get letters from Elsa and Mama.

Mama thinks I'll manage to make the trip.

Elsa and André[3] get on very well.

It's terribly boring without you!!!!!

I love you from your heads to your tails.

Write whether you got a setter, or else I'll bring one from England!

I feel grown up and independent, but I don't like it!!

Don't forget me!

Don't betray me!

Love me!

Give my regards to Annushka, Lyova, and the little piggy.[4]

Don't show anyone my letters.

I'm terribly happy that you're writing, Volosik. You absolutely must write something for my return! And Osik, that you and Arvatich[5] are winning — that's great!

Oslit! Don't fall in love with Lyubochka!!![6]

Volosit! Take care! Where are you living — on Myasnitskaya or in Lubyanskiy Passage???!![7] frightened!!!!!

I kiss all your little places sweetly,

your Lilya

Don't forget to collect the parcels from me and from Mama.

†34. Mayakovsky to Lili.
Letter from Moscow to Riga, 6 November 1921.

No. 3

My dear and sweet little Lisyok!

Yesterday I at last received two of your letters. One was angry (the one you sent three copies of — my luck was in, I got all three!), but the other one was sweet and nice, the one in which you ask whether Oska brought me grapes. In both of them you ask why I don't write. Silly kitten, how can you imagine that I might not write to you even once?! I write to you with every courier without fail, and sometimes I send letters with people too. You also write that you send something with every courier, but I hardly get a damn thing: out of the letters you list I haven't received either the one about stamps, or the one about Wolves.[1] In particular I'm very impatient to get an answer to the letter I sent with Vinokur.[2] Why don't you put the date on your letters and the number (did you get my letter in which I asked you to do so?).[3] Then at least we could always know how

69

many letters were sent but not received (my No. 3 means the third letter since Vinokur's departure). So far we haven't received a parcel either from you or from your mother. Lilyok! It seems Gay is leaving the People's Commissariat for Foreign Affairs, and so, dear kitten, if you can, write two copies of your letters, one through Gay (I think I can go on receiving them there even after he's left, and for the time being he's going to call in himself) and one through Lyova.

I spend the whole day thinking about one thing — will there be a letter soon, will there be a letter soon — that's why I have such a "Postal" style (I don't know if I'll manage to send a letter tomorrow (Monday), it's the anniversary[4] and the couriers' department will probably be closed).

I have no news. I live quietly, I love you and I wait. I lived the whole time with Oska, but the last few days I've spent at my place, because Mukha[5] has arrived and she had to be found somewhere to sleep so as not to turn Lyova out of his room — now Mukha's gone and I'll move back.

I kiss, I kiss and I kiss you, my wondrous kitten

your devil[6]

Shchen   6/XI 21

35. Mayakovsky to Lili.
Letter from Moscow to Riga, 6 (?) November 1921.[1]

No. 4
Dear and sweet Lilyonochek!

Lyova has just received the stamp letter. We'll send them. (If Lyova can get hold of them — he's just going now) How are things with you? Why don't you write about yourself? I kiss you all yours

My life doesn't change at all! Twice there was no courier. Along with this letter I'm sending you another full one.

6.XI.21

Volosik! Don't be sad, my puppy! I shan't forget you — I shall return without fail. I'm waiting for a telegram from Mama about the visa. If only I could get the trip over and come back!

Don't betray me in Kharkov!!!

Today I fondled a remarkable little Basavryuk[1] and I thought of you, and stroked it for you too — it wagged its tail terribly quickly and for a terribly long time. In general there are a very large number of dogs here and they're all wonderful!

Did you get my letter and parcel through Yastrebov?

In the cinema I've seen "20,000 Leagues under the Sea", "Lasso of Death", "A Woman's Revenge" and so forth . . . see what I mean!!

My acquaintances try all sorts of things to entertain me. It isn't worth talking about them — they're nice people. I'm waiting for London — can it really be no better there?

Everyone's looking after me. I have masses of flowers. I've already written that I'm absolutely faithful to you both.

Write and tell me whether Yastrebov gave you the liquid?

I feel as if I've been living here a year!

Write in detail about your appearances in Kharkov and everything to do with Kom-fut.[2] There are absolutely no Kom-futs here!

Can it really be that none of the letters I send by post get through? I wrote such a mass of them!!

I embrace you my little pup and sweetly, sweetly kiss you.

Your kitty Lilya

You swine of a kitten! Again you haven't written!

How do you get on without me? I get on very badly without you! Absolutely boo-hoo-hoo! There aren't any little kittens in the whole of Riga! There are lots of puppies but no kittens! What a shame!

I kiss your little tail, your wife

71

I sent off one parcel a long time ago. And three parcels just recently. For one of them call to see comrade Granik in the press department of the People's Commissariat for Foreign Affairs in Oska's name. The others — through the delegation. One's from me addressed to Osya; the other's addressed to Lyova from comrade Orlov.

37. Lili to Mayakovsky and Osip.
Letter from Riga to Moscow, 11 November 1921.

11.XI.21

My sweet little children, the courier didn't come yesterday, and I'm grief-stricken at not having a letter. Try using the post — <u>not</u> registered.

By the way, Volosik, are you going to Kharkov?

Yesterday I met a Jewish Futurist — a poet (I've forgotten his name).[1] They're soon going to have a collection out which will contain an article, in Yiddish, "about Mayakovsky". This evening he's coming over to get "Everything",[2] and he's going to read me his poetry. He promised to introduce me to the whole group. And today I'm going to eat at the Latvian Futurist dining-hall:[3] I'll try to find out about the Latvian Futurists. It's a pity I've wasted so much time, but Vinokur doesn't know a damn thing!

Did you receive the other cuttings? I'm sending you books: unfortunately odd volumes, since you can't get sets here. Elsa sent some music from Paris — <u>don't lose it</u>, I haven't played it yet. I've got a few more books — I'll read them first and then send them. I'm sending ten pounds of granulated sugar and two pounds of cocoa. Write, for God's sake, when you get something, otherwise it's boring sending it!!

As regards the visa — nothing new so far!!! . . .

Yesterday at the Latvian opera I heard "Cavalleria rusticana".

I went to the circus — it was a wonderful bill! Sweet little horses and remarkable clowns. I fed the little horses and ponies sugar. They have very sweet little lips and nostrils. Only the ponies bite, the beasts.

I love you frightfully and dreadfully!

Don't stop loving me!!

Your

Send me somehow <u>quickly</u> "Tvorchestvo", Chuzhak's articles[4] and "My Sister Life",[5] Kruchonykh and something else which would be interesting for abroad — something Kom-fut, of course. And, if you can, some fat cigarettes — they have terrible rubbish here.

What did Zhukov have to say? Write to me in detail!
Send articles to "Novyy put"[6] — you must! They pay in provisions!
Osik! Ask in the Cheka' how things are with Iosif Borisovich Fridman.

*38. Mayakovsky, Osip and Lev Grinkrug to Lili.
Letter from Moscow to Riga, 12 November 1921.

Dear kitten,
    Congratulations.[1] We kiss you and kiss you.

I drew them all. Shchen.
And I'm the one that kisses you most.

[Word in the drawings: Lev]

*39. Mayakovsky to Lili.
Letter from Moscow to Riga, 12 November 1921.[1]

No. 5
Dear Lilyok! Sweet Lilyok! Remarkable Lilyok!
    At last I've received your loving letters and immediately my heart felt at ease. (I've been walking around looking so gloomy these last few days that everyone's been asking me what's up with me. I drifted around cafés and various acquaintances' places, and came back gloomier still, but now I've calmed down a bit.) I was particularly alarmed that you wrote nothing about yourself. I was convinced that you <u>had reasons not to write about yourself.</u>

    I had a remarkable time on your birthday. I spent the whole day thinking of Kitty. I didn't go to any cafés, I just visited Nadezhda Robertovna's place[2] and drank your health in total solitude. Then I

73

walked around the avenues for a long time, on Tver Boulevard there was a telescope for some reason and I looked at the enormous moon for some time. I asked them to point it at Riga — they said they couldn't.

Kharkov's been postponed for some reason.

I'm writing badly — it's difficult.[3]

I kiss you, kiss you, kiss you, kiss you, kiss you, kiss you and kiss you. Write, write and write.

All yours

12/XI 21.

40. Lili to Mayakovsky and Osip.
Letter from Riga to Moscow, 14 November 1921.

14.XI.21   3

My dear boys, thank you for the postage stamps, but there are obviously some missing, since the quantities are quite uneven — maybe the second half will complement the first.

Yesterday I got a letter from Mama — she hopes to receive a visa for me any day. I've already been here a month!! The ten pounds I received turned out to be not from Misha but from Mama, but from Misha all I got was a telegram saying that money had been sent, but the money itself didn't arrive; yesterday I telegraphed him to say "Geld nicht erhalten".

I've put aside money for the trip, but I've spent almost all the rest, and you know I haven't the slightest idea what on, since I haven't bought a single thing apart from fifteen pairs of silk stockings and a pair of revolting shoes which I can't wear.

For God's sake write and tell me what you've received of the things I've sent: I sent a few parcels of sugar etc.; chocolate, a letter and a few other things through Yastrebov, books and a letter through Tennenbaum, who works in the Komintern. It's terribly miserable sending things and not knowing whether they get through!!!

I met some Jewish Futurists — they're great fellows. I visit them at the Jewish Arbeiterheim.[1] One of them, Livshits,[2] is translating "Man" into Yiddish and writing a big article "about Mayakovsky". They forced me to recite "The Flute" to them and went mad with delight about it; in a few days I'm going to read them "A Cloud" and so on.

I'm going to visit the Latvians tomorrow: the Jews gave me a letter for the main Latvian Futurist.[3]

I've been to the operetta — I now intend to go often.

I asked the Jews to transcribe something for me in Latin letters — then I'll send it.

<u>You must</u> send me permission for the importation of books into Russia — I think we'll manage to print anything we like here, and without having to pay immediately!

You absolutely must send me photographs of the posters, the posters themselves,[4] <u>"Everything Written"</u>, "Mystery", "150,000,000", "My Sister Life", Aseyev,[5] "Tvorchestvo", "Iskusstvo kommuny".[6] Please! Send them! Ask Velikovsky when comrade Galop[7] is travelling, and send them through him to comrade Alter,[8] in my name.

Send Volodya's cinema photograph[9] — it's in my drawer in Oska's desk.

I can't end up short of money, because everyone is offering to lend me as much as I want.

I'm not particularly "independent", since people are very solicitous about me.

If it weren't for my <u>terrible</u> pining for you, it would even be entertaining!

Every little dog and every little cat drive me to tears.

Write! Write! Write!

Your
Lilya

41. Lili to Mayakovsky.
Letter from Riga to Moscow, November 1921.

My little puppy! Volosit!

I very much want to be with you and I kiss you terribly!!!! And I bite the bridge of your nose.

How are your little teeth?

Are you going to Kharkov?

I am very true to you. I don't drink more than a single glass, and I do that rarely. <u>What about you?</u> I want you to love me terribly!

I stroke all the little dogs for you.

I love you definitively for my whole life.

Your Lilya

No. 6

Dear and sweet Lilyatik!

I got your letter about ponies, sugar and cocoa. I've also been at the circus and also stroked the little horses.

I'll go to Kharkov only around the 29th. Vladimir Aleksandrovich[1] was here, and he made me promise to live and eat at his place. I did promise, but I'll try to wriggle out of that tedium. The long poem[2] is advancing extremely slowly — a line a day! — I'll set aside Kharkov for writing. I live at home — it's very warm indeed — but not a single soul (regardless of sex) has crossed my threshold.

Oska and I go around together as much as we can, and all we do is talk about you (theme: the only person in the world is kitty).

He and I really are great friends. I draw and he reads me Chekhov.
Write
I kiss you 186 times
I'm waiting for you

your faithful

16/XI

My Volosyonochek! Thank you for the affectionate little letter, and for thinking about me on my birthday.

Write honestly — don't you sometimes live more easily without me? Are you never glad that I've gone away? — There's no one tormenting you! No one being capricious! No one wearing out your already worn out little nerves!

I love you, Shchenit!! Are you mine? Do you need nobody else?

I'm completely yours, my own child! I kiss all of you.

Lilya

17.XI.21   4

Dear little children!

First, about a very interesting matter: I've already written to you about the possibility of publishing books here. Yesterday I clarified the situation definitively: I spoke to a certain very important capitalist, the owner of a large printing-house; he agrees and is even very eager to publish our books at his own expense. We could publish monographs, collections, illustrated books — in hard covers, periodicals. Of course it would be good at the same time to publish a few textbooks — that would be to his advantage and to ours. He would like someone in Moscow to take exclusive responsibility for that. He proposes to supply that person with provisions and money. I would like you to agree to be that person, Volosik — in the first place it's very interesting, and in the second place it would give you the possibility of giving up the posters completely.[1] Bear in mind that this is no "bluff"!

The textbooks have also got to be privately published, without any links with the State Publishing House.

In order to get things going you need:

1) To call in at the transport and materials section of the People's Commissariat for Foreign Trade, and find out how to get permission to transport books from Riga to Moscow — for payment, of course (they'll pay in Riga).

2) To prepare the materials very thoroughly in the shape of books that are ready to be given straight to the printers.

3) To send these materials through comrade Granik, who works in the press department of the People's Commissariat for Foreign Affairs to the editorial board of the newspaper "Novyy.put" in the name of comrade Alter, who is the person who put me in touch with the publisher.

4) To work out carefully what royalties or what percentage of the profits, or a combination of both, authors should receive. (If it's difficult for you to calculate this, they'll try to do it here. In general your interests will be looked after here by comrade Alter, who is very interested in this publishing house.)

5) On what conditions would you, Volosik, agree to take this on?

It would be good to publish Mayakovsky, Khlebnikov, Pasternak and so on — as fully as possible; a collection of articles from "Iskusstvo kommuny";[2] a book under the title of "The Russian Poster" with an introductory article. In a word any book, however expensive it was to publish it.

You absolutely must find out about textbooks!

Take this very seriously, Volodik. It will give you the possibility of resting and writing.

I'm so attracted to the idea that if it works out I shan't regret the fact that I came here, even if I don't manage to get to London. In any case, I'll stay here till I get an answer from you.

———

The stamps you sent me are completely worthless if you don't send all the other values — a rouble, so many kopecks etc. In a word — find out from Olga Vladimirovna[3] what stamps have appeared since the inauguration of the R.S.F.S.R. and send them all.

[Notes in the margin:]

Am I a businesswoman?!

Ask comrade Granik if there's a parcel in Osya's name.

I'm sending books.

Write whether you've received anything. If you have, tell me precisely — what and through whom.

Give my regards to all the Komfuts and tell them that I remember them and am looking after their interests. They could also get paid in provisions.

I kiss all your paws tenderly

Your faithful Kitty Lilya

Did they allow you to publish the newspaper Krichevsky and Vinokur spoke to me about?[4]

If Regina[5] phones, give her the letter.

Has the debt to Lamanova[6] been paid? And Furmannyy Lane?[7]

If comrade Galop from the Foreign Trade Commissariat hasn't left, send me the peacock hanging. I need it badly.

Aren't you fed up yet that I ask for something in every letter?

*45. Mayakosky to Lili.
Letter from Moscow to Riga, 22 November 1921.[1]

No. 7

Dear Lilyok sweet Lilyok remarkable Lilyok beloved Lilyok

(aren't you fed up that I "repeat myself" so?)

I miss you very much, I love you very much and I can't wait for you to come.

78

We've started receiving your letters. The last one (which had bits for Shchen, Oska and Annushka) was so nice that I carry mine around with me all the time.

Yesterday Basias[2] phoned when he arrived from Riga and asked me to call in to collect books and a parcel. I ran round there like a man possessed three times, but he's never there. I'll run round again now. I think I'll also receive your old parcel today — they've already arrived from Riga but they haven't YET had time to sort through them.

My life doesn't change. I wrote a propaganda piece in four acts for the Political Enlightenment Committee of the Commissariat![3]

Foregger is staging it.[4]

I'm worried that I shan't be able to write a poem for you before you arrive.[5] I'm trying terribly hard.

Now I don't even love you but adore you.

Once it seemed to me (when the letters weren't coming) that you had left me. But after the latest letters I've bloomed. And my feelings for you are fantastic. Write. I kiss you 10000000 times.

I love you and I wait for you

your

22/XI 21.

As for permission to import books, apparently you have to talk to the State Publishing House, they won't do it for me. Sablin went.[6]

†46. Mayakovsky to Lili.
Letter from Moscow to Riga, 23 November 1921.

No. 8
23/XI 21.

Dear, dazzling and sweet Lisyonysh!

I've received your publishing letter.

I agree. I'd be happy to do only that. Today I'll go to the Commissariat for Foreign Trade and the Commissariat for Foreign Affairs and find out about the textbooks. In the next letter I'll write in detail about all the plans and possibilities. You must clarify the following

1) Who can we make an arrangement with in Moscow about the

financial side (both royalties and organisational funds etc.), and if not in Moscow, then with whom, where and how?

2) What textbooks? (Collections on the theory of poetic language are also almost textbooks!)

For the time being that's all about the publishing house.

Now about the most important thing.

In your letter to Volosit[1] you ask a series of little questions. Here are your answers:

1) I "honestly" inform you that not for a single second have I felt better without you than with you.

2) Not for a single second have I been pleased that you've gone away, but every day I grieve about it quite terribly.

3) Unfortunately no one is being capricious. For the sake of Christ come as soon as possible and be capricious.

4) My little nerves are worn out only because our mangy kitty's gone away.

5) I'm entirely yours.

6) I don't need anyone, anyone except you.

I kiss all of you, I'm all yours

 I kiss you, kiss you, kiss you,
kiss you, kiss you.

My child I'm impossibly delighted to get your letters. You write them so well that I carry them all in my waistcoat. A letter from you is a celebration, and when I've got one I walk around with my head held high as if to say look at us, we've got a letter from Kitty.

I love you I'm waiting for you. I kiss you and kiss you. Write

All yours Shchen

*47. Mayakovsky to Lili.
Letter from Moscow to Riga, 28 November 1921.[1]

Business.

No. 9

Dear and sweet Lilyonok.

Here is a report for you about the publishing house.

1) I went to Foreign Trade. Comrade Vasilev, who is responsible for importation, turned out to be an an acquaintance and promised to do all he could, but permission also depends on the Commissariat of Enlightenment (State Publishing House).

2) I went to Lunacharsky and while I was there he spoke to the State Publishing House (to Meshcheryakov),[2] there turned out to be no obstacles as far as they were concerned and Lunacharsky approved the list of books and asked Foreign Trade to give permission for importation.

3) My further plans are as follows: when I send out books to be printed I shall append each time the permit of importation.

4) The list of books proposed for publication (first series)

    1) MAF. Illustrated Journal of the Arts. Editors — V. Mayakovsky and O. Brik. Contributors — Aseyev, Arvatov, Kushner, Pasternak, Chuzhak and others.

    2) Mayakovsky. Verse collections.

    3) B. Pasternak — Lyric poetry.

    4) Book about Russian posters.

    5) Poetics (Collection of articles on the theory of poetic language).

    6) Khlebnikov: Works.

    7) Art in Production. Collection of articles.

    8) Anthology of modern literature.

Lunacharsky's directive: "I consider the idea of such a publishing house acceptable. I request you to allow the importation of books in accordance with the relevant statutes.

Lunacharsky"[3]

5) Krupskaya[4] will have to be spoken to about the textbooks. That's more difficult, but if the publishing house works out, I'll do even that.

6) So as to send out books it is necessary first here to get them into an absolutely acceptable state (as you wrote).

7) For that it is essential first to clarify the financial aspect (for organisation and for me).

8) I can speak to Granik only tomorrow.

9) I think I need (to make up for all the rest) no less than 20 mil. a month (in hard currency that's absolute peanuts).

10) For organisational expenses (typist, paper etc.) and also for paying out advances we absolutely need about 50 mil. more at the same time (also my opinion).

11) As soon as all this is clarified I'll send the books.

12) Half the money (minimum!) must be given to Kitty in Riga.

That's all the business for now
I kiss you my
    dear

        All yours   Shchen Mayak.

                                          28/XI 21.

†48. Mayakovsky to Lili.
Letter from Moscow to Riga, 28 November 1921.

No. 10

My sweet, dear and beloved Lilyonok.

I'm still your same Shchen, I spend my whole life thinking about you, I'm waiting for you and I adore you.

Every morning I come to Osya and I say "it's boring brother cat without Liska" and Oska says "it's boring brother pup without Kiska".

I received your parcel with tea, chocolate and oatmeal. Thank you my child.

I may leave for Kharkov tomorrow. I'm working at Political Enlightenment[1] and I'm rowing often with everybody. We're sending you a little through Lyova's aunt. Write, my sweet one, write, my little one, love me, my beloved one. I kiss you 150,000,000 times all yours waiting for you till death

28/XI 21

                    I love you terribly
                       terribly
                          All yours

†49. Mayakovsky to Lili.
Letter from Moscow to Riga, 28 November 1921.

No. 11

My dear Lilyonochek, my sweet Lilyonochek, my terribly beloved.

Besides you, my own one, there is no one in the world. I love you with all my soul and with all my heart. I'm waiting for you. Thank you for the tender little letters. I carry them around with me everywhere, so my side sticks out. I think I'll leave for Kharkov tomorrow. I'm glad. Otherwise I'm tired and too miserable. Come soon, my beloved. We're sending you a little. How are you living? Write. Somehow there aren't any letters again. None since the one sent through Basias. I love you, my own one. I kiss you billions of times all yours Shchenik.

28/XI 21

I kiss you, kiss you and kiss you
Yours yours yours
But are you mine?
Please!

I paid off Lamanova fully ages ago, the dacha too.
I'll finish paying Furmannyy on Saturday.

50. Lili to Mayakovsky.
Letter from Riga to Moscow, 30 November-1 December 1921.[1]

Wednesday
Volosik!

As regards the publishing house:

I've just got back from the theatre and I found your detailed letter, sent with Koltsov,[2] waiting for me. It's too late for me to see the publishing people today now, and tomorrow morning (tomorrow Thursday) I must send off this letter. I'll have to write to you definitively only on Monday.

I think they'll agree to your conditions and that you haven't asked for too much. But bear in mind that this enterprise is <u>purely commercial</u> and completely <u>privately owned</u>. Therefore I think even the textbooks must be printed without recourse to Krupskaya. Think about the textbooks (Krayevich, Malinin,[3] geography, arithmetic and so on) first, since that's the main source of income. <u>Our</u> books alone won't satisfy him. I don't know who you should talk to about this. Maybe it really ought to be done precisely through Krupskaya, in such a way that we receive in Riga an order for a particular quantity of particular textbooks. If it's simply a re-print, send a copy of the old edition and we'll send you an estimate of how much such a textbook would cost.

Think this all out soon, consult whoever's necessary and let me know the results quickly, since there's a great deal of money and a great deal of willingness to work with the R.S.F.S.R.[4] But profit is an essential condition. Work out how the writers will have to be paid — what rates.

83

Send, without delay, a book that's already ready to go to press, and with it an account: how much has to be paid to the author or authors, and how many copies of it must be printed. So that we can work out exactly how much each book will cost and what we can sell it for.

I like the list of books, only bear in mind — no politics. Since every manuscript has to go through the Latvian censorship. If I manage to see the publisher again tomorrow before I send this letter, I'll add a note. Is it correct that you're off to Kharkov now? You should settle the publishing house first. I'll see Koltsov tomorrow morning. Osyukha will have to be paid for the editing too, of course.

Thursday. I spoke to the publisher. He agrees to all your conditions. He only asks that you send a memorandum,[5] put together formally, explaining the shape you see the publishing house taking, and if possible send an order for textbooks. If nothing comes of the order for the time being, then find out from whom you can get a permit for the printing of textbooks privately, and send a copy of that permit. In a word — textbooks, textbooks, textbooks!

Send the books quickly so that we can send you an estimate of how much they're going to cost.

As soon as we receive the memorandum we're going to send the money.

You're happy. I'm very happy!

I kiss you

Osik! Mama has sent you a parcel: shoes, socks, underwear. Call in and collect it or it'll go missing.

I kiss you

†51. Mayakovsky to Lili.
Letter from Moscow to Riga, 1 December 1921.[1]

No. 11

Dear Lisyonysh, sweet Lisyonysh, remarkable Lisik and Lisit
  (Anyone would think there were a lot of you there)
Why have you gone silent again?

After the publishing letter with Basias there's not been a peep out of you again. Have you forgotten your puppies and kittens?

How are you living?

What news of England?

What news of the publishing house?

There's no need to talk about our life.

We amuse ourselves as best we can — but if you look at it closely it's all very boring. Life is only imaginable at all with you.

Once again I didn't go to Kharkov. They couldn't get me a first class ticket — they say I'll leave on Friday.

I'm having great difficulty writing. Though I'm thinking of things relatively well.

I've tried and failed to find Granik five times.

Write and tell me whether there are many numbers you haven't received of my letters.

And in general write more — your letters are a celebration.

I kiss you. All yours, waiting

I kiss you, kiss you
and kiss you

I kiss you and kiss you

1/XII 21.

*52. Mayakovsky to Lili.
Letter from Moscow to Riga, 5 December 1921.

No. 12

My dear and sweet Lisyonysh!

I'm in griefs.

Once again you don't write a damn thing. Lyova got a letter from you, but we didn't. Why, Kitty? The last one we've had is still the one through Basias.

I've had a savage couple of weeks: every day I intend to leave for Kharkov, and either there isn't a place, or there's no train, or no ticket, or no warrant, or no something else.

It's turned out harder than your trip.

They're doing Mystery in Kharkov.[1] They've already announced dates for my appearances five times, the tickets have been sold and I just can't find a way of getting there.[2]

How are the publishing plans?

For the last few days I haven't drawn a thing — I've started writing and I'd be glad to go on in this state.

I love you very much my sweet, and I miss you very very very much. I

85

am all yours. I'm waiting for you, kitten. I stroke all the cats. Write, soon, child, because I can't go on like this any more. I kiss you 10000000000000000000 times.

All yours

5/XII 21.

53. Lili to Mayakovsky and Osip.
Letter from Riga to Moscow, 8 December 1921.[1]

8.XI.21

To hell with it! I've only just found out that Dubinsky[2] is off to Russia! I shan't have time to send you anything. Only Matthias.[3]

You've probably received my second letter about the publishing house. Just in case once again: the main thing is the textbooks!

As soon as you send the publishing plan, set out in a formal manner, we'll send the money.

The publisher agrees to all conditions.

Damn all progress with the visa. I'm staying here only because of the publishing house . . .

Talk to Granik as little as possible — only what's absolutely essential.

For the publisher the main thing is profit! Best of all is orders from the government for textbooks.

Yesterday I sent three parcels: one personally to Lyovka from Alter, another to Osya from me, the third personally to Olga Vladimirovna, Head Post Office, from Orlov.

Dubinsky is an excellent fellow, give him dinners, don't let the Imaginists get hold of him. Get him to bring the "Satire Windows", "My Sister Life", Aseyev and "Mystery-Bouffe", and some fat cigarettes.

Answer quickly about the publishing house.[4]

I love you terribly, I miss you I kiss your eight little paws.
I want to kiss you!! Are you waiting?

Your faithful Lilya

12.XII.21

My little beasts!

Today I moved to Albert Street.[1] I'm waiting for the publisher's answer. Meanwhile the publisher's gone off to Berlin for 10 days! I'll have to sit and wait for him again!

Did you go to Kharkov, Volosik? Osik! Why do you write so little? I'm sitting at home since I'm bored with going out.

I'm waiting impatiently for Dubinsky. If he hasn't left yet — send him off soon and give him my regards.

As soon as the publishing business is clarified, I'm coming home. I'm sick to death of this place!

I love you!

A big kiss to all your little paws and so on.

Your

15.XII.21

Lights of my life!

Everything's changed again! Apparently I shall receive a German visa in about two weeks. I have decided to wait for it. That means I shan't get home for Christmas.

It's terrible!

Be very nice to the gentleman who gives you this letter and packet. I only met him today. He's on his way from England to feed Russian children.[1]

I'm not sending any clothes, as I think they're cheaper and better in Berlin.

I'm waiting for Dubinsky. Any publishing developments?

Volosik, did you go to Kharkov?

I yearn for you terribly.

I kiss all your little places.

Your faithful

Lilya

No. 16

Dear and sweet sweet Lilyonochek!

Yesterday (Sunday the 18th) I arrived from Kharkov and I immediately pounced on your letters, I got two sweet ones and all three business ones!

(Business on the next page!)

Did you get the letter from Kharkov No. 15?[1] I'm glad to have escaped from there — Kharkov is an absolutely terrible town. I read three times, there was quite a crowd of people.[2]

Lisyonok, I miss you terribly, what about you? I love you very much, what about you?

Don't forget me, my child, please. I am your faithful

I kiss you kiss you
and kiss you

I kiss you
and kiss you

[Page 2]

Here you are

Lisik	dear
Lisik	remarkable
Lisik	fine
Lisik	wonderful
Lisik	my little child
Lisik	marvellous
Lisik	little cat
Lisik	kitty
Lisik	little sun
Lisik	little redhead
Lisik	kitten
Lisik	little face
Lisik	sweet
Lisik	charming
Lisik	delightful
Lisik	my little one
Lisik	my beauty

Lisik	bewitching
Lisik	stunning
Lisik	fantastic
Lisik	little star

I love you

Shchen

[3rd page:]

Lilyok!

1) On Thursday I'll send both the memorandum and information about textbooks.

2) For textbooks you have to go to The Commissariat of Enlightenment on Ostozhenka Street.

3) I think I'll also get an order from David Petrovich[3] (I'll go there too tomorrow).

4) If there are orders from Political Enlightenment for posters and illustrated books, can they be published?

5) Isn't the publisher laying too much stress on textbooks?

6) Aren't our books just an unpleasant appendage to Yevtushevsky[4] for him? — and if that's the case, things aren't right.

7) <u>An important question</u> (asked by everyone): Will the Commissariat of Enlightenment have to pay <u>in gold</u>, or can we pay in roubles in the R.S.F.S.R.? Of course it would be easier to do the latter.

8) How will my books get past the Latvians? If they really want "art without any admixture", then my "collected works" won't get through, and nor will "Maf" or the book about posters.

Make more detailed enquiries about this.

9) I'll still try to send a book by Thursday (both for the printers and to estimate costs).

10) Why so much stress on textbooks, after all if he establishes a good literary publishing house (especially novels) that will also bring big profits.

On Thursday I'll send everything and weigh up everything in my mind finally.

Write.

I kiss you, your
VMayak.

With the text about posters, can we send big Rosta Window posters for them to make smaller in Riga, or should we (<u>or would it be better to</u>) do it here?

No. 17

Sweet and dear Lisyonysh!

I've only just cleared up the question of Maf. I append "In place of a memorandum". Show it to them. Answer. If they agree — how about some money?

How are you living, my dear? You've forgotten us. Even on letters you write tel. 5-06-52. But ours is 5-66-12! Poor us!

It's dull without you. I love you all the time, and I think about you all the time.

I rush like a train to the couriers.

I'm writing standing up at Rabis. I kiss you 1000000 56789 10 times.

your Your

22.XII.21

It's a terrible pity, Volosik, that Dubinsky missed you in Moscow.

Why isn't Osya living at home? And where should I address parcels and letters? I sent a letter and a little parcel through a certain Englishman. Does that mean you didn't get it? It had some tasty things in it.

I also sent three parcels by the ordinary route.

1) Personally to Olga Vladimirovna Mayakovskaya, Head Post Office, from Orlov.

2) To O.M. Brik, Vodopyanyy Lane, from Bramson.

3) To L.A. Grinkrug, from me, of which half is for Lyova, half for you. How was Kharkov?

Answer as soon as possible about the publishing house, I'm fed up of waiting!!!

Dubinsky gave me Osya's detailed letter.[1] And the books. Thank you! The photographs of the posters won't do at all — they're all old stuff! Write as soon as possible!

You've clearly quite stopped loving me and don't want me to come back.

I kiss you all the same.

Your Lilya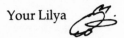

†59. Mayakovsky to Lili.
Letter from Moscow to Riga, 26 December 1921.

No. 18

My dear, My Sweet Lilyonochek

I miss you terribly, terribly. What about you?

Since my return from Kharkov I haven't received a thing from you.

Did you get my "In place of a memorandum" for the publishers? I'm waiting for an answer, I'm very eager to work on the books. Oska and I are alive. Alive and missing you.

Oska received from your mother the most amazingly long drawers, and he ties them almost under his chin — but he plays the dandy and shows off. Malkin has arrived for the Congress,[1] he's terribly insistent on sending you his regards. Zheverzheyev[2] has left after staying four weeks! with us!

Happy New Year, Lisyonysh. It's terrible without you.

What should I wish you? I don't know what you're like! For me, wish that I see you — soon! soon! soon!

I kiss you, my child, I am all yours. What about you? Somehow I've begun to have my doubts.

I kiss you and kiss you

your

26/XII 21.

28.XII.21

My little beasts!

First about business:

1) We'll pay for the textbooks in Soviet currency.

2) It's essential that we have official orders, i.e. with official stamps from The Commissariat of Enlightenment, Political Enlightenment etc.

3) a. — For the publisher our books are an appendage to Yevtushevsky.

b. — For us Yevtushevsky is an appendage to our books.

4) You can send the big windows — we'll reduce them here.

5) Don't forget that Latvia is a republic and the censorship is not that severe.

6) Stress is being laid on textbooks because an official order is something real and builds confidence.

7) I'm not going to speak about a salary of twenty million. The publisher agrees to pay sixty thousand Latvian roubles a month, but since it's customary here to conclude all deals in dollars (which fluctuate in value least), I'll get him to agree to dollars and to sending the money to you in foreign currency.

8) The main point: send orders and materials as soon as possible, so that you can start receiving money!!!

I'm waiting!

Why hasn't Olga Vladimirovna received the parcel from Alter sent at the same time as the parcels for Osya and Lyova, which they have received? Find out what's up!

I've sent another three parcels:

One: to Olga Vladmirovna from Orlov.

The second: to Osya from Bramson.

The third: to Lyova from me, of which half is for you and half for Lyova.

Why, Osik, weren't you living at home?

I sent a remarkable little parcel through one of the Nansen Englishmen. Have you really not received it? If not, make enquiries. Did you receive (some time ago already) three bottles of wine? (in a single packet). I ask you to reply, contrary to your base habit, to all my questions.

Did you receive the parcel in which there was four pounds of tea?

I'm now sending you material and linings for suits. Three yards for

Osik, four for Volosik, although he only needs three and a half. Half a yard for two books. Two and a half yards for Annushka for a skirt.

The suit material is amazing: it's English.

I'm taking the opportunity and sending you ten pounds of sugar.

If I don't get a visa in two weeks, I'll try to go via Danzig.

I'm hardly sending any books, because they're terribly expensive — I'll send them from Berlin or Danzig.

In any case I'll be home in Moscow in six weeks. After all, wasn't my leave for four months?

What terrible delays with the letters! Just think when I wrote to you about the publishing house, and not a damn thing's been done yet!

I get into a state of fury with these slownesses!! With visas! With publishing houses!

Send some fat cigarettes, damn it! How many times have I asked you!!! Tra-ta-ta-ta-ta! . . .

I kiss your eight little paws.

Yours till the grave

61. Lili to Mayakovsky and Osip.
Letter from Riga to Moscow, 29 December 1921.
29.XII.21.

Lights of my life, my little kittens, my little puppies!

I love you and I adore you. I wrote a really long letter, I prepared a parcel and — oh, horror! the comrade I was supposed to send them with isn't going!

Expect them on Monday.

I kiss your eight paws, your <u>faithful</u>

[On the reverse:]

Volosik!

On Monday we'll send you some money — the salary (250 dollars a month). We'll send you advances when you write more definitely.

Volosik, Shchenik, my little puppy, my little beast, I miss you unimaginably!

Happy New Year, my little sun!

You are my little hulk!

I want you! What about you?

If you're embarrassed to write in an unsealed envelope, write by post: it gets through very punctually.

I kiss the bridge of your nose, those dear little paws, and your little head, whether it's shaved or shaggy, and I kiss all the rest in general,

your Lilya.

No. 19   2/I 22.

Dear, dear, Lilyonok,

Are you writing? I don't receive anything. Lyova's got two letters. How is it you're not ashamed to write those foul things about us? We want, want, want you to come and quickly. And the rest is just comic:

what gave you the idea that Oska doesn't live at home? You gave the people who were coming here the telephone number 5-06-52 (whereas ours is now 5-66-12), and David[1] probably said that the Briks had moved ages ago! That's it!

The last letter I sent you (no 18) was about publishing matters. Judging by Lyova's letter you haven't received it — just in case I'm sending you the "memo" again. Galina Konstantinovna[2] is now working at the State Publishing House, which will be a big help with textbooks.

Vitya Khlebnikov's arrived: wearing just a shirt! We dressed and shod him.[3] He's got a long beard — he looks very good, only too intellectual. I was convinced that you'd be here by the New Year, and now I'm completely disappointed.

Write soon. I kiss you my dear child

I am your

No. 20

Dear, dear Lilyonok,

At last I've received your two letters. They made me terribly glad! The first one, about Oska's not living here (you funny thing!), and the second one about your sending a long letter on Monday (and also about the "salary", as soon as I get it I'll really get down to things. I'm convinced I can set things up).

You just can't imagine what joy I get out of your letters. I walk around in triumph and tell all my acquaintances to go to hell. This is how I live — 1) I feel miserable, miserable, miserable without you, 2) I write (I've only just started doing so seriously. Things have settled down), 3) I play, 4) The rest.

On the 8th I'm appearing at the Polytechnic "An evening of my satire".[1] And then in the same place with Oska — "A purge of poets".[2] Olya is terribly grateful to you. We too are all receivers of your benefience, I'm really moved by it. You are a remarkable person, Kitty. I love you alone. I'm waiting, your

I kiss you, kiss you, kiss you
Your Shchen
How are you living? I know nothing about you!

Volodik,

Yuliya Grigorevna Lenard has told me that you're drinking yourself sick, and that you're in love with the youngest Ginzburg girl,[1] that you're pestering her, and that you walk and drive around the streets with her in tender poses. You know <u>how</u> I react to that.

In two weeks I shall be in Moscow, and I shall pretend with regard to you that I know nothing. But I demand that <u>everything</u> which I might not like be <u>absolutely</u> liquidated.

There must not be a single telephone call etc. If all this is not put into effect down to the very tiniest detail, I shall have to part from you, which I absolutely don't want, because I love you. You're really fulfilling the conditions "not to get drunk" and "to wait" well. I have fulfilled both of them to this very day. As for the future — we'll have to see.

That Yuliya Grigorevna is a terrible bitch! What a malicious woman!

I had absolutely no desire to know the truth and didn't ask her anything!

Don't be miserable!

If you really do love me, then do everything I say and we'll forget about it.

I kiss you,

Lilya

66. Lili to Mayakovsky and Osip.
Letter from Riga to Moscow, beginning of January 1922.

Osik and Volodik,

I'm sending you letter No 1 without re-reading it — I can't be bothered! Despite the fact that it's considerably out of date.

I had a visit from Yuliya Grigorevna Lenard. The first time I laid eyes on her I took a strong dislike to her. Judging by her stories, you're having a very merry time, you have a large number of new lady friends, and I'm glad for you. She calls you all "our crowd" and mentions "Osya" and "Volodya" by name. Of course you understand that despite the fact that I'm very glad that you're having such a jolly time, you're going to have to open all the windows and disinfect the place before I get back. Microbes like Boba[1] and ladies such as Yuliya Grigorevna, just like the bedbugs in the wall, must be radically exterminated.

In general I am categorically against the new course in economic policy! Bear that in mind!!

In two weeks I shall be in Moscow. I'm terribly glad!

Write and tell me what you need most of all. Write without bothering about whether it's dear or cheap. What I can buy I'll buy.

In about two months I shall apparently be able to go to Berlin or Vienna. I'll tell you all about it.

Give a remarkable reception to comrade Bramson (whom you introduced me to at the station in Moscow) — he's very funny and a nice boy. If he gets an ice-cream mould, then feed him ice-cream till he can't take any more! He has one vice — he's terribly fond of an argument!

Don't get your suits made up yet. I'll bring some more material and then we can choose.

Osik! Write and thank my mother for the parcel immediately and send the letter to me — I'll send it on to London. You absolutely must go and see Tsilya Yakovlevna![2] If your teeth aren't in order by the time I get back, I'll give you a piece of my mind! I can see you both panicking!!!

Please hand on these little parcels to Rita and Malkin. If Malkin's left, eat it yourselves. I should like to catch him before he leaves Moscow.

I shall telegraph you about the day of my arrival. It will be good if you can get a van to come to the station, because I hope to bring a lot of provisions.

I received "In place of a memorandum". It's totally unsatisfactory: the whole affair must be carried out as officially as possible. There must be orders from an institution or from bookshops on the appropriate forms.

I shall try to bring the publisher to Moscow. That would be best of all. Because I'm so fed up with the delay with letters!

For the time being I'm sending you only fifteen thousand marks. "To make a start", as the publisher says. As soon as you send the order, we'll send off the rest.

My arrival too depends on how quickly you send the order. Whatever happens, I want to get this matter organised.

Hurry up!!!!

Lilya

†67. Mayakovsky to Lili.
Letter from Moscow to Riga, 9 January 1922.[1]

No 20

Dear Lilyochek

I got your letter about my pastimes. The information is extremely tendentious. In fact it's all fantastic nonsense. But all the same for the time being I'm very sad. My one consolation is that the very first time I met her I was myself convinced, and tried to convince others, that the woman was awful trash, the only one not to believe me was Lyova, and now with your help he's become convinced too. I'm no more a member of "this crowd" than you are.

It may be nonsense, but I'm very miserable.

On Thursday I'll send you a long letter.
On Thursday Elbert[2] is off to Riga. He's a great fellow!
On Thursday I'll send as much as possible about the publishing house.
I kiss you, my sweet and my own one. I'm waiting for you.

Your

9/I 22.

[Word in the drawing: Boohoohoo!]

68. Mayakovsky to Lili.
Letter from Moscow to Riga, 10 January 1922.

My dear and beloved Lilyok

I've received your two unpleasant letters. Very miserable. Especially the last one. In the first one all you did was to threaten "And then we'll have to see".[1] But the last one[2] no longer has any of your usual "Your"s, "I'm waiting"s and so on. Is the gossip of some trashy woman really enough to alienate you so quickly?

Of course I'm not going to boast that I live like a recluse. I go to see people and I go to the theatre, I go walking with and walk home. But not having any romance and I haven't had one.

None of my relationships goes beyond flirtation. As for the Ginzburgs, both youngest and oldest, they're not bad sorts, but since I've found a billiard hall, I haven't had to see them at all recently.

As for Yuliya Grigorevna's "crowd", I've never been a member, since I called her a bitch on the first day I met her, and remain convinced of same. I've always avoided her in every way.

When you arrive you'll see everything for yourself — what you don't like you can exterminate.

Well I kiss you my sweet and dear child, I'm your

Shchen

10/1-22.
For several days I've
been very sad.

98

I'm sending the letter to the publisher.

Elbert took some photos (of me), one of them is yours, the rest are my sisters', they absolutely mustn't go missing. Get copies made of them.

I kiss you

your Shchen.

69. Lili to Mayakovsky and Osip.
Letter from Riga to Moscow, first half of January 1922.

My dears,

I've sent you two parcels:

1) To L.A. Grinkrug, from comrade Orlov.

2) To O.M. Brik from me.

Each contains fifteen pounds of sugar, ten pounds of flour and five pounds of lard. Both parcels are for us. Lyova, I received your letter sent through the post.

From you, Volodik and Osik, there's been nothing since Bramson. This amazes me. Can you really not have received the money, material and so on?

I'm very glad that Vitya Khlebnikov's in Moscow. I wonder what new things he's written.

What's happened to the orders for textbooks? They're the reason I'm

sitting here!!

I've put on weight terribly again. Has Malkin left?

Have you received the English parcel? Has Olga Vladimirovna received her parcel?

I'm afraid that if I'm held up here any longer, they'll send the English visa and I'll have to go to London. I'd rather come to Moscow now, and then go to Vienna in about two months. I think that will be possible.

I give you all a big kiss.

Your Lilya

My Dear My Sweet My Beloved Lilyatik!

I love you. I'm waiting for you, I kiss you. I'm terribly, terribly melancholy without you. I'll write you a letter separately. I love you.

Your, your, your

We're sending you
a little
moneys.

My dear children, thank you for the letters, cigarettes and money.

Zivs[1] is now in Berlin. It's possible that I'll also get there in a few days. If not I'll wait for him here, he's supposed to be coming soon.

Bramson got it muddled — I got not thirty thousand marks from Zivs, but fifteen thousand, all of which I sent on to you.[2]

Since I again don't know when I'll get to Moscow, and you're probably worn threadbare, get your suits made up.

Osik, don't be envious of Volodya's lining, yours is much better and more expensive, unfortunately there wasn't one like it for Volodya's.

Tell Malkin that I'll buy everything in Berlin, if I get there. If not, I'll buy it here.

I'm sending some sheet music.

Volodik, if you want, send me the prologue to the Fourth International.[3] Bramson says it's very good. If you're afraid to, don't send it.

It's a terrible pity that the English parcel went missing. It had wine in it!

I'm very glad that Annushka is pleased with the skirt. I'll bring her some more of the same material for a jacket, so she'll have a suit.

I've sold a few of my rags and bought in their place a remarkable raincoat, a knitted suit, a knitted dress, two hats, shoes, boots, night slippers; I've had my fur coat mended and bought some material for dresses and underclothing. It's all terribly dear here. On the other hand I shall return very chic!!

The one trouble is that I've put on a terrible amount of weight! Everyone eats very well here, and I eat to keep them company.

My nerves are terribly much better. You won't recognise me!

I've become very friendly with a certain woman whom you know, Volosik. She met you at Runt's.[4] Her name is Yekaterina Vladimirovna Vystavkina. Both she and her husband are very nice. Unfortunately yesterday they left for Berlin. We were together from morning till night. I've never ever laughed as much as I did when I was with her — she's an exceptionally witty woman! Only she doesn't like Futurists much.

Oslit, next time I get the chance I'll send some books.

I'm also very taken with "Mon Homme"[5] — the whole of Paris is singing it, dancing to it, playing it.

Osik! Get your teeth seen to!!!!! They say you're off to Berlin?! Wait for me — we can go together in the summer.

There's a very, very great deal that we must talk about and discuss. I very much want to see you all. Osik, if some of the music is no good, sell it. Because it was very expensive — that's 1,800 Latvian roubles' worth.

Volodik, I've just spoken to Zivs's agent. All the prices will be worked out by Thursday.

I kiss you, my little beasts,
your Lilya

72. Lili to Mayakovsky and Osip.
Letter from Riga to Moscow, middle of January 1922.

My dear little beasts!

Dubinsky (he's also known as Sharik [little ball] because he's round) is a good fellow, a friend of Bramson's. Feed him dinners if you want to.

Volosik! He adores poker, but he plays so badly, that he never ever wins. Have mercy on him, Minos!

He has one terrible vice — he likes the Imaginists![1]

I sent you a pile of music. I hope you received it.

The book and the poster have been sent to Zivs in Berlin. Apparently everything's going to be printed there — it's incomparably cheaper.

I'm waiting for Zivs, any day now we're supposed to finish everything, go through the formalities and receive the money.

Even if I do get a visa, I shan't go anywhere. If I go, that'll mean at least about another six weeks. I must get home. I miss it all!

I think I'll leave in exactly a week, on Thursday. If there's some disaster (like Zivs being late — though I don't think he will), and I can't leave on Thursday, I'll send you a telegram. Otherwise — expect me! How joyful I am that I shall see you soon!!!

Don't write to me any more. Though you don't write to me anyway: that's two couriers without letters for me already.

I'm sending some of my material with Dubinsky, so I don't have to carry a lot.

1) Pink and blue cambric for underclothing.
2) Blue wool for a dress.
3) Black
4) Checked material

He's bringing something for you — I don't know if he'll manage to get it to you.

I've already written about Bramson getting it muddled — I got only 15,000 marks from Zivs, not 30,000 — and I sent it all to you, without keeping any of it for myself.

I've only just found out that Zivs is coming in two days. That means I'm leaving in exactly a week, on Thursday. Great!!!

I shan't write any more. Don't be amazed that I send sugar every time I get the chance. It really is very cheap!

I kiss you, kiss you, kiss you . . .

Your Lilya

I've just received your letters, Shchen, and Olya's letter.

Please send this registered letter to Kharkov.[2]

Keep the receipt.

*73. Mayakovsky to Lili.
Letter from Moscow to Riga, 17 January 1922.

No 21

Dear Lilyok!

I think this may arrive after you leave Riga. When is it you're leaving? We can't wait to see you. How's the publishing house? I'm dying to do some publishing.

Come

I kiss you and kiss you

all yours
17/I 22

102

Volodik,

They're offering you five appearances in March: two in Riga, two in Revel and one in Kovno. The journey and the hotel will be paid, and you'll get 50,000 Latvian roubles — ten thousand for each performance. On condition, of course, that you arrange the visa yourself. I don't think you'll say no to a little trip, and it won't be difficult to get a visa — I'll help you.

I'm getting all sorts of people coming to me all the time — newspapermen, journalists; they all ask about you.

You're a famous person!

I kiss you

No. 22

Dear and sweet Lilyonok

I got your two letters, one with the music and the other about the tour. Judging by both letters you've well and truly forgotten us (me).

How stupidly it turned out about the money. It didn't even occur to me that you would send it all to me. Is that too because you've become "alien"?

I was very glad to hear of the possibility of a tour. I'll go with pleasure[1] — I'm fed up here. And there's nothing to do. It's already about two months since I drew even half a poster. Great?!

And I was expecting you by the 16th. I licked your room clean!

For about five days after that I phoned home every half-hour!

So when will I see you? I miss you. I kiss you, kiss you and kiss you

Your

22/I 22

[On the reverse:]
Send the prices!

103

Come back, I kiss you! My dear, my sweet

I love and adore you

All yours

Puppy

This is the last letter.[1]

23.4.1922

Beasties!

I'm sending you:

1) A pair of sandals each for Cat and Shchen.

2) German magazines.

3) Music!

4) A few books.

5) For Cat, glasses with spare lenses.

6) A pack of cards each for Shchen and Lyova.

7) Chocolate, liqueur and four jars of preserves for Osik, Volodik, Lyova, Annushka, Rita and the Aseyevs, to be eaten together.

8) The book "The Reds and the Whites" for Natan Altman.

I hope to leave on the 6th of May. In the first place, I haven't done anything with Zivs yet, since he's terribly difficult to find. Secondly, I want to get a German visa for Alter.[2] He almost died. He's got tuberculosis, he was delirious for two weeks. He's still got a high temperature, but he's much better, and he'll recover completely if he's well looked after. He's in a nursing-home. He has a nurse.

Zivs is clearly not at all eager to hand over the money. Alter intends to have a talk with him!

I've been several times to the cinema, once to the circus, once to the theatre.

Deadly boring!

I can't manage to get anything done! — They won't give me material on credit!! And I can't get the money!! I don't want to borrow from Alter as he'll need it for his treatment.

All in all — I'm out of luck! My room is revolting!

Lyova! Pay Vinokur out of my gold money — ten pounds sterling — I still owe him it from my previous trip.

Ritochka! Thank you for the letter — it was very good!

I embrace and kiss everyone, everyone, everyone.

I'll be back soon and I'm never ever going anywhere away from you again!!!

Your Lilya

78. Lili to Mayakovsky and Osip.
Letter from Berlin to Moscow, 15 August 1922.[1]

Berlin. 15 VIII 22.

My little beasts,

I'm sending you permission to enter the country. Go to the German embassy, tell them you're ill, and if Aleksandr Mikhailovich[2] helps you you should get visas very quickly. On the way to Kissingen you can stop in Berlin, where you'll be able to get permission to stay as long as you need to.

I'm going to London on the 18th. I've already booked the ticket.

I'm sending you Busch,[3] Volosit; and Spengler[4] for Osik. A hat and hatpins for Rita,[5] and chocolate for all of you. Give Annushka some chocolate too.

I go riding at the riding-school. Like a man.

I've bought myself a few dresses and a wonderful leather coat. Come as soon as possible!!!! Bring as much money as you can! And you must fly!!!

I'm in a hurry. I must take this letter to the station.

Tell Rita to write.

I kiss you, my sweets.

Your Lilya

79. Lili to Mayakovsky and Osip.
Letter from London to Moscow, end of August 1922.[1]

90 Canfield Gardens,
West Hampstead,
London N.W.6

My own little beasts!

London is splendid, only I have little money!!!

Elsa's coming tomorrow — interesting.[2]

Telegraph, for God's sake, to say whether you got the visas, and when you expect to leave.[3]

105

Berlin 15. VIII. 22

Мои зверики,

посылаю вам ~~визы~~ разрешения на в'езд. Пойдите в немецкое посольство, скажите о том, что вы больны и, если Ал. Мих. вам поможет, то вам должны очень скоро выдать визы. По дороге в Россию вы остановитесь в Берлине, где вам дадут возможность жить столько, сколько вам будет нужно.

18-ого еду в Лондон. Уже заказала билет.

Посылаю тебя, Володя Буша; Осику Шпеллера. Рите Шийку, шпильки.

и всем вам шоколад
Алечушке тоже дайте
шоколаду
Я езжу верхом в манеже
— по-мужски.
Купила себе несколько
платьев и чудесное ро-
жовое пальто.
Приезжайте скорее!!!!
Берите денег побольше!
Обязательно летите!!!!
Торопитесь — надо везти
пальто на вокзал.
Скажите Рите, чтобы
писала —
Целую вас, мои са-
мые дорогие
Ваша Лиля

Letter No. 78, 15 August 1922.

Did Lyova tell you how we went on the spree in Berlin? Here I've seen Yevnin, Levidov and Shvets.

Osik, I bought some material for you from Bruni for a blue suit, and for an autumn coat (like Volodya's). And for Volosik, some grey material for a suit, what they have in Germany is terrible rubbish.

I miss you. Come soon, or else I'll get used to it!

How are Rita, Annushka, the Krasnoshchokovs, Malkin and so on?

Volosit, have you been hunting?

In Berlin I went to the zoo. In a few days I'll go here. You should see the little puppies here!!!

I kiss you, my dears. I love you.

Yours, true till the grave.

Lilya

There are such amazing things here — you want to buy everything! Bring as much money as you can!!!!

You can't buy a thing with the money I have!

I kiss your eight little paws.

80. Lili to Mayakovsky and Osip.
Letter from London to Moscow, 31 August 1922.[1]

Children! Why is it you don't leave and don't even write?!

Telegraph whether you've got your visas.

Telegraph a week in advance to Misha Grinkrug, so he can get rooms ready for you.

I embrace you, I kiss you. Your Lilya

[On the reverse:]

Why doesn't Rita write?

†81. Mayakovsky to Lili.
Letter, Moscow, 28 (?) December 1922.[1]

Lilyok

I see you've made a firm decision. I know that all my pestering you is painful to you. But Lilik what happened to me today is too terrible for me not to clutch at this last straw letter.

I have never felt so wretched — I really must have grown up too much. Earlier whenever you banished me I believed that we would meet again. Now I feel as if I've been completely torn away from life, as if there will never ever be anything else again. There is no life without you. I always said it, always knew it, now I feel it feel it with my whole essence, everything everything which I thought about with pleasure now has no value — it's revolting.

I'm not threatening, I'm not extorting forgiveness. I shall do nothing nothing to myself — I'm too terrified for Mama and Lyuda, somehow I can't stop thinking about Lyuda since that day.[2] Also sentimental adulthood. I cannot promise you anything. I know that there is no promise you would believe in. I know that there is no way of seeing you, of being reconciled that would not be a torment to you.

And yet I am not capable of not writing, not begging you to forgive me for everything.

If you made your decision with difficulty, after a struggle, if you want to try one last time, you'll forgive me, you'll write.

But even if you don't reply you are my only thought, as I loved you seven years ago so I love you this very second, whatever you may wish, whatever you may order I shall do it this very moment, I shall do it with rapture. How terrible it is to part if you know that you are in love and that the parting is your own fault.

I'm sitting in a café and howling, the waitresses are laughing at me. It's terrifying to think that all the rest of my life will be like this.

I'm writing only about myself, not about you. It's terrible to think that you are calm and that every second you are farther from me, and that it'll only take a few more for me to be forgotten completely.

If this letter causes you to feel anything other than pain and revulsion answer it for the sake of Christ, answer it immediately, I'm going to run home and wait. If you don't it will be a terrible terrible grief to me (30-32).[3]

I kiss you. Completely yours.

Me.

It's now ten o'clock. If you don't reply by eleven I'll know there's no point in waiting.

I sit here with moral satisfaction, but with ever growing physical torment. I shall be honest down to the smallest trifles for two months. I shall measure people by their attitude to me during these two months. My brain tells me that you shouldn't do a thing like this to a person. Despite all the conditions of my life, if this were to happen to Lichika, I'd put a stop to it that very day. If Lilik loves me, she'll (I feel this with my whole heart) put a stop to it, or alleviate it in some way. She must sense this, understand it. I shall be with Lilik at 2.30 p.m. on 28 February. If Lilik does not do anything even an hour before the end of my sentence, I shall know I am a loving idiot and for Lilik a rabbit being used in an experiment.

Vol.   28 December

Now I think that Lilik won't do anything. Happiness will be if it . . .[1]

Lilik

I'm writing to you now because I couldn't answer while Kolya[1] was here. I must write it to you this minute, so that my joy doesn't prevent me understanding anything at all in the future.

Your letter[2] gives me hopes which I absolutely dare not rely on, and do not wish to rely on, since every reliance based on your old attitude to me is wrong. And your new attitude to me can be formed only after you get to know the present me.

My little letters to you also should not and cannot be taken into account by you, since I must and can have whatever decisions there may be about our life (if we are to have one) only by the 28th. This is absolutely right — since if I had the right and the possibility of deciding something definitively about life this minute, if in your eyes I could guarantee that I would behave correctly, then you would ask me today and give your answer today. And a minute later I'd already be a happy man. If this thought is destroyed for me, I shall lose all strength and all belief in the necessity of enduring all my horror.

I grabbed your letter with a boyish, lyric frenzy.

But you must know that on the 28th you will meet a person who is completely new to you. Everything that comes about between you and him will begin to be constructed not on the basis of past theories, but on actions after the 28th of February, on your and his "doings".

I am obliged to write you this letter because this minute I feel a sense of nervous shock the like of which I haven't felt since we parted.

You understand what love for you, what feeling for myself this letter is dictated by.

If you are not frightened by a scarcely risky walk with a man about whom you have previously only known by hearsay that he is a fairly jolly and pleasant fellow, then drop me a line, drop me a line immediately.

I beg you and I'm waiting. Waiting for something from Annushka downstairs. I cannot not have your answer. You will answer me as you would an importunate friend who was trying to "warn" you about a dangerous acquaintance: "go to hell, it's not your business — I like it this way!"

You permitted me to write when I <u>very much needed to</u>[3] — that very much has now come.

It may seem to you — why does he write that, it's clear anyway. If that's the way it seems to you, that's good. Forgive me for writing today when you have people[4] — I don't want this letter to contain anything nervously far-fetched. But tomorrow it will be the same. This is the most serious letter of my life. It's not even a letter, it's:

"existence"

All of me embraces your one
    little finger

Shchen

The next note will be from a certain young man on the 27th.

†84. Mayakovsky to Lili.
Letter, Moscow, middle of January 1923.

Dear and beloved Lilyonok.

I have imposed the strictest interdiction upon myself from now on against writing you anything, or manifesting myself with regard to you in any way, <u>in the evening</u>. That is the time when I am always a little not myself.

After your little notes I feel "relaxed", and I can and want to write to you calmly for once.

When we meet[1] I look ghastly, I find myself pretty repulsive.

Besides, I know that they do me more harm than anything else. You understand that in such a state I'm no good for anyone or anything.

I understand that every time you're pricked by the thought, am I really going to have to waste my time on this lump of dead meat some day?

Лилик

Пишу тебе сейчас потому что при Коле я не мог тебе ответить. Я должен тебе написать это сейчас же, чтоб моя радость не помешала бы мне дальше вообще что либо понимать

Твое письмо дает мне надежды на которые я ни в каком случае не смею рассчитывать, и рассчитывать не хочу, так как всякий расчет построенный на старом твоем отношении ко мне — не верен. Новое же отношение ко мне может создаться только после того как ты теперешнего меня узнаешь.

Мои письмишки к тебе тоже не должны и не могут браться тобой в расчет — т.к. я должен и могу иметь какие бы то ни было решения о нашей жизни (если такая будет) только к 28-му. Это абсолютно верно — т.к. если б я имел право и возможность решать что нибудь окончательно о жизни сию минуту, если б я мог в твоих глазах ручаться за правильность — ты спросила бы меня сегодня и сегодня же б дала б ответ. И уже через минуту я был бы счастливым человеком. Если у меня уничтожится эта мысль я потеряю всякую силу и всю веру в необходимость пережить весь мой ужас.

Я с мальчишеским, лирическим бешенством ухватился за твое письмо.

Но ты должна знать что ты познакомишься 28 с совершенно новым для тебя человеком все что будет между тобою и им нач-нет слагаться не из пришедших теорий а из поступков с 28 февраля, из "дел" твоих

Letter No. 83, beginning of January 1923.

112

и его.

Я обязан написать тебе это письмо потому что сию минуту у меня такое нервное потрясение которого не было с ухода.

Ты понимаешь какой любовью к тебе, каким чувством к тебе диктуется это письмо

Если тебя не пугает не много рискованная прогулка с человеком о котором ты только раньше по наслышке знала что это довольно веселый и приятный малый черкни черкни сейчас же.

Прошу и жду. Жду от Анушка вкл. Я не могу не иметь твоего ответа. Ты ответишь мне как чаой либому другу который старается предупредить об опасном знакомстве: "йдите к черту не ваше дело-так мне нравится!"

Ты разрешила мне написать, когда мне будет <u>очень нужно</u> - это очень сейчас нужно.

Тебе может показаться - зачем это он пишет это и так ясно. Если так покажется это хорошо. Извини что я пишу сегодня когда у тебя народ - я не хочу чтоб в этом письме было что нибудь от первого наумленное. А завтра это будет так. Это самое серьезное письмо в моей жизни. Это не письмо даже это: " Существование "

Весь я обнимаю один твой мизинец

ИЦЕН

(следующая записка буду уже от одного молодого человека 27 ...

113

Don't worry, my child. I shall not be like that. If I am like that I shall not allow myself into your sight.

Another thing: don't worry, my beloved sunlight, that I extort notes about your love for me out of you. I understand that you write them mainly to stop me suffering unnecessary pain. I'm not building anything, any "obligations" for you, out of them, and of course I don't use them as a basis for any hopes.

Look after yourself, my child, and your peace of mind. I hope that one day I shall be pleasing to you again without any pacts and without any of my wild tricks.

I swear to you on your life, my child, that for all my jealousies, through them, beyond them I am always happy to learn that you're having a good time and enjoying yourself.

Don't abuse me more than necessary for the letters, my child.

I kiss you and the birdies[2]

> Your Shchen

85. Lili to Myakovsky.
Note, Moscow, middle of January 1923.

I'm glad!

I believe that you can be the kind of man I've always dreamt of loving.

> Your Lilya (of the 28th!)

But from then on — .

*86. Mayakovsky to Lili.
Letter, Moscow, 19 January 1923.

Moscow, Reading Gaol[1] 19/I 23

My beloved sweet Lilyonok, dear little sun,

Maybe (it's good if it was so!) stupid Lyova saddened you yesterday with some of my little nerves. Be merry! I'm going to. It's nonsense and trifles. I learnt yesterday that you frowned a little, don't, Luchik!

Of course you understand that an educated man cannot live without you. But if this man has the tiniest hope of seeing you, then he is very very merry. I am happy to give you a ten times bigger toy, if only you would then smile. I've got five of your little scraps, I love them terribly, only the last one saddens me — it just says "Volosik, thank you"[2] whereas the others have continuations — those are my favourites.

You aren't very angry about my stupid letters, are you? If you are, then don't be — they're my only celebrations.

114

I go around with you, write with you, sleep with your little kitty name and so on.

I kiss you if you're not afraid of being torn apart by a mad dog.

Your Shchen
also known as Oscar Wilde
also known as The Prisoner of Chillon[3]
also known as:
I sit — behind bars in the
dungeon — dry (I'm the one
that's dry, but when necessary
I shall be fat for you).

[Word in the drawing: I love you!!]

Beloved, remember me (. . .).[4] Kiss Crossbill.[5] Tell him not to climb out — after all I'm not going to!

*87. Mayakovsky to Lili.
Letter, Moscow, January 1923.

Sweet, sweet Lilyonok.

I know you're still worried, you're still frowning.

Treat your sweet little nerves, my child.

I think about you a lot and well.

Remember me a little.

We terribly need to live well for a while.

I infinitely want this to happen together.

If my head doesn't burst from the thought, I'll think of something.

Love the crossbill — he's like me: a big nose (only mine is red) and he keeps clinging to the bars (he's looking out of the window).

I'm already travelling round the globe with you.

The Prisoner of Chillon
Né Shchen

[On the reverse:]
Some time I'll kiss you personally. Can I?

115

Volosik! Puppy!

More than anything in the world I love you. Then the birdies. We'll live together, if that's what you'll want.

Your Lilya

Sweet, dear Lilyok,

Sending you a letter I knew today that you would not reply. Osya sees I wasn't writing. Even this letter is lying in a drawer. You won't reply because I'm already replaced, because I no longer exist for you, because you wish I'd never existed. I'm not extorting, but my Child you can stop me feeling unnecessary pain with two lines. The pain's too great! Don't be stingy, even after these lines I still have ways of tormenting myself. A line is not you! And yet I don't need any unnecessary pain, my child! If I'm talking jealous nonsense, drop me a line, please. If it's true, don't say anything. Only don't lie, for God's sake.

Kitty, am I really such crap that I'm no longer worth anything at all? You know I can only go on living if I don't think so. My child, drop me a line, please drop me a line, you're the richer one now, you can stretch a hand.

Lilik, don't let anyone else read this.

I'm not being stingy, Volodik; I don't want a "correspondence"! You are not replaced. That's the truth, although I am not obliged to be truthful with you. I embrace you and I give you a big kiss. Crossbill sends his regards, he flew away, but I caught him myself, stroked his little feathers and kissed him in your name.

I kiss my dear Kitty*

31/I 23.

*You don't even allow letters to get near you —
The disc of my head has set.
This is no "correspondence", Kitty,
It's just a corresponding CHEEP.

В. МАЯКОВСКИЙ

13 ЛЕТ РАБОТЫ

ДВА ТОМА

ПОРТРЕТ
Я САМ
ПОЧЕРН

[Book cover: V. Mayakovsky. 13 Years' Work. Two Volumes. Portrait. I Myself.
Handwriting. (Inscription translated above)]

92. Lili to Mayakovsky.
Note, Moscow, about 31 January 1923.

I embrace and kiss you, little pup!
Thank you for the "cheep".

Your Lilya

(translator-in-chief)[1]

93. Mayakovsky to Lili.
Letter, Moscow, January-February 1923.

Lichika.
Write some word here. Give it to Annushka. She'll bring it down to me.
Don't be angry.
Everything contains some sort of threat to me.
You already like someone. You haven't even spoken my name. You
have someone. Everyone's keeping something from me. If you write a
word before she disappears, I shan't pester you.

94. Mayakovsky to Lili.
Note, Moscow, January-February 1923.

I was terribly glad to meet the "working cats"
I kiss the kitty worker[1]

[drawing of sad puppy]

95. Lili to Mayakovsky.
Note, Moscow, January-February 1923.

I was very happy when I saw you, little pup!
We kiss you for the flowers.

Yours

[drawing of cat and two birds]

*96 Mayakovsky to Osip.
Letter, Moscow, January-February 1923.

Osik
You promised to phone, unfortunately my telephone doesn't work. So
that this final link has also been broken off. If something comes up, pop
round here.

I kiss you   Vol.
Thank Kitty for remembering me.

Osik

If you come down now I'll wait downstairs a minute — we can take a walk together if you need to have a talk.

V.

97. Lili to Mayakovsky.
Letter, Moscow, 7 February 1923.

Volosik,

do you want to go to Petersburg for a few days on the 28th?

If you want to, we'll meet at the station. Write to me on the 27th saying what time and send me a ticket.

If you have any money over, book a room at the Yevropeyskaya, so that various Chukovskys[1] don't know about our arrival.

Don't tell anyone about this, even Oska.

Lilya

98. Lili to Mayakovsky.
Note, Moscow, first half of February 1923.

Dear Volodenka, I'm ill. I've got a temperature of 38,1. I'm lying in bed.[1] How is your health?

I kiss you.

Lilya

99. Mayakovsky to Lili.
Letter, Moscow, first half of February 1923.

I kiss you, my child!

I'm terribly concerned about your 38,5.

I couldn't kiss you any way these last few days, because I've only got up today myself.

Get well, my own one, as soon as possible please!

Your little puppy.

It's miserable not being able to call in.

100. Lili to Mayakovsky.
Note, Moscow, first half of February 1923.

Little pup, you sent such a miserable note, it really makes me want to cry! I'm frightened to kiss you, I have such lousy Spanish flu, — I don't want you to get infected too!

All the same I kiss the bridge of your little nose.

Your Lilya

[drawing of lying cat]

119

Liska, Lichika, Luchik, Lilyonok, Lunochka, Lasochka, Lapochka, Little child, Little sun, Little comet, Little star, Little child, Sweet child, My beloved Kitty

Kitten

I kiss you and your Spanish flu (let's hope it's male because I don't want to kiss any Spanish females).

I'm sending you all sorts of nonsense I've written.

Smile, kitten.

I'm even sending the rubbish I wrote for Izvestiya.[1]

It just might make you chuckle!

I kiss you

Your

I can't bear the thought of you being "massaged".
And what about me?

Volosik, thank you for all the things. The flowers are wonderful. But the book's lousy — both the cover! and the table of contents![1] I'm angry as sin! But the Izvestiya verses are funny!

I kiss you

Your Lilya

I kiss Kitty

The book can't be lousy because it has "To Lilya" and all your things in it![1]

Your Shchen

Volodya, in view of the fact that when I wasn't there you "chatted up" Oksana,[1] just as you do all the other women (she herself told me about it), I have had to refrain from the orange.[2] This letter doesn't count. No one must know about it. Do not answer. If it weren't for my fever I shouldn't have written. This is of course nonsense, but I know of all your lyrical doings with all the details.

Lichika

Your note is more than an enormous unpleasantness for me, it's a sorrow from which there is no way out.

You ought to find out about my present life in order to have some idea about any "doings". What's terrible is not being suspected, what's terrible is that despite all my infinite love for you, I cannot know everything that may sadden you. What am I to do in the future? Only because I am absolutely ill do I allow myself to write despite your prohibition.

I'll withdraw into myself even more, understanding nothing, completely beaten.

Do you need me or don't you?

Your loving Shchen

Can you really have finished with me?

Volosik, I love you. Do as you wish. Get ready for the 28th. I'm so looking forward to it. I feel very bad and I couldn't stop myself — I wrote about the orange.

I embrace you and I kiss the whole of your head

Your Lilya

121

Lichika

It seems to me that you've changed your mind about seeing me, only for some reason you can't bring yourself to say so: — that's a pity.

Am I right?

If you don't want to, write now; if you tell me that on the 28th (without seeing me) I shan't survive it.

You absolutely don't <u>have</u> to love me, but tell me about it yourself. I beg you. Of course you don't love me, but tell me about it a little bit affectionately. Sometimes it seems to me that people have got together and thought of a punishment for me — to send me to the devil on the 28th! Whatever trash I may be, I'm still a little bit human. I'm simply in pain. Everyone treats me like a mangy beggar — give him alms if he asks and run off into another street. It's painful writing these letters and it's terrible sending them to you through the Grinbergs' servants.[1] But answer, my child (it is precisely "very necessary"). I'll wait downstairs. Never ever in my life will I be like this again. And I must not. Child, if you drop me a line, I'll calm down until the <u>train</u>. Only write the real truth!

I kiss you, your Shchen

Volosik, my child, my puppy, I <u>want</u> to go with you to Petersburg on the 28th.

Don't expect anything bad! I believe that things will be good.

I embrace and kiss you warmly.

<u>Your</u> Lilya

Lisichka Kitty

I can send you the ticket only on the 28th (they hand over tickets only on the day of departure) no later than five to three (I'll try), because the sentence ends at three and going on standing waiting for the signal to change[1] is utterly miserable.

Lilik, you absolutely must get yourself some sort of residence permit (maybe in the house committee), or else they won't register you[2] — I haven't been able to get any certificate for you. Just in case you intend to change your passport for a work-book, I'm sending you a note for Tomchin[3] — so you don't have to waste time waiting.

My child
I still feel you would be glad never to see me?
Let that not be the truth
I kiss Kitty and the birdies

Your

I've just seen comrade Tomchin — he promises not to lose it — but do as you think best. I'll still have to change or let the room if I leave Moscow.

The address is Petrovka, where the police-station is (in the yard), first floor on the left.

I kiss you again

Kitty my child!
I can collect the ticket only on the 28th (they hand them over on the day of departure).
When the train leaves I don't know yet, in the evening I think.
I'll send you the ticket before 3 o'clock, and at the same time I'll write precisely about the departure time.
I kiss you, my own one

Your

Dear Child
    I'm sending the ticket.
    The train leaves at 8.00 precisely.
    Let's meet in the carriage.[1]

I kiss you, your

28/II 23.

"The days of gloom are past
    The hour of atonement has tolled."
"Boldly comrades in step and so on"[1]

I kiss you, yours

3.01 28/II 23.

[Translated above]

Lichika, my little sun!

Today is the first of February. I have decided to begin writing this letter
one month before we meet. Thirty five days have passed. That makes at
least 500 hours of constant thinking!

I'm writing because I'm no longer capable of thinking about it (not to
say because my head is spinning), because I think that everything is clear
even now (relatively, of course), and in the third place because I'm afraid

124

of being simply overwhelmed with joy when I meet you, and you may be in for, or more precisely I may foist my old rubbish upon you, with a garnish of joy and wit. I'm writing this letter very seriously. I'm going to write it only in the mornings when my head is still clear, and I'm free of the tiredness, spite and irritation I feel in the evenings.

In any case I'm leaving margins so that if I change my mind about something I can make a note of it.

I shall try to avoid any "emotions" and any "conditions" whatsoever in this letter.

This letter is only about what I have verified absolutely, what I have thought over thoroughly during these months, — only about facts. (1 February) /. . ./

You absolutely will read this letter and think about me for a minute. I feel such endless joy at your existence, at everything about you even without reference to me, that I don't want to believe that I myself am unimportant to you /. . ./

<u>What to do with "the old"</u>
Can I be otherwise?
I find it incomprehensible that I have become like this.

I, who for a year threw even the mattress, even the bench out of my room, I, who three times have led such a "not quite ordinary" life as today — how could I have, how did I dare be so moth-eaten by a flat?

This is not a justification, Lichika, it's only a new piece of evidence against me, a new confirmation that I really have sunk low.

But, my child, whatever faults I may be guilty of, I have been punished enough for each of them, not even by these months, but by the fact that neither the past nor the distant past exists for me now, but only, from 1917 to the present day, a continuous, unmitigated horror. Horror is not a word, Lichika, but a condition — I could now provide a flesh and blood description of all forms of human grief. My punishment is earned and I shall endure it. But I do not want to have any occasion to repeat it. The past for me before the 28th of December, for me with regard to you until the 28th of February, does not exist, either in words, or in letters, or in actions.

There will never be anything routine about anything! No aspect of the old routine will insinuate itself — I give you my firm word about THIS. That at least I guarantee. If I turn out to be incapable of doing that, then I shall never see you; if I am seen and even caressed by you and I see again the beginning of routine, I shall run away. (It cheers me to speak of that

125

now, as I live through two months with the single aim of setting eyes on you on the 28th of February at 3 p.m., without even the certainty that you'll allow it.)

My decision to spoil your life in no way, not even by my breathing, is the main thing. The fact that you feel better off without me for even a month, even a day, is a good enough blow.

That is my desire, my hope. At the moment I do not know how strong I am. If I don't quite have enough strength, help me, my child. If I'm a complete rag, use me to dust your staircase. The old is finished† (3 February, 1923, 9.08.)

Today (it's always the same on Sundays) I'm still in a pretty bad way after yesterday. I shall refrain from writing. There's something else which oppresses me: I said something stupid to Oska about the ending of my poem — and now it seems like some kind of blackmail about "being forgiven" — an absolutely stupid situation. I shall purposely not finish the thing for a month! Besides, it's also some sort of poetic routine-mongering to make some sort of special interest out of it. People who talk about the poem think that he must have thought up some way of making it intriguing. An old device! Forgive me, Lilik — I only mentioned the poem because of my bad mood. (4.II.)

Today I'm in a very "good" mood. Even the day before yesterday I thought that life could not be more foul. Yesterday I became convinced that it could be even worse — which means that the day before yesterday it wasn't that bad.

The one advantage of all this is that the following lines, which until yesterday were conjectural, have now become firm and immutable.

About my sitting here
I have sat here up to now with scrupulous honesty, and I know that I shall go on sitting here just like this until 3 o'clock on the 28th of February. Why am I sitting here — because I love you? Because I am <u>bound</u> to? Because of our relationship?

Absolutely not!!!

I'm sitting here only because I myself want to, I want to think about myself and my life.

Even if it isn't like that, I want and intend to think that it is precisely like that. Otherwise there is neither name nor justification for all this.

It's only by thinking so that I could write little notes to you without dissembling that I was "enjoying sitting here" and so forth.

Is it possible to live like this at all?

126

It's possible, only not for long. Anyone who lives like this even these 39 days can boldly accept his certificate of immortality.

Therefore I cannot form any notions about the organisation of my future life on the basis of this experience. I shall not repeat any one of these 39 days ever in my life.

I can speak only of the thoughts, the convictions, the beliefs which are taking shape in me as the 28th approaches, and which will be the point from which all the rest begins, the point from which it will be possible to draw out as many lines as I shall wish, and as shall be wished of me.

If you hadn't known me earlier, this letter would be completely unnecessary, everything would be decided by life. It's only because your notion of me has become encrusted with millions of shells — habits and other muck — during earlier voyages, that you need, in addition to my name when we're introduced, this guide too.

Now about what has been established:

Do I love you? (5.II.1923)

I love you, I love you, despite everything and because of everything, I have loved you, I love you and I will love you, whether you're foul to me or affectionate, whether you belong to me or to someone else. All the same I love you. Amen. It's ridiculous writing about it, you know it yourself.

I wanted to write a terrible amount here. I purposely set a day aside to think it all through precisely. But this morning I have an unbearable sense of all this being unncessary for you.

Only the desire to have it all down in the record for myself has made me carry on.

It's hardly likely that you'll ever read what I've written here. And there's no need for me to spend much time convincing myself of it. It's painful that in the daytime when I wanted to be strong for you this endless pain now afflicts me in the mornings too. If I don't get complete control of myself, I shan't write any more. (6.II) /. . ./

Again about my love. About my notorious activity. Is love the sum total of everything for me? Yes, only in another sense. Love is life, love is the main thing. My poetry, my actions, everything else stems from it. Love is the heart of everything. If it stops working, all the rest withers, becomes superfluous, unnecessary. But if the heart is working, its influence cannot but be apparent in all the rest. Without you (not without you because you've "gone away", without you inwardly) I cease to exist. That was always the case, it is so now. But without "activity" I am dead. Does this

127

mean that I can be any way at all, as long as I can "cling" to you? No. The situation you spoke to me about when we parted "what can I do, I'm not a saint either, I just like 'drinking tea'". If you're in love this situation is completely ruled out /. . ./

About your invitation

I wanted to write about whether you loved me, but your letter[2] completely agitated me, I shall have to pause over it again for myself.

Can this letter be a <u>continuation</u> of relations? No, absolutley not.

Understand, my child! We separated in order to think about life in the future, the one that didn't want to prolong our relationship was you, suddenly you decided yesterday that you can have a relationship with me, so why is it that we didn't go off yesterday and we're only going in three weeks' time? Because I'm not allowed to? This thought should not even occur to me, or my sitting here will become not something voluntary, but an incarceration, something I will not agree to even for a single second.

I shall never be able to be the <u>creator</u> of relations, if you can just crook your little finger and I'll sit at home howling for two months, and then you'll crook another one and I'll break out without even knowing what you think, and rush off abandoning everything. Not through words but through actions I'll prove to you that I think about everything, myself included, before I do anything.

I'm going to do only what results from my own desires.

I'm going to Petersburg.

I'm going because I've been busy working for two months, I'm tired, I want to have a rest and have some fun.

It was an unexpected joy for me that this coincides with a desire on the part of a woman whom I like terribly to do a little travelling.

Can there be something between her and me? It's hardly likely. She's never paid me very much attention at all. But then, I'm not completely worthless either — I'll try and make her like me.

And if she does, then what? We'll see when we get there. I've heard it said that this woman tires of everything quickly. That she's surrounded by heaps of tormented lovers, that just recently one of them almost went off his head. I'll have to take every precaution to protect myself from such a fate.

So that I too can play some part in all this, I shall designate the return date in advance (you're thinking, anything for a quiet life, all right, I'll start with that), I shall be in Moscow on the fifth, I shall arrange everything so that I have to be back in Moscow[3] on the fifth. You will understand that, my child. (8.II.1923)

Do you love me?

It's probably a strange question for you — of course you love me. But do you love me? Do you love me in such a way that I can sense it constantly?

No. I've already said so to Osya. You don't feel love towards me, you feel love towards everything. I too occupy my place in it, (perhaps even a large place) but if I come to an end I'll be removed, like a stone from a stream, and your love will go on washing over all the rest. Is this bad? No, for you it's good, I'd like to love in that way /. . ./

My child, you read this and you think — it's all lies, he doesn't understand a thing. Luchik, even if it's not like this, this is still the way I sense it. It's true, my child, you sent me Petersburg, but how didn't it occur to you, my child, that that means lengthening the sentence by half a day! Just think, after travelling for two months, to spend two weeks driving up to the house and then to wait another half a day for the signal to change![4] (14.II.1923) /. . ./

Lilyatik, I'm not writing all this to reproach you, if it turns out otherwise I shall be happy to change my mind about it all. I'm writing in order to make things clear to you — and you must think a little bit about me.

If I don't have a little "lightness", then I shan't be fit for any life at all. All I shall be capable of is proving my love by some sort of physical labour, as I'm doing now. (18.II.1923) /. . ./

There are no ideal families. All families break up. All there can be is ideal love. But you can't establish love through any sorts of "musts" or "must nots" — only through free competition with the entire world.

I cannot endure "must" come!

I love you endlessly when I "must" not come, hang around outside your window, wait for even a glimpse of your hair as you drive by.

Routine

All the routine is my fault, but not because I'm some sort of mediocre lyricist, who loves his family hearth and his wife who sews on his buttons! No!

The difficulty of my routine sitting down to 66 was that it was some sort of unconscious "sit-down strike" against family relations, this humiliating caricature of myself /. . ./

129

I feel absolutely abominable, both physically and spiritually. My head aches every day, I have a nervous tic, it's got so bad I can't even pour myself a cup of tea. I'm absolutely exhausted, since in order to take my mind off all this to even some slight degree I've been working literally sixteen and twenty hours a day. I've done more work in this period than I've ever done before in six months.

My character

You said I should think about it and change my character. I've thought about myself, Lilik, and whatever you might say I still think my character is not at all bad.

Of course, "playing cards", "drinking", and so on are not my character, they're chance — quite important trivialities, but trivialities all the same (like freckles: when there is a solar cause for them they come, and then this "triviality" can only be removed by cutting the skin off, but if you take measures in time they won't exist at all, or they'll be completely unnoticeable).

There are two main features to my character:

1) Honesty, keeping my word to myself (is that funny?).

2) Hatred of all forms of constraint. This is the cause of all the "squabbles", hatred of domestic constraints and . . . of the poetry, hatred of general constraints.

I'll do anything at all with pleasure of my own free will, I'll even stick my hand in the fire, [but] even the forced bringing home of some purchase from the shops, the very tiniest chain, brings on feelings of nausea, pessimism and so forth. So is the conclusion that I must do just what I like? Nothing of the sort. What is necessary is just not to establish any externally noticeable rules for me. You must do exactly the same with me, but without my having any sense of it /. . ./ I kiss Kitty. (27.II.1923).

What sort of life can we have, what sort will I agree to as a result of all this? Any sort. I'll agree to any sort. I miss you terribly and I terribly want to see you /. . ./

*114. Mayakovsky to Osip.
Letter, Moscow, end of April 1923.

Osik!

1) Comrade Meshcheryakov has approved the cover, only he wants "Long live the 1st of May" at the bottom (we can use a smaller type-face for the No. 2 at the top).[1]

2) I didn't manage to get the announcement-advertisement passed (they were having a meeting); let's leave it till the number comes out.[2]

3) On the cover itself we'll just put a block with lines through it (the number will become general purpose).[3]

Vol.

P.S. If the large block is unsuitable, we can grudgingly put a small one

Resp. ed.[4]

Volodenka,

Stupid as it may be to write, but you and I can't talk to each other for the time being:

You and I cannot go on living the way we've lived up till now. I absolutely refuse to! We must live <u>together</u>; we must travel <u>together</u>. Or, we must part — a last time and forever.

Which I do not want. We must stay in Moscow now; get the flat sorted out. Do you really not want to live a human life with me?! And then, starting from our shared life, everything else will follow. If there's some money left over, we can make a trip together in the summer, for a month; we'll get a visa somehow; then you can try to make arrangements for America too.[2]

We should start doing all this straightaway, if, of course, you want to. I want to very much. It seems both fun and interesting. I could like you now, I could love you, if you were <u>with me</u> and <u>for me</u>. If, regardless of where we had been and what we had been doing during the day, we could lie side by side <u>together</u> in the evening or at night in a clean, comfortable bed; in a room with fresh air; after a warm bath!

Isn't that right? You think I'm complicating matters again, or being capricious.

Think about it seriously, like an adult. I've thought about it for a long time, and <u>for myself</u> I've decided. I would like you to be glad about my desire and my decision, and not simply to go along with them! I kiss you

Your Lilya

My dear Lisyonok

I'm writing from the carriage. I think I'm about to get three whole places to myself. For the time being I'm standing. There are two impossible fat men sitting here, knocking back the beer, smoking, they've undressed and are sweating the place out with their woollen winter socks.

Kitty: get a receipt from Sharik for 65 dollars, that'll make it easier for me to get the screenplay through in Moscow. Otherwise they'll say: just Mayakovsky again.[2]

I miss you, I kiss you, your

[Russian word in the drawing: she-bear.]

My dear and sweet Lilyonochek!

I feel so terribly miserable without you!!!!

Come as soon as possible!

Did you get the letter I wrote on the way[1] and my telegram from Moscow?

It's completely impossible without you here!

Here's some advice for the journey:

1) You absolutely must get from the Embassy (comrade Dmitriyev) permission for the importation of your things a) a certificate that you're returning from an official trip, b) an exact list of the things you're bringing in (that's for our border. I don't think I said this to you in Berlin).

2) In any case send a telegram to Riga to order you second class sleeper places.

3) In Riga, use porter No. 8, he did everything for me quickly and well (I spoke to him about you). That's all!

The little squirrel,[2] is alive, her backside and half of her tail are already turning grey.

Lyova's still in the Crimea. Malkin's arrived.

I saw Kolya.

Arvatik is very bad.[3]

Tell Oska that Inkhuk is getting a real drubbing, and there's no one to speak up for it. Babichev's ill and in the Crimea.[4] I went to see Anatoly Vasilevich and today I'm going to see Lev Davidovich.[5] It all has to do with Lef. Everyone is terribly terribly looking forward to your arrival. And everyone is distressed to see me. I'm writing on a scrap of paper at the Commissariat for Foreign Affairs. So as to catch the plane with the post.

Come as soon as possible, my child.

I kiss you all (Kitty + Osya) and you I also embrace a lot.

all yours

*118. Mayakovsky to Lili.
Note, Moscow, 1923 (?)

Delil (dear Lilyok)

It turns out I'm expected at Sverdlov University today. I'm going and in an hour I'll be in Press House.

†119. Mayakovsky to Lili.
Letter from Kharkov to Moscow, 15 January 1924.[1]

My own dear dazzling little sun, Lisik

I miss you very horribly!!

Yesterday I arrived in Kharkov, and in half an hour I'm going back to Kiev.

I can't say the trip has been excessively comfortable. And yesterday I found an animal on my neck eating me. I killed the animal, but I sit and count the days. And please don't you chuck me if the animal was poisonous!

133

I'm finishing this on the train. Clearly I shan't manage to get to Rostov — all the halls are occupied by congresses of Soviets.

In Kharkov it was full but with a slight thinning in the boxes; in Kiev, on the other hand, there was such a Tower of Babel that there were even two casualties. I can't arrange anything about the books since I never stay in a town more than half a day.[2]

That's all of my life.

In Kharkov I called in on the Karelins; their life is preternaturally colourless, but on the other hand their grey cat gives you its paw. I stroke all the cots and dags I meet. In the hotel in Kiev there's a big ginger one with white specks. I shall probably come back even earlier than I calculated.

I kiss you always and everywhere.

Your Amerigo Vespucci Sven Hedin and other traveller Shchen

120. Lili and Elsa to Mayakovsky and Osip.
Telegram from Paris to Moscow, 13 February 1924.[1]

My address 41 Rue Laugier. We kiss you.

Lili.   Elsa.

*121. Mayakovsky to Lili.
Letter from Moscow to Paris, 14 February 1924.[1]

Dear dear
beloved beloved
sweet sweet
Lisyatik!

I'm writing to you with some discomfort as I'm off this minute to Odessa and Kiev to read and this very minute I've received your little letter[2] and Sharik's.[3]

Thank you.

We sent you a telegram at the address you gave us, but they sent it back "not known", so that Lyova's writing the address on this letter, having ascertained the real one. Our life doesn't change. So far I've been at Lysistrata[4] but I fled after the first act.

It was such trash!

I'm glad to be going to Odessa. Here it's terribly windy and cold!

Write from Paris, child, and as quickly as possible!

I kiss you warmly warmly

all yours

122. Lili to Mayakovsky and Osip.
Letter from Paris to Moscow, 23 February 1924.

23.II.24

My dear cats, dogs and squirrels, what's happened about the American visa?[1] Volosik, did you get my letter and Sharik's? Have you already got a telegram from him?

It wouldn't do any harm to write to me one little time!

I shan't go to Nice: there's a conference of the Russian emigrantern there. If I get a visa I'll go to Spain; if not, somewhere in the south of France, to bake in the sun for a week or so.

Here we're completely on a spree. Elsa has instituted a notebook in which she writes down all our rendezvous ten days in advance! I'm beginning to dream of a quiet life!

I go dancing, but the only Gertsman is Gertsman!!![2] Not one of them can hold a candle to him, and his friend, René, is an absolutely revolting creature.

Our more or less regular cavaliers are Léger (the artist) and Shalit (from London, apparently Gertsman knows him). They're both very fine fellows. They take us everywhere, from the most chic of places to the worst of dives inclusive.

Nice clothes are very expensive here too. If you win some mad sum of money, you can send it through the bank, by telegraph (which is very profitable!) or through Liber,[3] if it isn't very much (. . . . !!!! . . . .)

What news of A.M.?[4]

Very many of the books and journals which Elsa has sent haven't got through. I'll bring everything myself.

It's very late now — I want to go to bed and the ink's run out in my pen.

I'll write in detail in a few days. Hallo to everyone, everyone, everyone. I love you terribly, I embrace you, I kiss you.

Your Lilya

I'm writing to Lyova separately.

123. Lili to Mayakovsky and Osip.
Telegram from Paris to Moscow, 29 March 1924.

My English visa's run out. In week leaving for Moscow. Worried about Osya. Telegraph. Kiss you.

Lili

124. Lili to Mayakovsky.
Telegram from Paris to Moscow, 30 March 1924.

Volodya telegraph Hotel Iéna where you're going. I'll wait. Kiss you.

Lili

125. Lili to Mayakovsky.
Letter from Paris to Berlin (?), 14 April 1924.[1]

My own little puppy Volosit! Terrible disaster: I received your telegram that you were setting off on the same day as I got my English visa! I can't not go to London for a few days, Mama's ailing all the time and implores me to come. I can leave only the day after tomorrow because of business to do with visas and clothes.

I'm bored insensate with Paris! I desperately don't want to go to London!

I miss you so!!!

You can't imagine how humiliating it was to be turned back at the English border. I have all sorts of theories about it, which I'll tell you about when I see you. Strange as it may seem, I think they didn't let me in because of you.[2]

I haven't lost weight at all, the food is too tasty! I want to know how your paunch is getting on.

Yet another woe: I was given a puppy! (I'm sending you photographs of his mother, en face and in profile.) But now it turns out that the importation of dogs into England is forbidden! Besides which everyone advises me to buy one in England, because that's where they come from (the Basavryuks)[3] and there's a good choice. So expect us both!

I love you and terribly want to see you.

I kiss all your little paws and bridges of noses and your muzzle.

Your Lilya

Leaving for London today. Telegraph 90 Canfield Gardens Kiss you.
Lili

We can leave 24th.[1] We kiss you.
Shchen[2]   Lili

Please send by telegraph fifty pounds.
Lili

My dear Lisyonysh

No one is glad to see me because they were all waiting for you. When you telephone they first say "Ah!" and then say "Ooh!" I'm reading yesterday, today, tomorrow and either Thursday or Friday.[2] So I'll arrive on Saturday or Sunday. There's nothing going on because all the leaders have left for Moscow.[3] Tomorrow Rita's going to take tea at my place at 5.00, and then at 7.00 all the linguists.[4]

How melancholy it is here on you own. This is the hardest of towns. Tomorrow I'm going to eat at Menshoy's. He's a terribly nice lad, Some creatures were standing by my posters and saying "Yes, but it doesn't touch the soul-strings".[5] It's the real backwoods. I kiss you strongly strongly terribly terribly your Shchen.

Kiss Scotty and Oska if they don't have worms.

Volosit,

I know that I mustn't give you a present: you'll throw it away or hide it in a drawer.

Congratulations and warm kisses.
Your Lilya

My own dear and sweet little whale, I miss you terribly terribly.

I grieve that I can't come to the dacha today, but Roshchin almost burst into tears when I refused.[2] Tomorrow I'll wait for you at Vodopyanyy, if I'm not there yet phone me

All yours
Shchen

Dear Lilyok,

Unfortunately I have to run.

I waited for you for two hours, but alas. I'd wait a bit longer, but I'm afraid they'll close all the artists' materials shops and I'm out of paper and paints[1] — the more so since I don't know when you'll drop by.

Tell them at home that you've left — I'll phone — or else I'll be anxious that something may have happened to you.

Please tell Oska to forgive me if I don't come tomorrow, as I have to be in town around 5-6. I'll try to come in the morning.

I kiss you very much

We're well. Why do you kiss only Oska? I embrace you, kiss you.
Lilya

To Shchenik till we meet in America or Chukhloma
Lilya

23.X.24 Moscow

138

Dear dear sweet sweet beloved beloved Lilyok

I've already been in Paris a week, but I haven't written because I don't know anything of what's happening to me — I'm not going to Canada and they won't let me go, in Paris for the time being they're letting me stay two weeks (I'm trying to arrange an extension) and whether I should go to Mexico I don't know as it seems pointless. I'll make another attempt to contact America[2] about a trip to New York.

How I'm living while this is going on I don't know myself. My basic feeling is unease, unease to the point of tears and complete absence of interest in everything here (tiredness?).

I terribly want to go to Moscow, if I wasn't ashamed before you and the editorial boards I'd leave today. Although — what is there for me to do in Moscow, I cannot write, and as for who you are and what you are I still have absolutely, absolutely no idea. Because there really is no way to console myself, you are dear to me and I love you, but all the same you are in Moscow and you're either someone else's or not mine. Forgive me — but I feel so wretched.

I live in Elsa's hotel (29 rue Campagne Première Istria Hotel),[3] I didn't telegraph the address as Elsa says that letters sent to her old address get through excellently. They'll even reach me — if you write. I'm terribly uneasy about you. Both about your affairs of the heart and your circumstances. How are things with the books and the contracts?[4]

Ask Kolya to tell Pepper[5] that I'm not writing anything, not from a desire to cheat them out of the advance but because I'm terribly tired and I'm consciously giving myself 2 or 3 weeks rest — and then I'll write for everywhere at once.

No one met me at the station in Paris since they got the telegram only ten minutes before my arrival and I set off in search of Elsa independently with my knowledge of French. Nevertheless I settled in Elsa's hotel because it's the cheapest and the cleanest little hotel and I'm saving money and trying as much as possible not to gad about.

I'm very friendly with Elsa and André, we've arranged a fur coat for her from you and me, we always have dinner and breakfast together.

I wander around with Léger[6] a lot, I called in on Larionov[7] but he was out. Otherwise I haven't been anywhere except at the theatre. Today I'm going to eat with Elsa, Tamara[8] and the Khodaseviches.[9] Not with the poet of course![10] Zdanevich[11] dropped in once, but he's in love and spends his time under some lady's wing.

I'm gradually getting kitted out under André's direction, and I've even got myself a corn from trying on shoes. But I don't feel any enthusiasm for the enterprise.

We devoted my very first day here to your purchases, we ordered you a spendid little case, and bought hats, which we'll send as soon as the pigskin case is ready. I sent the perfume (only not a litre, I couldn't manage that), a bottle, if it gets through in one piece I'll gradually send more the same. Having managed the aforementioned I'll get down to the pyjamas!

I'm collecting advertising material and posters for Oska.[12] If I get permission I'll do a bit of travelling around small French towns.

It's terribly bad if you don't speak the language!

Today I saw a little scotty in the Bois de Boulogne and I almost burst into tears. I'm afraid of getting the reputation of being a provincial, but how I wish I could not go, but come back and read meine Verse![13]

Without you I'm miserable, miserable, miserable, miserable.

It's not up to much without Oska either. I love you both terribly!

Every similar intonation of Elsa's plunges me into melancholy sentimental lyricism.

It's probably a long time since I've written such colourless letters, but in the first place I'm milked completely dry as regards literature, and secondly I don't feel any jolly life-asserting self-confidence.

Write my little sun.

I've whipped your letter from Elsa (you write that you're miserable, and will go on being miserable till I'm with you) and locked it in my case.

I'll write to you and telegraph too (you too!) I hope as the days pass to feel more cheerful. And my letters will get more cheerful too.

I kiss you, my child, kiss Oska, all yours, Vol.

Kiss Lyova, Kolya, Ksanochka,[14] Malkin and Levin,[15] they're all a hundred times cleverer than all the Picassos.

> V. Mayakovsky
> Paris (that doesn't mean I'm Paris!)

9/XI 24.

136. Mayakovsky to Lili and Osip.
Telegram from Paris to Moscow, 17 November 1924.

29 Rue Campagne Première Hotel Istria. Write. Kiss you.

> Your Steven

140

I'll write. Love kiss you.

Your Lilya

Volosit,

Thank you for the note asking me to eat jam in your room.

I am now Mayakovsky: I go round the editorial offices with Kolya, I wait for the money, I dictate to the typists, I correct the proofs. Then I buy wine and sweets and I take Kolya home by cab.

Write to me.

What good timing for your trip to Paris. Just in time for the recognition.[1]

I kiss you.

Your Lilya

Lubyanskiy Passage, <u>19.XI.24</u>

Volosik, I was terribly glad to get the letter, because I was already beginning to think you'd decided to stop loving me and forget me.

What can be done about it? I cannot give up A.M. while he is prison.[1] It would be shameful! More shameful than anything in my entire life. Put yourself in my place. I can't. Dying would be easier.

I'm in town a lot. I stay at your place.[2] When I say home, I don't understand myself where I mean. I love you, I miss you, I want to come to you.

Scotty's got the plague. You can't look at him without crying. I'm afraid he may die.

Your family are well. Lyuda's in love and she's happy. Ksanochka is jealous about Kolya and me — I'm a replacement you for him.

Beskin's in love with me.[3] Mosselprom's been renamed Mosselbrik or Oselprom.[4] Shmidt has been removed at the State Publishing House;[5] it'll probably be Ionov,[6] and in the Moscow section Malkin (!!). He'll also join the editorial board of Lef (!!!).

Where are you going? Alone? To Mexico? Doesn't it make your hair stand on end? Get me a Mexican visa and we'll go together in the Spring. (Shall we take Oska along?)

141

Anyway, do as you wish, but we're miserable here without you.
I kiss your little puppy muzzle.

Your Lilya

140. Lili to Mayakovsky.
Letter from Moscow to Paris, 21 November 1924.

21.XI.24

Volodenka,

I've been crying for more than a day — Scotty's dead.
It's so sad! . .
I kiss you, my own little one.

Your Lilya

Don't bring a dog.

141. Lili to Mayakovsky.
Telegram from Moscow to Paris, 26 November 1924.

Worried. Telegraph immediately in detail. Kiss you.

Lili

*142. Mayakovsky to Lili.
Telegram from Paris to Moscow, 27 November 1924.

Waiting American visa. If don't receive month or six weeks return
Moscow. Telegraph and write more often. Kiss you love you.

Your Schen

†143. Mayakovsky to Lili.
Letter from Paris to Moscow, 6 December 1924.

Dear Lilyonok

I yearn for you terribly. Every day I almost howl. It's difficult to write
about it and unnecessary.

Your last letter is very painful and incomprehensible for me. I didn't
know how to reply. You write about shame. Are you really trying to tell
me that that is all that binds you to him and the only thing that prevents
you from being with me? I don't believe you! — And if that is the case, it
really is so unlike you — so indecisive and so immaterial. This is not a
clarification of non-existent relations — it's my sorrow and my thoughts
— pay no attention to them. Do what you like, nothing will ever change
my love for you in any way.

142

Your latest telegrams are so lacking in tenderness — no "I love you" no "your" no "Kitty"!

I know nothing about you, Elsa doesn't show me your letters although she swears they contain nothing either about you or about me. She reads me extracts! Your "forbidden" letters!! It's utterly wretched!

I know nothing nothing nothing about you!

Write more, Lilyok, or at least more often — telegraph! I grieved terribly over Scotty. He was the last thing you and I did together. Well, that's enough about grief — I believe want to believe that we'll still have a lot of things together. I've come up with a few things while I've been here. They seem good. Please don't completely stop loving me — I need it very much!

What's this nonsense with Lef? Has the issue with the first part come out at least?[1] Oughtn't I to do something? If the issue hasn't come out you're probably in a terrible state financially. Write in detail. How are things with Lengiz?[2]

This is not
a small tear,
this is me!
Is it anything
to brag about?

If you haven't any money, don't send any to Elsa for the time being. I'll arrange it somehow myself. Where did you manage to place extracts?[3] If Lef needs me to, I'll return to Moscow immediately and not go to any Americas.[4]

There's almost nothing to write about me. I haven't done a thing the whole time, now I'm starting again. Unfortunately I'm drawn towards poetry again — It's the lyric in me![5]

I sit here in Paris because I've been promised an answer about the American visa in two weeks. I almost hope they don't give me one — then I can leave for Moscow that very second, pay off my advances and not go anywhere for about three years.

I miss you and all of you completely inexpressibly. That's even despite my exceptional poetic imagery.

I'm very fed up here — I can't stand having nothing to do. Now that our people have arrived I go and unburden my Soviet soul.[6]

So far I haven't read anywhere. Except at home — under my breath and to one person at a time.

If there are any new books of mine or extracts printed somewhere, send them.

Boris Anisimovich[7] is still not here.

Your things are lying here, but there's no one to send them with and I can't send them by post — they're rather heavy. Of course your entire list will be carried out exactly. With the addenda in your letter to Elsa.

I no longer go to the theatre, or to bars, I'm sick of them, I sit at home gnawing at chicken legs and eating goose liver and salads. All this is brought by the landlady Madame Sonnet — it's an amazingly aesthetic town!

Did Osik get the linen from Berlin? I'll bring him a chess-set and a belt from here. What size shirts does he wear? I think it's a 39 collar? Tell Osik that I miss him very very badly and also that I love him very very much. Kiss him. Ask him to add a few lines to your letter (if of course you write one).

Who are these foolish women who phone up to say they've had letters from me? Note down their names and write them to me. I really do hope no one believes these lies?! Can you imagine me sitting scrawling young girls letters? It's some sort of Faustian fantasy!

Kiss Kolya and Ksana from me, Lyova, Malkin and anyone you wish.

Lilyok, answer this letter as quickly as possible please, both by letter and by telegram. Or else I'll order collar size 41 — whereas earlier when I was calm and plump I wore 43! And even 44!!

I kiss you my own sweet and beloved little Sun.

I love you.

Your (forgive me for foisting such old-fashioned goods on you)
Shchen —

Paris
6/XII 24.
Love me a little, my child! !

144

Telegraph immediately health doings. Worry miss you love you kiss you.
Your Shchen

8.XII. 24

My dear, my own Volosit, I'm still in Sokolniki. Today Alter brought
me a doberman pinscher bitch. She's terribly jolly and clever — she's
going to be our guard-dog. Her owners have had their living-space
reduced and they had to give her up. I already love her, but I'll never
forget little Scotty.

Lef has already been almost closed down — they won't even let them
print the issue that's already been set. So that I didn't get anything from
them for "Lenin". Osya's going to go and try to persuade Ionov
tomorrow.

There's been a chapter of accidents with the fur coat. They put the nap
on the wrong way, and when I wore it for the first time I aroused
rapturous applause on the tram for my bare knees, and I came home with
my dress turned up round my neck like a muffler! I'll have to have it
altered again.

Tell Elsa that she wrote me a shockingly undetailed letter: what lace did
Tamara give her? What new fur coat? What have you had made, and what
have you bought yourself? and so on . . .

I'm glad that you're having a good time. It would be good if you did
manage to get to America.

Osik works and gads about. Lyova spends the whole day at the co-
operative publishing house (!) and then has rendezvous in the evening.
Malkin rings up: he's turned down the State Publishing House. I can't
stand Kolya. Ksana has some sort of women's illness. All the other card-
sharps are in place (in Vodopyanyy). Yesterday Alter, Kolya and
Kruchonykh played poker till 7 a.m.; Kruchonykh twice ran up to the
seventh floor for money.[1]

It's a pity you don't write to me.

What kind of a haircut have you got?

Thank you for the perfume and the pencils. If you're going to send any
more, make it Parfum Inconnu by Houbigant.

I kiss all your puppy muzzle.

(Lilya)

146. Mayakovsky to Lili.
Telegram from Paris to Moscow, 13 December 1924.

Paid off Elsa. Any day leaving Moscow.[1] Telegraph immediately do you want even a little see me? Kiss you.

Volodya

147. Lili to Mayakovsky.
Telegram from Moscow to Paris, 13 December 1924.

Very much want see you. Miss you. Kiss you.

Lilya

148, Mayakovsky to Lili.
Telegram from Berlin to Moscow, 25 December 1924.[1]

Leaving Berlin 25th. Kiss you, love you. Your Schen. Volodya copycat kisses your head.

149. Lili to Mayakovsky.
Note, Moscow, winter 1924/25.[1]

Volosit, I'm sending you some things. She (Mama)[2] couldn't carry the blanket and pillow as well. If you need them, she'll bring them tomorrow. Have we forgotten anything?

I kiss you my own one.

Your Lilya

†150. Mayakovsky to Lili.
Note, Moscow, winter 1924/25.

My own Lilyok

Thank you for the things. Let the blanket and pillow stay in the dacha — after all I still want to come out there! I've spent the whole night dreaming about something at Levashovo.[1] You were on your way there and I was arranging a big house for you (although in Levashovo it was the other way round).

I kiss you

Your loving

[On the reverse:]

I kiss you, I kiss you.

146

To Kitty

1) Keep a watch on Oska about the agreement and scold him every day so that he hands everything in on time.[2] Don't trust him.

2) Choose a photograph straightaway for the collected works. If you need an enlargement, I had them taken on Tver Street just before Strastnaya Square to the right of Stoleshinikov Lane at the old "John Bull" booth.

3) Chivvy along my sister, Osya and everyone with Lef.[3]

4) Chivvy along the Surf Publishing House (Sofiika Passage) about the tale.[4]

5) When the tale comes out, collect the money according to the agreement.

6) About the 15th of July go to the Moscow Worker Publishing House on Great Dmitrokva Street, to see comrade Kantor about a second edition of the Tale of Petya,[5] and if they can re-issue it, collect 12% royalties.

7) Between the 15th and the 20th of June, go to Moscow Worker and collect from comrade Kantor 250 roubles for Paris.[6] Give a hundred of them to Lyova.

8) When you get the second tale, hand it in to Surf and collect 150 roubles.

1, 2, 10, 100, 200) Don't get ill!

9) Hand all the poems you get from me to editorial boards, send me half the money and keep the rest for yourself.

10) Take care of the books (my auto collection) and add to them any new ones that appear.

11) If you get asked for extracts give them any extract from The Flying Proletarian (paying half the fee to comrade Gurevich, Air Force Herald, Yushkov Lane).[7]

Landed. Kiss you.
        Shchen

Lots of kisses.

Volodya Elsa

Dear dear sweet and most beloved Lilyonok!

I'm terribly glad that in your letter to Elsa you're keeping an eye on me to make sure I get enough sleep, behave like a member of the family and carry on my journey as soon as possible — that means I'm still our little pup and then everything's all right. I'm writing to you only today because on Saturday, Sunday and Monday everything was shut and I couldn't find out a thing about Mexicoes[1] and without Mexicoes I couldn't make up my mind to write. Unfortunately my ship leaves only on the 21st (that's the earliest). I'll get the ticket tomorrow. The "Espagne", a transatlantic liner, 20,000 tons. A nice old boy, even though it's only got two funnels. It's expensive. I try not to spend any money and to live off our paper, where they give me two francs a line.[2]

I try to do all I can to make Elsa leave as soon as possible.[3] I went to the Consulate. Tomorrow I'll send Elsa and then they'll ask Moscow by telegraph.

I don't write that I'm terribly wretched only so that you don't swear at me for moaning.

The exhibition is a very tedious and pointless place.[4] Unimaginable bad taste.

The so called "Parisian Spring" is quite worthless, since nothing blooms and all they do is mend the streets everywhere. The first evening we drove around a bit, but now I've stopped going anywhere, I sleep twice a day, have two breakfasts, wash and that's all.

Tomorrow I'll start writing for "Lef". I don't meet any of my old acquaintances and of the new ones the best of all is "Bouzou", Elsa's friends' dog.

They tell him "die!" and he lies on his back with his legs in the air; they say "eat!" and then he wolfs down anything you like, and when they take him out on a lead he tears along so fast that his owners have to run, and he runs on just his back legs.

He's white with one black ear — a fox terrier but with a long coat and a very long nose. He's thick as bricks* (*Urechin)[5] but he absolutely refuses to run down the middle of the road, he sticks to the pavements.

I've run out of ink.[6]

The flight was fine. Opposite me a German was sick, but over Kovno, not over me. The pilot Shebanov[7] is fantastic. It turns out that all the German directors themselves try to fly with him.[8] He dropped his tail at every border, waved his wings when we met other planes, and in Königsberg he taxied right up to the doors of the customs hall, with everyone absolutely petrified, but it turns out he's won first prize for precision landing.

If you're going to fly, then only with him.

He and I then loafed about Königsberg the whole evening.

Kitty, write, my little one so as I get it before we sail. Write everything everything precisely about your splendid belly, tell me all Braude's words precisely.[9]

The whole of your list of things has been given to Elsa and everything will be delivered to you in full. We'll start sending things tomorrow.

And the suit for Oska.

Write whether Oska received the money for the collected works.

I kiss you my own sweet Lilik

Love me a little all yours

Shchen

Kiss Osik

2/VI 25

Please write!

†155. Mayakovsky to Lili.
Letter from Paris to Moscow, 9-10 June 1925.

Dear beloved sweet and amazing Lilyonok

As you yourself know — not a line from you. You promised a niggardly answer (only!) to all my writings. I've already sent you 2 telegrams and 1 letter and there hasn't even been a line out of you at the end of your letters to Elsa! Little one, write quickly and write more since on the 19th I'm already leaving. The steamer "Espagne" leaves St. Nazaire (eight hours from Paris) and will spend a whole 16 days crawling to Mexico! That means an answering letter from you via Paris (if it arrives on time for a steamer) will take 40 days! It really is the back of beyond. Even beyond the back of beyond!

My little sun, write to me more before that! I insist! Write everything everything everything. Without a letter from you I won't go.

Describe the whole of your belly to me in the minutest detail.

What are you doing, what are you going to do?

Kitten, don't take on any work till my return. Rest so that you become the picture of health in a steel carcass.

I live here more tediously than ever. I'm sick to death of the exhibition, especially of the conversations going on around it. Everyone wants to display his chef d'oeuvre to the best advantage, and harnesses his entire knowledge of French into saying a couple of ardent words about himself.

Today I had a visit from Morand on his return from Moscow — he's obviously a particularly vile piece of work.[1]

I haven't been to a single theatre. All I've seen is Chaplin once at the cinema. The heat is unbearable. The only place is the Bois,[2] and that only towards evening. Today I'm going to the Legation, I'm reading my poetry in the evening and then I'm going with Elsa to the Welters.[3]

I'm putting all my efforts into travelling to all the places I intended and still getting back to you no later than the autumn.

Out of all the people in the world the only ones I'm envious of are Oska and Annushka because they can see you every day.

How are you off for money? Has the State Publishing House paid Oska? Are people writing for Lef?

Give Oska a very very big kiss.

And an enormous kiss for you, I love you and miss you

Forever yours

Puppy

Write! Write! Write!
Immediately!

*156. Mayakovsky to Lili.
Telegram from Paris to Moscow, 10 June 1925.

I kiss dear Kitty. Don't worry and don't send me money. Only chivvy State Publ. House. Ticket not stolen.[1] Kiss you.

All yours Shchen

157. Lili and Osip to Mayakovsky.
Telegram from Moscow to Paris, 15 June 1925.

State Publ. House sent telegram.[1] We kiss you.

158. Lili and Osip to Mayakovsky.
Telegram from Moscow to Paris, 17 June 1925.

Telegraph health things. Kiss warmly love.

Your Lily Osya

150

Healthy. Things fine. Going Mexico. Thankyou. Love kiss dear Kitty sweet Osya.

All yours Shchen

Osya received money.[1] Lili's belly quite healthy. What Elsa's visa?[2] Happy journey. Embrace kiss love dearly.

Your Lili Osya

My dear beloved and sweet Lilyatik!

I haven't had a single letter from you, you're no longer kitty but a web-footed goose. How did you manage it? It makes me terribly miserable — it means I now shan't get any letters from you before I leave! All right — I'll take the telegrams with me — they're sweet, but there aren't many of them.

Tomorrow morning at 8.40 I'm leaving for St. Nazaire (Brittany) and twelve hours later I'll spend the night on the steamer. I sail on the 21st!

Thank you very much for the State Publishing House, and forgive me for putting you to the trouble. Last Wednesday (the day I sent you my last letter) I was, as you know, robbed down to my last copeck (they left me three francs — thirty copecks!) The thief took the room opposite mine in the Istria and when I popped out for twenty seconds on business connected with my stomach he extraordinarily skilfully swiped all my money and wallets (with your photo and all my papers!) and skedaddled from the room in an unknown direction. All my statements to the authorities had no effect, only they said that all the signs pointed to its being a thief who is notorious for this sort of thing. I'm young enough not to care too much about the money. But the thought that my journey would be curtailed and that once again I'd come back like a fool to be made a laughing-stock by you put me into an absolute frenzy. Now everything's been sorted out with your help and the Publishing House's.

I purposely asked you to send me the November and December payments[1] so that it didn't cause you any problems now, and then when I get back I'll earn some more.

Lilyok I'm sending for "Surf" (it's on your list) a sheet with a text.[2] Give it to them, please.

151

Elsa's visa can be arranged only in Moscow.

Today I got a telegram from Lyova, he's arriving just a few hours after I leave.[3]

How's the Volga?[4]

It's funny that I learnt about that by chance from acquaintances. Because I'm interested in knowing it, if only from the point of view of learning you must have recovered!

My child I'm now adding a few lines in the morning and in ten minutes I have to leave for the station. I kiss you, sunray.

I kiss Oska.

I love you both terribly and I miss you.

All yours Mexican Shchen

*162. Mayakovsky to Lili.
Letter from the steamer "Espagne" to Moscow, 22 June 1925.

22/VI 1925

Dear Linochek

Since Spain has appeared I'm taking this opportunity to inform you both that I am now successfully skirting round her and shall even call in at some little port look on the map Santander.

My Spain isn't a bad little steamer. I haven't discovered any Russians so far. There are men wearing both belt and braces at the same time (they're the Spaniards) and some women wearing enormous ear-rings (they're also the Spaniards). Two short little dogs run around. They're both the same, Japanese but ginger.

I kiss you my own one and I run off to learn how to send off a letter in French.

I kiss you and Oska

all yours Shchen

[Words in the drawing: Atlantic Ocean]

152

1. Standing, from the left: Roman Jakobson, his brother Sergey, Lili, Elsa, I. Volpert. Sitting: M. Volpert. Moscow, 1903.

2. Lili. Friedrichroda, summer 1906.

3. Osip, Lili, the poet Konstantin Lipskerov (?) and a young Turkmen, during their trip to Turkestan, autumn 1913.

4. Lili and Mayakovsky. Petrograd, September 1915.

5. Mayakovsky. Portrait of Lili Brik. 1916.

6. "Pasya" Dorinskaya, ballerinia in Diaghilev's Ballets russes. Friend and ballet teacher of Lili Brik.

7. Below: Lili Brik in the flat in Zhukovsky Street, 1917.

8. Lev Grinkrug, Elsa, her friend Tamara Beglyarova, Yelena Kagan, the mother of Lili and Elsa, Lili. Moscow, 1918.

9. Still from the film *Fettered by Film*, spring 1918.

10. Dedication to Lili on the first edition of the poem *Man*, February 1918: "To Lilinka, the author of my verses — Volodya."

В. МАЯКОВСКІЙ.

Автору стихов моих
Лилинкѣ — Володя

ЧЕЛОВѢКЪ.

11. Lev Grinkrug. About 1920.

12. Fialka Shterenberg, daughter of the artist David Shterenberg, the dog Shchen, Lili Brik, Lev Grinkrug. Moscow, Poluektov Lane, 1919-20.

ВЕЩЬ.

13. Lili Brik. Riga, 1921-22.

14. Lili and Elsa with their mother, London, 1922.

15. Lili Brik in Berlin zoo, 1922. This is the picture referred to by Mayakovsky at the end of *About This:* "Perhaps, perhaps, one day, along a path of the zoological gardens, she too — for she loved animals — she too will enter the zoo, smiling, like that, like in the photograph on my desk."

16. Photograph of Mayakovsky with a dedication to Lili Brik: "For my beloved red-haired Kitty/I shall see her in two weeks." Berlin, 17 November 1922, the day before Mayakovsky left for Paris.

17. Vodopyanyy Lane, seen from Myasnitskaya Street. "Shuffling the windows with the palm of the corner,/I fanned out pane after pane from the edge." (*About This*).

18. Vodopyanyy Lane. The windows of Lili Brik's flat. "All my life/was staked on the cards of the windows./One pip of a pane/and I shall lose." (*About This*).

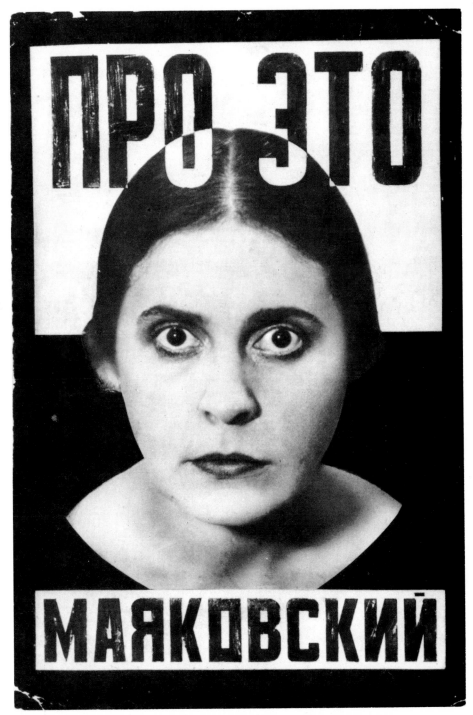

19. Cover to Mayakovsky's poem *About This* (Moscow 1923) by Aleksandr Rodchenko.

20. Photo montage to the poem *About This* by Aleksandr Rodchenko.

21. Photo montage to the poem *About This* by Aleksandr Rodchenko.

22. Photo montage to the poem *About This* by Aleksandr Rodchenko.

23. Lili Brik with a copy of *About This* in her hand. Moscow, 1924. Photograph by Aleksandr Rodchenko.

24. Lili, Osip, Roman Jakobson, Mayakovsky. Bad Flinsberg, July 1923.

25. Opposite: Photographs taken at Norderney, on the North Sea coast, in August 1923.
They show Mayakovsky and Lili with Lili's mother, Yelena Kagan; Raisa Kushner, the wife
of the writer Boris Kushner; and Viktor Shklovsky.

26. Mayakovsky with the dog Scotty, 1924. Photograph by Aleksandr Rodchenko.

27. Lili and Mayakovsky in Vodopanyy Lane, 1924.

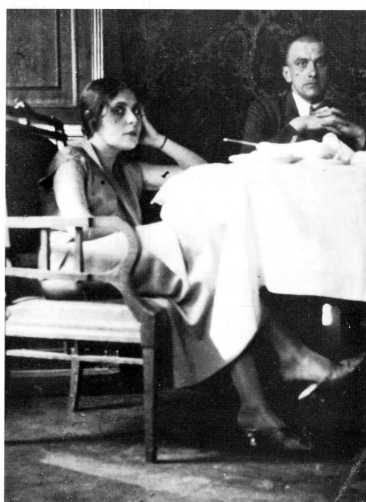

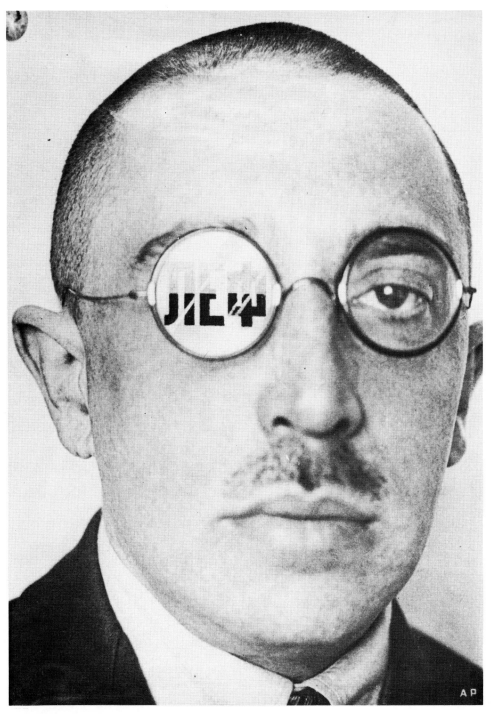

28. Osip Brik with Lef eye-glass, 1924. Photo montage by Aleksandr Rodchenko.

29. Aleksandr Krasnoshchokov, early 1920s.

30. Lili Brik and Llewella
Krasnoshchokov, 1926.
Photograph by Aleksandr
Rodchenko.

31. Lili and the dog Bulka in the
flat in Gendrikov Lane. Late
1920s.

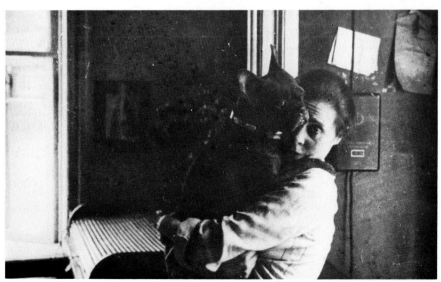

32. Mayakovsky in New York,
October 1925.

33. Lili with an Italian friend in
Salsomaggiore, October 1925.

34. Elsa Triolet, Moscow, 1925. Photograph by Aleksandr Rodchenko.

35. Back row: Mayakovsky, Osip Brik, Boris Pasternak, Sergey Tretyakov, Viktor Shklovsky, Lev Grinkrug, Osip Beskin, Pyotr Neznamov. Front row: Elsa Triolet, Lili Brik, Raisa Kushner, Yelena Pasternak, Olga Tretyakova. Sokolniki, November-December 1925.

36. The house in Gendrikov Lane. The flat belonging to Mayakovsky and the Briks is on the first floor.

37. Gendrikov Lane. The dining room and Mayakovsky's room.

38. Gendrikov Lane. Lili's room with the hanging she was given by Mayakovsky. First publication.

39. Lili and Mayakovsky. The Pension Chaír, Crimea, August 1926.

40. Lili Brik, Yevgeniya Zhemchuzhnaya, Osip Brik. Late 1920s.

41. Elly Jones with Elly, her daughter by Mayakovsky, born in New York in 1926. Nice (?), 1928.

42. Portrait of Elly Jones by David Burlyuk. Drawn in the "Nit Gedaige" workers' summer camp near New York, autumn 1925.

43. Tatyana Yakovleva, Paris 1932. Photograph by V. Shukhayeva.

44. Lili Brik with the Renault which Mayakovsky had bought in Paris. 1929 (?). Photograph by Aleksandr Rodchenko.

45. Veronika Polonskaya in Lili Brik's film *The Glass Eye*, 1928.

46. Lili Brik with a lion cub in her arms. Berlin, March 1930.

47. Telegram to Lili and Osip Brik in Berlin, 14 April 1930: "This morning Volodya committed suicide. Lyova, Yanya [Agranov]."

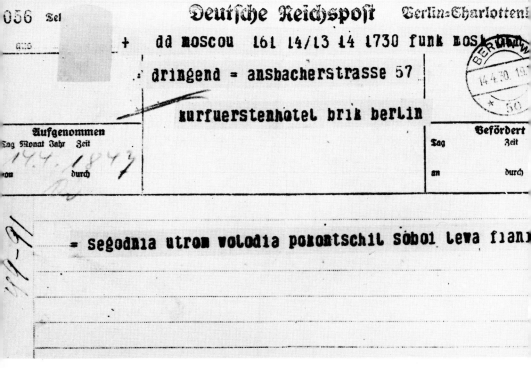

48. Lili Brik by Mayakovsky's coffin. Moscow, 17 April 1930.

49. Lili Brik with the compiler of this book at the "Twenty Years of Work" exhibition, Moscow, July 1973. (Mayakovsky's retrospective exhibition of 1930 was recreated to celebrate the eightieth anniversary of Mayakovsky's birth. The exhibition was shown in Edinburgh, Oxford, Sheffield and London in 1982.)

50. Lili and Mayakovsky during a break in the shooting of Mayakovsky's film *Fettered by Film*, June 1918.

51. The same photograph without Lili Brik (see the Introduction, note 7).

52. Lili Brik at the "Twenty Years of Work" exhibition. Moscow, July 1973. Photograph by Bengt Jangfeldt.

3 July 1925.

My dear dear sweet sweet sweet and most beloved Lilyonok!

Are you getting my (2) letters sent en route?[1] We're now approaching the island of Cuba — the port of Havana (whence the cigars). We'll spend a day or two there. I shall take the opportunity of yet again despairingly shoving a letter into the box.

The heat's unbearable!

This minute we're crossing the Tropic.

Capricorn[2] herself however (in whose honour this tropic is named) I haven't yet seen.

To the right we're beginning to be able to pick out the first real land, Florida (if you don't count trifles like the Azores). I shall have to write a poem about Christopher Columbus, which is very difficult, since in the absence of any Odessans it's difficult to ascertain the diminutive of Christopher.[3] And to find a rhyme for Columbus (a difficult enough task at the best of times) at random in the tropics is a heroic feat.

I can't say I've had a very jolly time on the steamer. Twelve days of water is fine for fish and professional discoverers, but for landlubbers it's too much. I haven't learnt to speak French and Spanish, but on the other hand I have perfected the expressiveness of my face since I communicate by miming.

My own one, telegraph me without fail about your health and how things are. Unfortunately I don't know our Embassy's address. Find out in the Commissariat for Foreign Affairs. I think their telegraphic address is Mexico City, Sovgovdel (Soviet government delegation).

I'm doing a lot of work.[4]

I miss you both inexpressibly.

I kiss you 1000 times and Oska 800.

All yours

(Columbus)[5]

Shchen

3 July 1925

My dear my own my beloved little Kitty

I dropped my letter in the box during the day, but now it's evening and I already miss you horribly horribly again.

I walked along the upper deck where there are already only machines and no people and suddenly towards me came a very young little grey cat that I had never seen before.

I went to stroke her for you but she ran off behind the lifeboats.

Kitty will you run off from me behind the lifeboats too?

My beloved you mustn't run off from me behind the lifeboats!

It's terrible terrible how much I love you.

Two yellowish little Japanese dogs and one Spanish whippet send you their regards, they all speak very good Russian and talk to me in it.

The bell is going for dinner.

It's terribly boring going to dinner.

Every day when I get up I think why does everything turn out so abominably for me, why aren't you getting up from a bunk in empty cabin No. 104?

I horribly want to see you.

I kiss you, my own one and I love you

all yours Shchen

*165. Mayakovsky to Lili.
Telegram from Mexico City to Moscow, 10 July 1925.

Healthy. Arrived. Address Whin 37 Mexico.[1] Kiss you.

Shchen

166. Lili and Osip to Mayakovsky.
Telegram from Moscow to Mexico City, 10 July 1925.

Miss you. Warmly love you kiss you.

Lili Osya

167. Lili, Osip and others to Mayakovsky.
Telegram from Moscow to Mexico City, 15 July 1925.

Congratulations kiss you.[1]

Lili Elsa Osya Mama Lyuda Olya

*168. Mayakovsky to Lili.
Letter from Mexico City to Moscow, about 15 July 1925.

Dear, dear a million times sweet and once and forever beloved Kitten,

I've already been in Mexico a week. I spent the first night at a hotel and then I moved to the embassy. First it's more pleasant because the house is nice and it differs from other embassies by the extraordinarily small number of people working here — only four (after the departure of Volynsky[1] and his wife). Secondly it's convenient since I don't know a word of Spanish and still keep mixing up gracias — thank you — and escusada,[2] which means a water-closet.

Thirdly, I don't have any monies and here I only have to put two pesos (two roubles) a day into the kitty, which since Mexican prices are so high is just fantastic.

About Mexico:

First of course it differs from other abroads mainly by sorts of palms and cactus, but that thrives properly only in the south beyond Vera Cruz. The town of Mexico City itself is oppressive, unpleasant, dirty and infinitely boring.

I've arrived out of season (season is winter), it rains regularly here for half the day, it's cold at night and the climate is very lousy, since it's 2400 metres above sea level, therefore it's terribly difficult to breathe (the first two weeks, they say) and you get palpitations. Which is quite awful.

I wouldn't stay here more than two weeks. But in the first place I made arrangements with the "Transatlantic" line for a ship (and if you order your return ticket too you get a 20%! reduction), and secondly I'm bombarding the United States with telegrams for a visa.[3] If the United States doesn't come off, I'll leave for Moscow about the 15th of August, and arrive between the 15th and 20th of September. In a few days the embassy secretary and I are going deep into Mexico[4] — to tropical forests, the only bad thing is that there's yellow fever there and we'll obviously have to limit ourselves to the train.

My child! What are you doing and what are you thinking of doing? I'm constantly afraid of not finding you at home and if you go to Italy[5] I'm afraid that I shan't manage to because of the damn theft!

I obviously shan't be in Mexico City any more when you get this letter, since after the trip up country I'll go straight to the ship. So you absolutely must write and tell me everything at the Paris embassy by the first of September so that there's a letter from you waiting for me when I arrive. Only please don't write that you don't love me. I miss you all terribly without any of your news. How is Oska? How is Lef? How is my collected works?[6]

My child I'm sending you some poems and I'm going to bother you with some terrible requests.

1) Give "The Discovery of America" to Lef.
2) Give Spain to "Ogonyok"
3) Try Izvestiya for "The Nuns" ⎫ I'm sending warrants.
4) "The Atlantic Ocean" to Prozhektor ⎭ Or the other way round

155

5) Offer the whole lot to Radio Rosta.[7]

Don't take any money from Lef, obviously. From the others take one rouble a line, and from Radio Rosta (comrade Galitsky)[8] twenty or thirty roubles a poem. I beg you terribly to transfer this money (I calculate there should be about 450 or 500 roubles, but if there's less there's less) to Elsa's André from whom I borrowed money before I set off, and I must pay him back before the first of September. If you can't get hold of all the money or you don't get any at all, please don't send your own money, just telegraph, and I'll arrange to borrow it somehow.

Thank you, my child for the little telegrams, they're terribly, terribly good and they lie at my breast in wonderful pigskin.

I'm not sending you anything now because in the first place things get lost, secondly I haven't had a chance to look around, and thirdly I want to bring you something myself.

My dear and beloved kitten I kiss you terribly, terribly. All yours with all four paws, Shchen.

I kiss Oska on his whiskers.

I kiss Elsa.

Greetings to Yelena Yulevna.[9] Please give this little letter to my mother.

[Words in the drawing: Kitty. Sokolniki. Moscow.]

169. Lili to Mayakovsky.
Letter from Moscow to Mexico City, 26 July 1925.[1]

26.7. 25

My beloved Puppy-Volosit, I do receive your letters, and bitch that I am

I don't write back! At first, I don't know why myself, and now, it's such a very long way!

In the first place — I love you terribly and I'm suffering terribly. Secondly — I'm being offered a splendid little dog (an affen-pinscher), he's grey, shaggy, with a tousled muzzle — I just don't know whether to take him! In the third place, Oska's become dreadfully keen on amateur photography.[2] He has captured the dirt under his nails once and forever in his tone-fixing bath and he's quite delighted. He snaps everything he claps eyes on, but mainly beautiful views and he says that he's now a landscape-photographer.

I'm writing on the terrace and Sharik is sitting next to me licking himself. I've adopted all the neighbourhood kittens, and they come over in the morning to eat eggs. Annushka gets angry and says they've got fleas. But I caught one and killed it on the spot.

I thought I'd quite recovered on the Volga, but I got back and fell ill with children's disease: I've got aphthae in my mouth — they're a kind of little sore children get from unboiled milk. I lay in bed for a week with a temperature neither drinking nor eating and they disappeared. Now I am utterly healthy in all respects.

But I'll still have to go and take the mud-baths — the Italians have promised me a visa in six weeks.

Oska's received the money from the State Publishing House,[3] but I, can you credit it, haven't had a copeck! So that I live in debt. Moscow Worker only gave me 150 roubles.[4] And as for Sima and Petya, the first edition hasn't sold out yet.[5] They took the tale at Surf and also gave me 150 roubles.[6] They asked me to give permission for their artist to illustrate it. I did. Is that all right? And Denisovsky's done "What is good" very sweetly.[7] "Paris" is coming out with a cover by Rodchenko.[8] Material is being typed for Lef.[9] Oska's doing everything that needs to be done.

Mama and Elsa are here. Mama's leaving the day after tomorrow. Elsa bought me everything — thank you, my own one. She told me how you'd been robbed — it nearly had me in tears. By the way — they've got it in for us! — Lyova was robbed too, and in the most brazen way! — They came up to him in the street and took 1000 francs from him.[10] Oska hasn't received his suit yet — they're bringing it any day now.

I'm sending you 15 photos. I've sent three telegrams to Mexico. When you get this letter, telegraph to say you've received it. Nothing will come of the flat in town — there's no money. I'm looking for something a bit better here or in Serebryanyy bor (the bus goes there).[11]

Your mother's had a very good rest in the sanatorium. Everyone looked after her there because of you, and she was terribly pleased. Lyuda's gone off to the mud-baths.

It would be good if we could meet in Italy. I wonder if you'll get into the United States! Write in detail how you're living. (With whom you can omit). Do you like it? How are you off for money? Are you going to Japan?[12] Are you writing the novel?[13]

Everyone misses you.

Let's meet somewhere not in Moscow, abroad, if you're not completely fed up of it there already.

Yes! It's very bad that you didn't call in on Vionnet.[14] If you get any money, send them something without fail: 50, Av. Montaigne, Madeleine Vionnet, Paris, Mr. Louis Dangel.

If you don't have any money, don't worry about it. It's not so dreadful. It's just a pity you didn't call in and have a chat.

Our cat is completely worn out. He only comes home to eat and he hits everyone with his paw.

I embrace you heartily, I kiss all the bridges of your puppy noses.

I kiss you, kiss you, kiss you.

Your Lilya

---

170. Lili to Mayakovsky.
Telegram from Moscow to Mexico City, 27 July 1925.

Worried. Telegraph. Love you kiss you.

Your Kitty

*171. Mayakovsky to Lili.
Telegram from New York to Moscow, 31 July 1925.

I kiss you from New York.[1] Beginning August Volynsky bring poems Lef. Telegraph health. Address Three Fifth Avenue. Kiss you love you.

Your Shchen.

172. Lili to Mayakovsky.
Telegram from Moscow to New York, 31 July 1925.

Healthy. Wrote Mexico. Telegraph details. Kiss you love you.

Your Kitty.

Dear Kitty no details yet. Just arrived. Kiss you love you.

Your Shchen.

3.8.25.

My dear and beloved puppy, it's absolutely dreadful if you haven't received my long letter with the photographs.[1] I wrote you a mass of details about dags and cots.

I was terribly surprised and delighted that you're in New York. Please send me a visa and moneys.

I really don't know what to write about — I wrote it all in my other letter. Telegraph to Mexico to have it sent on.

Oska's received the suit and walks around looking very proud of himself.

Write or telegraph to your family, because they're very distressed and offended.[2]

I'm healthy, but it would still be good to get to the mud-baths. I handed in my forms to the Italians. There'll be a reply in 6 weeks. I want to send a telegram to Kerzhentsev.[3]

Mama's already left. Elsa's here. They're not paying up the money anywhere. Seryozha's arrived, with the most incredibly interesting stories![4]

Give my regards to Burlyuk. How is he? Don't dare to forget me!!!

I love you and kiss you and embrace you.

We're terribly looking forward to Volynsky's arrival with the poems. Please don't ever go off anywhere again, or I'll get terribly angry.

Your Lilya

I've received all your letters and telegrams.

Everything seems to be all right with Lef. I shall force Oska to write to you.

Very much want come New York. Kiss you. Telegraph.

Your Kitty.

Trying hard get visa.[1] If can't will self come home. Miss you terribly.
Kiss you love you.

Your Shchen.

Don't hurry. Need money for flat Vionnet. If you don't send visa will go
Italy September. Telegraph often. Kiss you love you.

Your Kitty

Miss you love you. Telegraph.

Lili.

Where have you got to?

Lili

Dear Kitten tragedy Khurgin[1] upset visa business plans. Tenth start
lectures America.[2] If month don't arrange everything about tenth October
come home. Answer tenderly please. Love you kiss you.

Your Shchen.

My sweet Puppy I love and miss you.

Your Kitty

State Publ. House hasn't paid three months. Mass of debts. If can
immediately telegraph money. Telegraph. Kiss you.

Your Lilya.

Dear Kitten upset by news. Telegraph immediately reasons delay. Whom telegraph. Tomorrow send money by telegraph. Finish lectures immediately come to you. Forgive looked after you badly. Couldn't have foreseen it. Love you kiss you.

Your mangy Shchen

Puppy State Publ. House found publication unprofitable. Clarified end month.[1] Telegraphing pointless. Thank you. Kiss you love you.

Your Kitty.

Puppy received money. Kiss you warmly. Essential immediately send whole debt André[1] 43 Boulevard Capucines Lloyds bank. Telegraph. Miss you love you.

Your Kitty

Received Italian visa. What to do. Embrace you kiss you.

Lili

Lilyonok you must go treatment. If go send fivehundred dollars fourth. About fifteenth coming home. So far things very mediocre. If earn come with you Italy. Otherwise must go straight Moscow print written. Telegraph immediately. Twenty ninth going Chicago lecture.[1] Kiss you love you.

Your Shchen

Volosit I miss you. Please please come Italy. Love you kiss you.

Your Lili

Kiss you from Chicago. Miss you. Love you. Try Italy.
All yours Shchen.

Dear little sun telegraph when leaving. Tell Italian address. Miss you
love you kiss you.
Your Shchen

Transferred telegraph Amtorg fivehundred dollars. Kiss you.
Your Mayakovsky.

Received money Volosit. Hope leave sixteenth. Try to come. Miss you.
Love you kiss you.
Your Lili. Osik kisses you.

Terribly worried. Why no reply fourth telegram. Immediately today
telegraph health things. Kiss you love you miss you.
Your Schen

Transferred telegraph threehundred fifty dollars. Ask Amtorg
Kuznetskiy most. Telegraph. Kiss you.
Your shchen Mayakovsky.

Today leave Italy Salsomaggiore poste restante. Waiting kiss you.
Your Lili.

Miss you badly. Two three weeks clarify visa day. Most likely going home. Here revolting. Kiss you love you.

Your Shchen.

Telegraph immediately whether coming. Address Salsomaggiore Hotel Central. Love you kiss you.

Your Kitty

Dear kitten tearing to you. Stopping only for visa. Going Europe not later than third. Miss you horribly. Love you kiss you.

Your Shchen

Twenty eighth leaving Le Havre Paris.[1] Must ask Italian visa Paris. Telegraph immediately Elsa's address. I kiss Kitten. Till we meet.

Your Shchen

Elsa's address Moscow Sokolniki Bolshaya Olenya 14. Telegraph me money. Telegraph. I kiss you Puppy.

Your Kitty.

Telegraphing third time. Please send money express. Very worried. Telegraph immediately. Kiss you.

Your Kitty.

Sent by telegraph hundred dollars. Till we meet. Kiss you.

Your Shchen.

4.XI.25

My dear, beloved, my own Pup, tomorrow morning I'm going to Rome and I'll try to send you a visa from there. If I can't do it quickly, then let's meet in Berlin and return to Moscow together.

I haven't received the hundred dollars you sent me! I had to telegraph Lyova. All in all there was a nonsense about my money: it's too long to write — I'll tell you about it. Telegraph whether you have any money. I'm completely in rags — I've worn everything into holes. We should buy everything in Italy — it's much cheaper. It would be good if I could get you a visa, so you could come and fetch me here! I think there's a direct train from Paris to Rome. I miss you incredibly! We could spend about ten days travelling round the Venices — and then go home!

I've got a splendid present waiting for you in Moscow.

Volosit, my sweet, let's meet as soon as possible! I love you terribly.

Your Lilya

Telegraph: Lili Brik. Roma. Ambasciata Reppublica Sovietica.

This minute arrived Paris.[1] Telegraph in detail Hotel Istria. Kiss you love you.

All yours Shchen

You must wait Italian visa three weeks. Telegraph immediately details what I must do how long you'll stay Paris. My address Via Principe Amedeo 11 Hotel Genova. Miss you. Love you.

Your Kitty

Dear Kitten, let's meet soon as possible. Come Berlin Saturday fourteenth.[1] Telegraph immediately precise day hour which station arrive. Very little moneys. Sent telegraph twohundred fifty dollars bank Credito Italiano. Kiss you love you miss you.

Your Shchen

164

207. Lili to Mayakovsky.
Telegram from Rome to Paris, 10 November 1925.

Horribly anxious. Telegraph immediately details.

Lili

208. Lili to Mayakovsky.
Telegram from Rome to Paris, first half of November 1925.

Very much want see you. Miss you. Kiss you.

Lili

209. Mayakovsky to Lili.
Telegram from Kharkov to Moscow, 25 January 1926.[1]

Tomorrow 6.30 going Kiev. Address Kharkov Red Hotel. Kiss you.

Your Ochen

210. Mayakovsky to Lili.
Express telegram from Kharkov to Moscow, 26 January 1926.

Dear Lilik worried. Telegraph immediately Kharkov Red Hotel. Kiss you.

Your Schen

211. Lili to Mayakovsky.
Telegram from Moscow to Kharkov, 26 January 1926.

Everything fine. Kiss you.

Your Lilya

212. Mayakovsky to Lili.
Express telegram from Kiev to Moscow, 27 January 1926.[1]

Telegraph Kiev Hotel Continental. Kiss you.

Your Schen.

213. Mayakovsky to Lili.
Express telegram from Kiev to Moscow, 29 January 1926.

Own one why no answer. Telegraph express about flat money.[1] Worried. Kiev Hotel Continental. Kiss you.

Loving Schen

214. Lili to Mayakovsky.
Express telegram from Moscow to Kiev, 1 February 1926.

Living Lubyanskiy Passage.[1] Waiting kiss you.

Your Lilya

165

Rostov Don hotel Delovoy dvor. Leaving Tuesday. Kiss Lisik.

Your Schen

Dear Lis telegraph Krasnodar First Soviet Hotel. Here till Sunday. Kiss you.

Your Schen

Telegraph more often. Everything satisfactory. Waiting money. Kiss you.

Your Lilya

Transferred Lyova fourhundred. Rest from Baku. Kiss you.

Your Schen.

Telegraph Baku Hotel New Europe. Kiss Lisik.

Your Schen

Received money. Telegraph Lubyanskiy Passage.[1] Kiss you.

Your Lilya

<u>20/II 26.</u>

My own dear Kisitsa!*

*(I made that out of Kisa and Lisitsa)

I'm living at this minute in Baku where I have seen (as also on the way) much of interest about which I hasten to write to you.

First from Krasnodar all the way to Baku we were accompanied on the train by a large and ancient monkey. The monkey sat in the window chewing all the time. Often he would pause before he had finished chewing and look long and seriously at the hills, in hopeless sad amazement like Levin after he has lost at cards.

And before that in Krasnodar there were lots of little dogs about whom I'm now writing a poem.[1]

Baku is also not without its beasts. In the first place two days ago eleven (precisely) camels rushed past my window together right into a tram. In front of them there was a man in a Circassian coat who raised his hands, jumped backwards and shouted at them, trying to persuade them to turn back.

With immense difficulty he talked them into it.

And also there's a nice little donkey with fruit who takes up position down the road every day at nine o'clock. But as for Regina Fyodorovna,[2] she wasn't here, she'd already left for Moscow.

I'm having a merry time: given half the chance I read "Left March" and I give faultless answers to questions such as what is futurism and where does David Burlyuk live now.

Lucky Osya, he too is living a full and beautiful life: I read about his speech at the House of Unions[3] and also his furious article about cinema posters in Soviet Screen.[4]

Give him a big kiss. I don't kiss him in my telegrams because express telegrams may arrive at night and I don't want to disturb him at night over trifles.

On Tuesday or Wednesday I'm off to Tiflis and when I've finished reading there it's back to Moscow as soon as possible.

I'm sick of it — it's muddle after muddle. The organisers are young. There are huge gaps between the readings, and not a single lecture has been coordinated with convenient trains. So instead of travelling first class I go from place to place resting against my unoriginal enormous star-ticked ear. Even without the ticks it would be more comfortable, but I can't be bothered to comb out the ticks, especially out of 20,000 copies.[5]

It's spring here. They're selling mimosa in the street. You can walk around without a coat but then it's very cold. There's a little street to the left of me with a barber's called "Aelita". Everything's in Turkish here but it looks horribly foreign because they now use the Latin alphabet: Chemist's and then straightaway in their language — "Aptiq", and anyway they have their Sundays on Fridays. On my right is the Caspian Sea, which the Volga pours into day after day, though there's nowhere for it to pour out from since this sea is a lake and it's in a situation with no way out.

Dear sunray I'm very sorry for you having to deal with all the bother

167

about the flat on your own. And I'm envious of you because that kind of bother is interesting.

My own one, I miss you very much. Everyone needs to have someone, and for me that one is you. It's true.

I kiss you with both lips and moreover with both of them an infinite number of times.

All yours Schen the First (of Azerbaidzhan)

222. Mayakovsky to Lili.
Express telegram from Baku to Moscow, 21 February 1926.

Transferred Lyova fourhundred. Wednesday going Tiflis. Kiss you.
Your Schen

223. Lili to Mayakovsky.
Telegram from Moscow to Baku, 23 February 1926.

(Money /?/)[1] received. Very warm kisses.
Your Kitty

224. Mayakovsky to Lili.
Express telegram from Tiflis to Moscow, 26 February 1926.[1]

Telegraph Tiflis Palace Hotel. Kiss Kitty
Your Schen

225. Lili to Mayakovsky.
Express telegram from Moscow to Tiflis, 26 February 1926.

Volosik please transfer more money. Embrace kiss warmly you and all little beasts. Osya kisses.
Your Kitty

226. Mayakovsky to Lili.
Telegram from Tiflis to Moscow, 1 March 1926.

Transferred Lyova threehundred. Today depart Moscow. Will telegraph arrival date from Baku. Kiss kitties.
Your Schen

227. Mayakovsky to Lili.
Telegram from Mineralnyye vody to Moscow, 3 March 1926.[1]

Arriving Friday[2] five p.m. Kiss you.
Your Schen

Ordered drizzle stop. Kiss you love you.

Schen Cat

15.V.26

My dear beloved beasties, I had a very good journey. There was a pleasant woman travelling with me. We drank tea and talked all day, and at night we slept the sleep of the dead. The male population of the compartment spent a long time vainly chatting us up, but they were out of luck! I even feel sorry for them — the poor things, they were so delighted to see us and so obviously hopeful!

The journey from Moscow to Tuapse is splendid: at some station, on the platform, there were cages (they were taking them to Petersburg) with two wolves, two wolfcubs, two eagles and two storks. The storks were pecking at and inspecting each other's feathers. I had a little chat with all of them.

But that's not yet all the sights: in addition out of the window I saw masses of bull calves (all the spit and image of Osya!), and young goats and enormous herds of young rams.

The journey from Tuapse to Sochi was like in "Our Hospitality".[2] Fifty miles in 5 hours! On the way the passengers got out to pick flowers. We crawled our way out of tunnels completely black. And all the way we whistled, blew the horn and rang the bell like madmen.

In the Riviera[3] there's also fauna, by the name of "bedbugs".

My room gives straight out on to the sea. And moreover, not from a window but through a door. The door has no railing round it and the room is quite tiny, so running into it is not recommended — you might not be able to stop yourself and you'd fall into the sea!

Every day I eat shashlyk and strawberries.

The sea is noisy and changes colour every minute. You just can't keep up with it! And in the evenings there's a healthy smell of subtropical plants.

Tell Lyova that tomorrow I'll write to him with all the details about Matsesta. I think that without a bath you can live there for 200 roubles a month.

I very much want to take the steamer from here to the Crimea. But I'm a bit afraid of it pitching. I'll only go if the sea is absolutely calm.

It's very warm, but it drizzles all the time (despite your instructions). Yesterday the sun clambered its way out for about three hours and I immediately burnt my back and legs. Today I can't sit and I can't lie down!

Cat! Puppy! Don't forget me!!!

I kiss with all my strength your little muzzles, your necks and all your eight little paws.

Your

I kiss Annushka and Olya.

230. Mayakovsky to Lili.
Telegram from Leningrad to Gagry, 18 May 1926.[1]

Will send by Saturday no less than 150. Kiss sweet Kitty from Leningrad.

Schen

231. Osip and Mayakovsky to Lili.
Telegram from Moscow to Batum, 26 May 1926.[1]

Kiss you waiting love you

Osya Vol

*232. Mayakovsky to Lili.
Telegram from Odessa to Moscow, 24 June 1926.

Revelling in Odessa.[1] Monday sail Yalta on some Hawk.[2] Many kisses Kitty Osya.

Your Schen

233. Lili and Osip to Mayakovsky.
Telegram from Moscow to Odessa, 25 June 1926.

Why no telegrams? Very anxious.

Lilya Osya

*234. Mayakovsky to Lili and Osip.
Telegram from Yalta to Moscow, 30 June 1926.

Kiss dear Kitty and Osik. Miserable as horse. Address Yalta Hotel Rossiya.[1] Write telegraph!

All yours Schen

Healthy. Everything fine. Kiss you warmly.

Congratulations.[1] Kiss you warmly.

Lili Osya

My own dear dear beloved and sweet Kit

Strange as it may seem I'm writing from Simferopol.

Today I'm going to Yevpatoriya and in two days I'm going back to Yalta (where I'm going to wait for your telegrams and letters).

The money from Odessa has finally run out, and I'm having to do some readings to earn more.

Unfortunately that too hardly earns you a thing. For example in Sevastopol not only did they refuse to pay me according to the contract (the organisers maintaining that they were members of the International Organisation for the Assistance of Fighters for the Revolution) but then the lecture was wrecked and cancelled, and I was publicly called various names which I don't find very nice. I had to waste a whole day convening a meeting of the secretariat of the regional party committee against this rabble, and the secretary of the regional committee tore the high-handed local bobby to shreds. Complete moral satisfaction but an empty pocket. And in addition instead of writing poems I have to spend my time writing letters to editors.[2]

I haven't got a tan yet but the third layer of skin is already peeling from my nose and I carry it before me like a crimson flag. You can imagine how ugly I look.

The most unpleasant thing for me is that you're probably sitting without a single copeck, everyone is badgering you and Osik doesn't have any money for his trip to the Volga. If it goes on like this I'll come back to Moscow in a week or two.

Without you, my own dears, it's quite impossible and miserable. Even here I have absolutely no news — nothing happens on Chetyrdag and Ai Petri apart from beautiful sunrises, and even the newspapers have· stopped writing about those.

If you don't write me absolutely all your news I shall immediately start dying of boredom. I kiss all your little paws and little heads, both yours and Oska's bald patch. Love me, please, and don't forget me, and I'm all yours

Schen 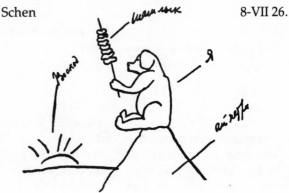 8-VII 26.

[Words in the drawing: Sunrise. Shashlyk. Me. Ai Petri.]

*238 Mayakovsky to Lili and Osip.
Telegram from Yevpatoriya to Moscow, 10 July 1926.
Living Yevpatoriya Hotel Dulber.[1] Twelfth depart Yalta.[2] Crazed with boredom. Write telegraph more oftener please. Warmly kiss Kitty Osya.
All yours Ochen

239. Lili to Mayakovsky.
Letter from Moscow to Yalta, 12 (?) July 1926.[1]
<u>2.7.26</u>

My beloved Puppy, why are you such a spendthrift and prodigal? Why are you bored?

We live luxuriously, merrily and variously: on Mondays the cream of literary, artistic, political and financial Moscow gather at our place — Tikhon Churilin,[2] Pertsov,[3] Malkin, Grinkrug!![4] On Sundays we drive to the races — in style! changing buses on the way! On the other days Osya visits his women friends (Oksana, Zhenya),[5] and I go to Serebryanyy bor to visit one of the "bigwigs" living there — Tayye or Alter. Now try to avoid envy, Volosit!

We've given Tobka away. But the puppies are splendid! They're always together and they're waiting for us no matter what time we get back. We love them terribly and we feed them. They also love us but they don't feed us; we're fed, unfortunately, by Olya.

The most important news is that I'm working in "Ozet" (The Society of Jewish Worker Farmers). If you can, go and see the colonies in the Crimea.[6]

In a few days Vitya Shklovsky is going there to make a film with Roóm[7] and Yushkevich (from Goskino). So far I have very little to do and they don't pay me.[8]

Martynych[9] has left for Sochi. When he left I gave him a fantastic bulldog puppy. I've never seen anything so sweet in all my life! He's French, small, black, two months old. He's terribly pure-bred — both his mother and father have won prizes and medals. His ears are cocked, he's all wrinkled and he grunts!

The State Publishing House has postponed signing the contracts for volume five and for Lenin by a month.[10] Don't worry about us, my sweet. Rest until you get bored. When you get back we'll send Oska off for a rest. He doesn't want to leave me on my own.

There's a cat with five tiny little kittens living on the back stairs. The kittens live in a little basket on the window-ledge.

Some child in your family's flat on the Presnya[11] has got scarlet fever; they've taken him off to hospital, but they're afraid to come and visit us.

It's cold. You have to wear a coat, so you don't feel like going anywhere.

How's the play?[12] And the romance? (by which I mean the novel!)

Write to us and telegraph more often. Make a little cap for your nose to stop it burning up.

I kiss the bridge of your nose and all your enormous muzzle.

Your

Dear Volodya! Come back soon!

Your Osya

Dear Puppy it's dull here. Please rest. Kiss you love you very warmly.
Your Kitty

My own sweet Child

I'm living just like the shipwrecked Robinson: I cling to the wreckage
(of a ten rouble note), all around is uninhabited (by you and Oska)
Yevpatoriya, and there's already been one Friday and tomorrow will be
another.

But the main thing we have in common is that you neither write nor
have written a single word either to Robinson or to me.

To tell the truth there is one answering telegram but I don't even count
it since it has no signature and so I tell myself: maybe it's from Kitty, but
maybe it's from Drapkin.[1] Maybe it's my own fault and there's a whole
armful of letters and telegrams waiting for me in Yalta. But even there I'm
not to blame since I've been stuck here for a whole week because I've had
terrible flu. I've only got up today, but whatever happens I'm going to
leave this filthy place for Yalta tomorrow.

Three lectures, arranged once again with such difficulty in Sevastopol
and Yevpatoriya, have had to be cancelled.[2]

A merry little story! Well bis with it (bis meaning the devil in Ukrainian,
and not bis as in "bravo").

Kitty, if you haven't written yet, write to Yalta. Don't be a pig,
especially since such a little Kitty couldn't make a nice big pig anyway.

What's happening about Oska's holiday?

He should come to Yalta.

For reading to the patients in the sanatorium I've been paid two weeks
board and lodging in Yalta.[3] Oska could arrange the same thing.

It would of course be dazzling to see Kitty on a little balcony in
Yalta!. . But the wreckage of the ten rouble note is crumbling, there aren't
any more and I don't know when there will be.

In my own estimation I've become a terribly proletarian poet: I've got
no money and I don't write any poetry.

My own Lisik please answer immediately.

You probably can't imagine how miserable I am without any lines from
the two of you.

I kiss and embrace you, my own one, and I love you. All yours
Schen

[Words in the drawing: moulting.]

I kiss Osik terribly   15/VII 26

242. Lili to Mayakovsky.
Telegram from Moscow to Yalta, 19 July 1926.

Wednesday depart Yalta. Will telegraph precisely. Till we meet. Kiss you.

Your Kitty

***243. Mayakovsky to Lili and Osip.**
Telegram from Yalta to Moscow, 19 July 1926.

Infinitely glad. Friday Saturday giving lectures Yalta.[1] Come straight Yalta. Best steamer from Sevastopol. Car shake you to bits. Bring Osik. Telegraph. Till we meet. Kiss you.

Your

244. Lili to Mayakovsky.
Telegram from Moscow to Yalta, 21 July 1926.

Leaving today Wednesday ten twenty from Sevastopol by car. Kiss you.

Lilya

245. Lili to Mayakovsky.
Letter from Yevpatoriya to Yalta, 23 July 1926.

<u>Friday</u>

My own puppy, we're hard at it filming, but we're not using your script.[1] <u>The colonies are dazzlingly interesting!</u>

I shall be in Yalta on the 5th or 6th. Please, please wait for me. I want to go from there to Bakhchisaray for the day. If you want, we can meet there, in which case telegraph me immediately, and I'll tell you when precisely I'll be there and in which hotel. I'll come with Vitya.[2]

Though you're a little swine for never telegraphing me, I kiss your boundless muzzle and neck horribly tenderly.

Your Lilya

I forgot the most important thing!

I'll send you money by telegraph on Monday.

Please, please phone Solovyov[3] immediately and ask him to get hold of some film (two cans) immediately. We haven't got enough. We sent him a telegram.

246. Lili to Mayakovsky.
Telegram from Yevpatoriya to Yalta, 27 July 1926.

Shklovsky missing. Telegraph immediately time cameraman's departure. Kiss you.

Your unhappy Lilya.

*247. Mayakovsky to Lili.
Telegram from Yalta to Yevpatoriya, 28 July 1926.

Shklovsky cameraman left 1.00 p.m.[1] Evidently arrive Wednesday morning.

Your Shchen

*248. Mayakovsky to Lili.
Telegram from Yalta to Yevpatoriya, 29 July 1926.

Promised send film Monday.[1] Lectures probably prevent trip Bakhchisaray. Will wait Yalta. Telegraph arrival. Kiss you.

Your Schen

249. Lili to Mayakovsky.
Telegram from Yevpatoriya to Yalta, 2 August 1926.

Check film sent. Telegraph express.

Lilya

*250. Mayakovsky to Lili.
Telegram from Yalta to Yevpatoriya, 2 August 1926.

Film sent today steamer. Kiss you warmly.

Your Schen

Arrive Yalta Tuesday evening.[1] Kiss you

Your Lilya

Arrive Saturday. Kiss Kitty. Greetings Bulka.[2]

Your Schen

Telegraph Rostov Don Hotel Delovoy dvor. Depart Krasnodar
Saturday.[2] Kiss you warmly.

Your Schen

My own dear dear sweet and beloved

Kitty child Lis*

I miss you savagely and I terribly miss all of you ("terribly miss you
all"?)**

I'm travelling around like a madman.

I've already read in Voronezh, Rostov, Taganrog, Rostov again,
Novocherkassk and twice more in Rostov,[1] now I'm sitting in Krasnodar,
this evening I shall not so much read as wheeze — I'm begging the
organisers not to take me to Novorossiysk, but they're begging me to go
to Stavropol as well.

It's rather difficult reading. I read every day: for example on Saturday I
read in Novocherkassk from 8.30 in the evening until 12.45 at night, and
they asked me to appear again at 8.00 in the morning in the university and
at 10.00 at the cavalry regiment, but I had to refuse because at 10.00 I left
for Rostov and read at RAPP from 1.30 till 4.30, and then at 5.30 in the
Lenin workshops, which I absolutely couldn't refuse: it was for the
workers and free! Rostov is no bed of roses either!

A local reporter said to me as we were walking down the street:

"They say that genius and evil are incompatible, but here in Rostov
they've merged." In translation that means that a few months ago the
sewage and water pipes burst and joined together! Now they don't drink
unboiled water, and they advise you to drink boiled water within four
hours of boiling it — or else, they say, there's some sort of "sediment".

You can imagine what I did in Rostov!

I drank Narzan mineral water and washed in Narzan mineral water and kept myself clean in Narzan mineral water — I'm still all fizzy even now.

I didn't touch any teas or soups for the whole three days.

Such is my intellectual life.

From the spiritual and romantic point of view things are also pretty awful.

There's only been one romantic interlude, and that was rather strange. After my lecture in Novocherkassk I was invited back to his study by the local professor of chemistry who zealously plied me with his own wine from his own vines out of measuring-glasses and test-tubes to the accompaniment of a recitation of his 63-year-old verses. Since the wine was remarkable but there was nothing to help it down apart from various "manganeses and anhydrides", I had no option but to get merry exceedingly fast and exchange kisses with the poetry-loving chemist.

Distilling phials are very fragile and if you just stand them on the table it turns out they smash, I realised that quickly and reached for my travelling glass[2] but saw only the case, the students had snaffled it as a keepsake, so there was no loss to the university but on the other hand I'm even more afraid of Rostov and I'm completely disarmed.

I shall have to boil Narzan and wash the dishes with it, but how can you tell whether Narzan is boiling since it's always hissing and letting off bubbles?

Life is dangerous as the writer Elsa Triolet says.[3]

That's all that's happened. Did you receive the moneys? I sent them by post so that they could be brought straight to your bed.

I don't know yet if I'll go to Kiev. I really ought to and I really don't want to.[4]

If I don't I'll be in Moscow Sunday Monday, if I do Tuesday Wednesday.

Don't forget me my own one — I love you terribly and I'm terribly yours
SCHEN

Kiss Oska —

Osik, look after Lef.[5] I kiss you.
                    Your deputy Vol
*The so-called "little sun". — Mayakovsky's note
**Ask Osya to proof-read. — Mayakovsky's note.

Krasnodar 29/XI 26.   [Word on the bottle: Narzan]

178

Arrive Moscow Sunday.[1] Kiss you
Your Schen

Train late. Kitty spent night Warsaw. Probably arrive Vienna today.
Kiss you.
Osya

Kitty's address Vienna Hotel Bristol. Kiss you.
Osya

Kiss you warmly
Schen

Nothing new. Kiss you
Osya

Telegraph Samara Hotel National about Kitty Lef[2] Federation.[3]
Thursday depart Saratov.[4] Miss you kiss you.
Vol

Lef printing. Federation wrangling. Kitty asking money. Miss you.
Come back soon. Kiss you.
Osya

Second arrive Moscow. Immediately receive permission send money.
Miss you.
Your Schen

179

Telegram from Moscow to Vienna, 3 February 1927.

So far permitted 205 dollars. Sent telegraph Arbeiterbank poste restante. Trying anyday send rest. Thanks parcel. Kiss you

Schen

264. Lili to Mayakovsky and Osip.
Telegram from Vienna to Moscow, 4 February 1927.

Received ten pounds twohundred five dollars. Waiting rest. Miss you. Kiss you.

Your Lilya

265. Lili to Mayakovsky and Osip.
Telegram from Vienna to Moscow, 6 February 1927.

Why silent as grave. Hundred ninety five.

266. Mayakovsky and Osip to Lili.
Telegram from Moscow to Vienna, 7 February 1927.

Doubling efforts. You'll receive money anyday. Love you kiss you.

Schen Cat.

267. Mayakovsky and Osip to Lili.
Telegram from Moscow to Vienna, 10 February 1027.

Money sent. Waiting miss you love you kiss you

Schen Cat

268. Lili to Mayakovsky and Osip.
Telegram from Vienna to Moscow, 13 February 1927.

Leaving Sunday 2.40.[1]

Your Kitty

269. Mayakovsky to Lili.
Telegram from Kharkov to Moscow, 23 February 1927.[1]

Dear Kitty transferred twohundred. Thursday arrive Kiev Continental. Telegraph. Kiss you Osya

Your Schen

270. Lili to Mayakovsky.
Telegram from Moscow to Kiev, 25 February 1927.

If can transfer more moneys. Kiss you.

Your Kitty

*271. Mayakovsky and Roman Jakobson to Lili and Osip.
Telegram from Prague to Moscow, 19 April 1927.[1]

Kiss you. Prague Václavská 22 Hotel Julius.

Schen Roma[2]

272. Lili and Osip to Mayakovsky and Roman Jakobson.
Telegram from Moscow to Prague, 23 April 1927.

Kiss you Romik tenderly.

Your Lili Osya

273. Lili and Osip to Mayakovsky.
Telegram from Moscow to Prague, 25 April 1927.

Telegraphed healthy. Embrace kiss you.

Kitty Osya

274. Lili to Mayakovsky.
Letter from Moscow to Paris, 25 April 1927.[1]

<u>25.3.27</u>

Volosit, nothing's happening here. We haven't yet been to rent the dacha. The Easter bread and cakes are excellent. Oska's writing an introductory article for Kolya's collected works.[2] There wasn't a Tuesday last week but there'll be one tomorrow.[3] It's really warm.

I'd very much like a little car. Bring one please! We've thought about the make a good deal. And we've decided that best of all would be a little Ford. 1) It would be best of all for our roads, 2) it's the easiest to get spare parts for, 3) it's not smart, it's a working car, 4) it's the easiest to drive, and I absolutely want to drive it myself. <u>Only you absolutely must buy</u> a Ford <u>of the latest model, with the stronger re-inforced tyres;</u> with a complete set of all the instruments and as many spare parts as possible.

In addition Bulka and I ask you please, please, if you can, to buy everything I noted down for you for the motorcycle, as we do a great deal of driving on it.

Please write to me, Puppy! I kiss the bridge of your nose. Stay healthy. Please rest, and come back as soon as possible.

I embrace and kiss you with all my might. Your

If there exists in nature some sort of cinematic tooth-make-up — to make them white, bring some back for Shura.[4]

181

Please spoil Elsa terribly. Write to me about her in detail. I'll write to her separately.

Kiss her on both cheeks for me.

Dear, sweet Volodya, we feel very miserable and very orphaned without you. Lef No. 4 has already been set in type and will come out any day.[5] You absolutely must send some material for No. 5, or there'll be nothing to print. There's no interesting news; it's all trivia and gossip. Lavut[6] keeps phoning you all the time; he doesn't believe you've gone away; he says you've been seen in the street. Tomorrow we'll have a Lef Tuesday in the flat and discuss material for No. 5. Send poetry and prose, even in the form of letters, we'll print them.[7] I kiss you very warmly and miss you very badly.

Osya

*275. Elsa Triolet and Mayakovsky to Lili.
Telegram from Paris to Moscow, 30 April 1927.

Congratulations kiss Kitty

Elsa Schen

*276. Mayakovsky and Elsa Triolet to Lili.
Telegram from Paris to Moscow, 2 May 1927.

Eighth depart home stopping Berlin Warsaw.[1] Kiss you

Your Schen Elsa

277. Lili and Osip to Mayakovsky and Elsa.
Telegram from Moscow to Paris, 3 May 1927.

Embrace kiss you Elsa

Your Lili Osya

278. Lili to Mayakovsky.
Telegram from Moscow to Paris, 3 May 1927.

Essential talk Vionnet

Your Kitty

*279. Mayakovsky to Lili.
Letter from Paris to Moscow, 7 May 1927.[1]

My amazing dear and beloved Lilik

The moment I tumbled into the Istria they brought me your letter[2] — I hadn't even had time to take my hat off. I went wild with joy and from then on I led my life according to your instructions — I looked after Elsa, thought about the car and so on and so forth. My life is utterly repulsive

182

and unbelievably boring. I'm doing everything I can to curtail the time I spend in these rotten abroads as much as possible.

I've got a major reading in Paris this evening.[3] Flakserman's going to call in (he's here in connection with various auto-aero matters).[4] We'll have dinner and then we'll go and read. On the ninth I'm leaving for Berlin (there weren't any tickets for the eighth), on the tenth I'm reading in Berlin[5] and from there to Moscow via Warsaw (so far they won't give me a visa — only a transit visa).[6]

In Prague I signed so many copies of my books I completely wore my hand out. The Czechs are manic collectors of autographs, it's their equivalent of stamps. I had a splendid reception from the Czechs, they arranged a tremendous evening reading before a thousand people — they sold all the tickets and then started selling the ticket stubs; they sold half of them, but then people started leaving because there was no more room.[7]

*280. Mayakovsky to Lili.
Telegram from Berlin to Moscow, 11 May 1927.[1]

Dear child depart Thursday Warsaw. Miss you infinitely. Completely forgotten how write. Kiss you Osik.

All yours Schen

281. Mayakovsky to Lili.
Telegram from Warsaw to Moscow, 13 May 1927.[1]

Kiss you. Telegraph Warsaw Embassy.

Your Schen

282. Lili and Osip to Mayakovsky.
Telegram from Moscow to Warsaw, 14 May 1927.

Miss you waiting love you

Your Kitty Osya

283. Mayakovsky to Lili and Osip.
Telegram from Warsaw to Moscow, 20 May 1927.

Coming home Saturday.[1] Kiss you.

Your Schen

284. Lili to Mayakovsky.
Telegram from Moscow to Warsaw, 21 May 1927.

Worried.

Lili

Congratulate my own Puppy. Kiss you
Your Kitty

Received money. Hotel Oriant.
Your Kitty

Depart today week by sea.[1] Will send address. Kiss you
Your Lilya

Congratulations,[1] embrace kiss you. Telegraph Batum Makhindzhauri
dacha Roshchet.
Your Kitty

Thanks telegrams. Kiss you love you.
Your Schen

Volosik transfer money Batum Statebank. Telegraph Gagry poste
restante. Terribly love kiss you Osik.
Your Lilya

Puppy essential leave extra twohundred. Owe Kuleshov.[1] Leaving
Friday. Try wait me.[2] Telegraph. Anxious. Miss you. Kiss you.
Your Lilya

Transfer not less threehundred. Embrace kiss you
Kitty

Monday twenty fifth lecture Kharkov. Your train Kharkov Monday twelve thirty night. Meet station.[1] Miss you. Kiss you.

Your Schen

Warmly kiss you love you.

Your Kitty

Depart Yalta. Many kisses

Your Schen

Telegraph immediately health state. Terribly anxious. Yalta Hotel Rossiya. Kiss you.

Schen

Anxious. Telegraph Yalta Hotel Rossiya. Kiss you love you.

Your Schen

Healthy. Embrace kiss you. Sixth Lef printing.[1] Urgently send material seventh.[2]

Your Kittens

Bulka successfully given birth two black three white. Love you miss you. Return soon.

Your Kitty

My own dear beloved Lichik

How are you? How is Osik? How are the respected sons of bitches of our bulldog?

185

I'm living in Yalta or rather I'm said to be living in Yalta because I go off to read in all the directions there are.

I've read twice in Lugansk, once in Stalino, Simferopol, Sevastopol, Alushta and so on.[1]

I'm living in Yalta with Gorozhanin,[2] and he comes on most of my train trips. Though I went to Alushta with Llewella, who was visiting some Valya Shakhor who she'd thought was called Shakher, so that the first time she laid eyes on her she yelled piercingly to the entire kursaal dining-room: "I'd always thought you were a 'her', but it turns out that you're a 'hor'." I lowered my eyes in shame.

I'm reading in Yalta on the 15th, then on the 19th and 21st in Yevpatoriya and Simferopol, and I think from the 1st to the 10th the Caucasus, from the heights of which I shall come to Moscow.[3]

My child I have a number of requests to make of you.

1) Get four hundred roubles from Molodaya gvardiya (you must collect them no later than the fifteenth, or else they'll send them to me in the Crimea) and take the money for yourself. (I'm including a warrant.)[4]

2) Find out whether Molodaya gvardiya has received my second part of the poem.[5]

3) Please find out from Beskin whether my sixth volume of the collected works has got into the editorial plan.[6]

4) How are things at the State Publishing House with regard to the publication of my October poem?[7] Please, please get Oska to check the proofs of this poem with particular care.

5) How are tings in general with flats, repairs, dachas and so forth?[8]

6) Ask Osik to compare the State Publishing House copy of the poem with the extract sent for Lef[9] and to make any appropriate changes in the Publ. House copy. And that's all.

Is it a lot?

My own one please answer all these points in a detailed letter to Yalta.

I kiss you and I miss you all yours Schen

10/VIII 27.

[Words in the drawing: Kiss Osik on the]

Collect four hundred Molodaya gvardiya. Sent poems Lef warrant money express post. Love you miss you. Kiss Kitty Osya puppies.

Your Schen

17.8.27

My dear Volosit, Puppy.

Our little bulldogs are amazing: blind, pot-bellied, shouters, gluttons and fighters. Bulka is absolutely ecstatic about them, despite the fact that they suck at her day and night.

The repairs only started on Monday, before that I just couldn't find a good craftsman. It'll come to about 400-500 roubles. We can't have a gas bath. I'll find out about an electric one. Or else we'll have to squeeze in a water-heater somewhere, — it's really very bad with the storage tank.

The second part is being printed at Molodaya gvardiya — they haven't received anything from you from the Crimea. Yermilov[1] sends his regards.

The sixth volume has passed through into the editorial plan.[2]

The whole poem is set up in type at the State Publishing House: there haven't been any proofs yet.[3]

Oska has signed the last proofs of "Lenin" as ready for printing.[4]

Everything's fine at the dacha. The Tiflisites[5] have left. We have Lyova and Syoma[6] living with us; the Rodchenkos[7] are always coming round; people come and go. The little goat has died — he caught a cold — I was very sad, he'd been terribly sweet lately, chasing after everyone and asking for bread and sugar with his hoof.

I'm writing a screenplay for International Workers' Aid from a story by Nekrasov[8] — I'll get 600 roubles!!

I've arranged for Elsa's "Tahiti" to appear in the State Publishing House's Universal Library series.[9]

I haven't yet got the money from Molodaya gvardiya. I'll get it only on the 22nd.

Annushka's made masses of jam — of all different sorts.

Rodchenko and Kuleshov haven't left yet — they weren't at all keen and Varvara[10] was trying to persuade them not to.

Everything's fine with the Mayakovskys.

We play Mah-jong for money and ping-pong (table-tennis).[11]

If you have any, send some more money, or I won't have enough for the repairs. If you haven't got any, I'll borrow some.

We'll live in the dacha till the 15th of September, the repairs in Moscow won't finish till about then.

Osik is crazy about the puppies — he sits watching them, he shouts at them all, gives them orders. He doesn't let Bulka out of his sight, he won't stop feeding her. It's hilarious! His leave's already over and he hasn't had a rest at all. I keep trying to persuade him to go to the Crimea, but — I don't have to tell you! . .

The extract for Lef is amazing!!! Oska's asked me to tell you he's waiting for some prose.

Telegraph more often. Where are you going in the Caucasus?[12] Bring back a wooden box of nougat, especially if you're in Batum. There's a special sweet-shop on Lenin Street. Though you don't have to bring it.

Telegraph and let us know if you've had a rest. I kiss you, my own one. Although I now have five little puppies, you must still come as soon as you can — I really need the sixth one!

I love you terribly strongly. Please don't get seriously married, because everyone is assuring me that you're terribly in love and will definitely get married! All three of us are married to each other and to get married any more is a sin.[13]

Your

---

303. Mayakovsky to Lili and Osip.
Telegram from Yalta to Moscow, 26 August 1927.

Tell State Publ. House name October poem "Good". Subtitle October poem.[1] Don't divide parts. Give individual poems Arabic numerical order. But penultimate poem last.[2] Third going Kislovodsk lecture. About fifteenth joyfully be Moscow. Kiss my only Kitty Osya family.

All yours Schen

---

304. Mayakovsky to Lili.
Telegram from Yalta to Moscow, 31 August 1927.

Sent telegram. Transferred threehundred. Third going Kislovodsk. Anxious saddened absence news. Everyone forgotten me. Telegraph express. Kiss you miss you love you.

Your Sven[1]

188

Received money. Miss you love you.

Your Kitty

Arrive fifteenth six evening. Telegraph Kislovodsk Grand Hotel. Kiss
you miss you.

Your Ochen

Waiting kiss you

Your Kitties

Sent onehundred fifty telegraph. Arrive fourth. Many kisses

Schen

Osik.

I'm sending a little article and a chronicle.[2] Please arrange them, and it's
essential that I see Lef in manuscript.[3] It's not difficult and it won't cause
delays.

Your Vol

Everything fine except Lyova. Kiss you with all might.

Your Lilya

Telegraph express Baku Hotel Europe health state. Kiss you Osya.

Your Schen

Miss you kiss you.

Your Kitty

Miss you terribly love you terribly kiss you terribly but depart Tiflis.
Your Schen commercial traveller

Miserable out when you phoned.[2] Love you kiss you.
Your Kitty.

Telegraph express things health Sverdlovsk Market Committee Hotel.
Kiss you miss you.
Your Schen

Very anxious. Telegraph oftener. Kiss you.
Your Kitty

Going Perm. Arrive Moscow about fifth. Kiss you love you. Miss you
badly.
Your Schen

Transferred telegraph fivehundred. Telegraph express health things.
Perm First Hotel. Miss you badly kiss you.
Your Schen

Arrive Sunday midday. Many kisses.
Schen

Sent Elsa's hundred. Essential telegraph express Dnepropetrovsk
Hotel Spartacus. Kiss you miss you.
Your Schen

Express telegram from Moscow to Dnepropetrovsk, 1 March 1928.

If possible send Elsa hundred fifty more please. Glad that home[1] but miss you badly. Telegraph. Love you.

Your Kitty

322. Mayakovsky to Lili.
Telegram from Dnepropetrovsk to Moscow, 2 March 1928.

Sending hundred. Rest sixth. Leaving fifth.[1] Kiss you miss you.

Your Schen

323. Mayakovsky to Lili.
Telegram from Zhitomir to Moscow, 8 March 1928.[1]

Telegraph immediately express health Kiev Hotel Continental. Ninth depart Odessa.[2] Sending Elsa fifty. Kiss you miss you love you.

Schen

*324. Mayakovsky to Lili.
Telegram from Kiev to Moscow, 20 March 1928.[1]

Going Vinnitsa.[2] Transferred fifty. Ask Lyova call Tuesday six Pravda cooperative.[3] Papers on my desk. Kiss you.

Your Schen

325. Mayakovsky to Lili.
Telegram from Vapnyarka to Moscow, 21 March 1928.[1]

Telegraph Odessa Hotel London. Love you kiss you.

Your Schen

326. Lili to Mayakovsky.
Express telegram from Moscow to Odessa, 22 March 1928.[1]

Love you kiss you much.

Your Kitty

327. Mayakovsky to Lili.
Telegram from Odessa to Moscow, 25 March 1928.

Going Kiev Hotel Continental.[1] Arrive Moscow twenty ninth. Kiss you love you.

Your Schen

328. Lili to Mayakovsky and Osip.
Telegram from Berlin to Moscow, 16 April 1928.[1]

Arrived very well. Address Kurfürstenhotel. Telegraph health. Kiss you.

Your Kitty

Getting better.[1] We love you kiss you.

Schen Cat

Telegraph often health. Kiss you.

Your Kitty

Hurrying get better. Hope leave about three days. Love you kiss you.

Schen

Sunday

Dear beasties! I'm terribly anxious about Volodik!

Volosit, when you leave, bring: 1) some *soft* caviare; 2) 2-3 boxes (square metal ones) of fruit drops; 3) 2 pounds of sunflower-seeds and 4) a hundred (4 boxes of 25) "Mosselprom" cigarettes.

My cinema business depends entirely on Moscow, that is to say on money.[1]

I saw Chaplin's "The Circus" — I was utterly disappointed! And the Piscator's so boring that it was even difficult to fall asleep! It was deadly![2]

I've bought myself a dark-blue knitted suit, shoes, a little watch and four handkerchiefs, on account of my cold.

Mama is leaving tomorrow.

Oslit! Think about my cinema business!!! It'll be a shame if I can't manage to buy anything! After all it isn't that much money! Persuade the board.

Tomorrow I'll receive the manuscripts, go to Malik,[3] and find Gasbarra.[4] Ruttmann isn't in Berlin. All in all it's a good thing Mama's leaving!!

Berlin is splendid. The taxis are cheap.

I sent you a neckerchief with Misiano,[6] Oslit, and driving gloves for Kuleshov. He didn't want to take anything else.

I love you both and Bulka terribly.

I kiss all your little paws, your

¡ I'm expecting Volodik!

Doctor ordered sit home week. Hope leave first days May. If ill longer telegraph. Miss you badly. Kiss you.

Your Schen

Telegraph immediately details Volodya's health. Wildly anxious. Have transferred Vionnet. Rayechka[1] sent nothing. Love you.

Your Kitty

Nothing special. Cough remains slight temperature. Essential stay home. Raya promised send twenty third. You dispose Cleopatra.[1] Love you kiss you.

Your Schen Cat

Don't forget Elsa's money. Anxious. Telegraph daily. Kiss you.

Your Kitty

My own dear sweet and beloved Kit

I'm having monstrous luck: I still haven't recovered fully from my flu. I always have exactly the same temperature — 9 o'clock 36,6; 2 o'clock 37,1 and 7 o'clock 37,3 and a slight cough. I'm being treated again by Yefim Yurevich[1] — he told me it was because of my left lung, and at the bottom of my left lung he found what they call a "trick". Yefim Yurevich says there's nothing wrong and there's no danger, but it's all very long-winded. Y.Y. has just been here again today and said that I must stay in bed for a minimum of a week.

Given the slow pace of my present flu, there's absolutely no guarantee that that minimum will be the maximum.

And then I'll have to stay at home for four days after I've recovered, and then there's work, and then and so on, in a word you can work out how long yourself.

I think you should go on to Paris without waiting for me. I may appear only as an unexpected joy.

(I've already scoffed 24 chickens!)

I spoke to the local committee today — and they'll send Elsa the money the day after tomorrow.

Telegraph saying where and about the 4th I'll send you as much moneys as they'll allow and as much as there is.

There are no other newses.

Forgive me for not recovering, dear child, I'm doing all I can — I scoff pills all day long, I wind myself into compresses and apply cupping-glasses, but the main thing is the two thermometers, and I still find it difficult to drive off each quarter of a degree.

Dear child write and telegraph. Loving my own Kitty and all yours

[Word in the drawing: Schen.]

338. Lili to Mayakovsky and Osip.
Telegram from Berlin to Moscow, 30 April 1928.

Absolutely distressed and confused. Telegraph possible wait Volodya or immediately come Moscow.

Your Kitty

339. Mayakovsky and Osip to Lili.
Telegram from Moscow to Berlin, 30 April 1928.

Upset your distress. Come Moscow because me unnecessary. If recover this week immediately come. If continue ill you immediately telegraph where send three hundred. What news Cleopatra. Love you kiss you.

Your Schen Cat

340. Lili to Mayakovsky and Osip.
Telegram from Berlin to Moscow, 1 May 1928.

Send money Berlin. Cleopatra clarified Friday. Love you.

Your Kitty

Telegraph health. Have you transferred money. Will you come.

Your Lilya

Still lying ill. Temperature remains. After such illness must convalesce well arrange visas earn money. Impossible even approximately suggest time my trip. Sad. Miserable. Adamovich[1] telegraphed trade delegation Grigory Arkus transfer fourhundred. Inquire. Kiss you.

Schen

Received money. Depart Paris today in complete despair Volodya's illness.[1] Telegraph.

Your Kitty

Elsa over month no money. Unbearably anxious about Volodya.

Your Kitty

Health better. We'll send Elsa.[1] Kiss you miss you.

Schen Cat

Very worried. No news. Telegraph immediately health plans. Volodya started going out. Miss you badly waiting. Kiss you warmly.

Your Schen Cat

Volodya recovered started going out. Many kisses waiting.

Your Schen Cat

Dacha robbed. Moved to town. Love and kiss you.

Your lonely Kitty

Miserable anxious. Telegraph immediately Yevpatoriya Dulber. About 15 will definitely come relax best resort Pushkino.[2] Kiss you.

Your Schen

If revolver[1] stolen permit number 170 given Kharkov. Please tell GPU publish newspaper. Telegraph express Yevpatoriya are you barefoot? Shall hurry to defend own Kitty. Kiss you love you.

All yours Schen

Revolver safe shoes too. If can send moneys. Rest. Love you kiss you.

Your Kitty

Anxious. Telegraph Yalta Hotel Rossiya. Reading fifth sixth Yevpatoriya[2] eighth fifteenth Yalta.[3] Kiss you love you.

Your Schen

Insufferably bored. About tenth coming home. Tomorrow send hundred. Till eighth Yalta poste restante. Kiss you love you.

Your Schen

Kiss you love you miss you.

Your Schen

Arriving eleventh nine morning.[1] Kiss you.

Your Schen

Sent fivehundred. Arrive fifth. Kiss you.

Your Schen

Telegraph. Kiss you.

Berlin Schen

Kiss you.

Your Kitties

Dear Kit,

Please cherish dear comrade Khaykis[2] — he's my best Mexican friend.
He'll bring you "dr"[3] etc. — I'm carrying out all your Berlin errands 100%.

The Magalifs[4] (I'm just having lunch with them) send their regards.

I kiss you all yours

Kiss Osik.

<u>14.10.28</u>

My beloved Volosit-Puppy!

I hardly miss you — I'm in the factory assembling the film from 4 till 11
at night.[1] Let's hope that the Berlin telegram in which the first word was
telegrafte was from you: all the other words were so garbled that we
didn't understand a . . .! "telegrafte zelniu schen cerlius kue"???[2]

<u>About the car</u> don't forget 1) bumpers front and back, 2) an extra
searchlight at the side, 3) an electric wiper for the front windscreen, 4) a
light at the back with the word "stop" on it, 5) it absolutely must have

electric arrows showing where the car is turning, 6) a warm covering so the water doesn't freeze, 7) don't forget about the trunk and the two spare wheels in the back. About the clock that is wound up once a week.

The colour and shape (closed . . . open . . .) I leave to your and Elsa's taste. Only it mustn't look like a taxi. Best of all would be a Buick or a Renault. Only not an Amilcar! Tomorrow morning I'm starting driving lessons.

Osya's going to read his lecture "What the devil do we need poetry for?" at the Polytechnic. After which Aseyev and Kirsanov will read their poems![3]

Malkin left for Berlin today. He wanted to send you a telegram. I wonder whether he caught you.

It's terribly cold. The windows have been sealed. We're well. Bulka's a terribly sweet little calf. I'm bankrupting myself on taxis because of the rain and mud.

Write a long letter. Go and rest somewhere!

I kiss all your paws, the top of your (eau de Cologned) head, one little eye and all your cheeks.

Kiss Elsa, tell her to send you off for a rest and to write.

Your

361. Elsa and Mayakovsky to Lili and Osip.
Telegram from Paris to Moscow, 16 October 1928.

We kiss you.

Elsa Schen

362. Lili and Osip to Mayakovsky and Elsa.
Telegram from Moscow to Paris, 17 October 1928.

We kiss you.

Kitty Osya

*363. Mayakovsky to Lili.
Letter from Paris to Moscow, 20 October 1928.

My own dear sweet amazing Kit

Unfortunately I'm in Paris which has bored me to the point of insensibility, nausea and revulsion. Today I'm off to Nice for a couple of days (lady acquaintances have turned up)[1] and I'll decide where to have a holiday. I'll either base myself in Nice for four weeks or I'll go back to Germany.

198

I can't do any work at all unless I get a break!

It goes without saying that I shan't stay a day over two months in these places, which as far as I'm concerned have croaked.

My affairs aren't working out so far.

For the time being Piscator has fallen through.[2] There's nothing auspicious on the Parisian horizon (some trivial little lectures), all my hopes are pinned on Malik — they want to sign a contract with me — depending on the quality of the play (which I'm making strenuous efforts to finish).[3] In view of this I've only been licking my lips at cars so far — I had a special look round a car show.

I just can't get hold of Ruttmann, they say he's out of town. I gave Herzfelde the caviare[4] so that he'll deliver the cigarettes to Ruttmann.

Shalyto promised to send the newsreel although he raised his little hands in bewilderment suggesting some entire culture film instead of bits.[5]

The only one of the arts I can watch is kinos, where I go every day.

The artists and poets are more repulsive than slippery oysters. Rotten ones. As a pursuit it has completely degenerated. Earlier factory owners would make cars so as to buy pictures, now artists paint pictures only so as to buy cars. For them a car is anything you like, only not a mode of transport. But as a mode of transport it is indispensable all the same.

Did comrade Khaykis visit you? He's so very nice. I love and kiss you my own one.

I embrace Oska and kiss Bulka, your Schen

In the telegram it was Berlin Schen.[6] Thank you for the letter.

20/X 28.

Write, child!

364. Mayakovsky to Lili.
Telegram from Paris to Moscow, 25 October 1928.[1]

Write telegraph. Miss you badly kiss you love you.
Your Schen

<u>28.X.28</u>

Puppy! BOO-HOO-HOOOO-HOOOOOO! . . ! . . ! . . Volosit!
Boohoohoohoohoohoohoohoo-hoo-hoo-hoo-!!!

Are we really not going to have a little car?! But I've learnt to drive so brilliantly!!!

Please! Let Malik like the play!

Please bring back a little car!!!!!!!!!!!!!!!!!   !!!!!!!!!!!!!!!!!

Khaikis came to see us. He's terribly sweet — like a Pekinese.

Everything I'm wearing is new.

I'm checking the proofs of your "volume".[1]

In Molodaya gvardiya the last time they paid 169 roubles instead of 350 — there turned out to be fewer lines than you thought.

The foreign extracts for "the Glass Eye" have arrived. I'll finish the picture any day now.

Before you buy the car consult me by telegraph if it isn't a Renault or a Buick.

Boo-hoohoohoohoo-hoo-hoo. . . . . . .!

Where are you living? Why do you telegraph so little? You write: I'm off to Nice but there aren't any telegrams from Nice.

We're healthy. Oska's busy with Katanyan[2] and developing his photographs. I'm assembling the film and learning to drive. Bulka's grunting. A very sweet little kitten (a grey one) has taken up residence with us, only he's very ill and so he makes a mess everywhere. But it would be a pity to chuck him out — maybe he'll get better. He was lying around looking very miserable yesterday, but today he suddenly started playing with a fly! Bulka loves him, but teases him. We all kiss you and love you terribly. And I most of all.

Your Lilya

Telegraph car news. Kiss you.

Your Kitty

Having talks filmscript René Clair.[1] If conclusive hope car possible. Kiss you.

Your Schen

2.11.28

Puppy! Yesterday Osya, Kolya and Syoma gave a reading.[1] There were lots of people. Kolya was terrible! You couldn't understand what he was getting at! And when he started reading his poetry, the public left in droves! Syoma read splendidly. But Oska's lecture was brilliant! People clapped themselves senseless; they kept interrupting him with applause (the whole hall)! He spoke for exactly an hour and I've never seen anyone listened to with such attention. I was terribly pleased!

I've finished my film — apart from one part, which still hasn't been sent from Berlin. I showed it to the management, they were all pleased with it. Arustanov[2] says that the film is "brilliant" (I don't find it so), he's rushing me on with the next screenplay (he's ecstatic about the subject),[3] so I'm ensured work. The management don't want to show it at the "Artes", but at the "Colossus" and the "Ars". Tomorrow morning I'm going to show it to the commercial section — I don't think they'll agree to that!

Oska too likes the film very much. He says it's very "elegantly" made and that the "montage" is remarkable, and Kuleshov says he couldn't have cut it better himself. (I did all the montage myself — without Vitaly.)[4] In a word, total success. I'm terribly glad, although (word of honour!) I consider the praise profoundly unwarranted!

Please read all the above to Elsa. Why doesn't she write to me?

You wrote that you were off to Nice but all your telegrams are from Paris. Does that mean you didn't go? When are you going to get a rest then? You're a really naughty Shchen! And I'll completely stop loving you!!!

What happened with René Clair? If there isn't enough money then at least send (through Amtorg) 450 dollars for a little Ford with no spare parts. If the worst comes to the worst you can even get spare parts for a Ford here.

Boo-hoohoo-hoohoohoo - - - - - - - - - - - - - - !!!?

Tell Elsa to buy me more of the stockings I gave you to show her, and three pairs of absolutely brilliant ones, in the sense that they should flash magnificently and yet not be too bright. Buy another three dr in different sizes, and ask Elsa to buy a bottle of Nyuta's red perfume.[5]

Why don't you write? I'd like to know!

The Pudovkins[6] are leaving for Berlin any day now.

Please, please, Volosenka, get even a little rest somewhere!

I embrace you, my own little beasty, and I kiss you terribly tenderly.

Your

Kiss Elsa's little muzzle. There was an announcement in the paper that her book had come out, but it isn't on sale yet.[7] I'll phone Tikhonov tomorrow.[8]

*369. Mayakovsky to Lili.
Telegram from Paris to Moscow, 10 November 1928.

Buying Renault. Handsome grey brute 6 horsepower 4 cylinders conduite intérieure. Car departs Moscow twelfth December. I arrive about eighth. Telegraph. Kiss you love you.

Your Schen

*370. Mayakovsky to Lili.
Letter from Paris to Moscow, 12 November 1928.

My own dear Kitty

I've delayed with this letter since I telegraphed to you "buying" and I still haven't transferred it into the past tense "bought". But now it seems that nothing else will prevent it, and the moneys I'll scrape together and earn with the help of some good souls. It's an attractive car, you probably know what it's like yourself:

Of course the drawing is clumsy but I handed over the photograph from the catalogue with the order and I haven't got hold of another one yet.

I asked them to make it a grey one, they said if they can manage it, if not it'll be dark blue.

I'll stay on a while in Paris so as to collect the car from the factory myself and get it crated up and sent off or else it'll drag on for months.[1] But for the time being I'm sitting here dragoning out the play and the screenplay,[2] that'll be the first petrol Renoshka tries to wolf down.

I was wildly happy to read your letter about "Cinema Eye".[3] By the way I don't know where from but they say that on her way through Paris Shatova[4] also praised this eye terribly.

Kitty please telephone Kostrov[5] and tell him that I'm writing poetry with benefit and with pleasure but that for the sake of much convenience I'll send or bring them a little later.

Lisit, please transfer by telegraph thirty roubles to Lyudmila Alekseyevna Yakovleva,[6] Penza, 52 Krasnaya Street, Flat 3.

Lilyok, if you got the volume for proof-reading with the slogans and the advertisements,[7] discuss with Osya how best to print the advertisements, because there's no sense in churning them out in verse type! Perhaps we could use poster heading type right down the page? Think about it please.

My life is rather strange, with no events but many details which are not material for a letter and can only be talked about as I sort through my cases which I am going to do no later than the 8th or 10th.[8] You must write and telegraph a lot.

I kiss you, my own sweet and beloved little one
your Schen

Stroke Osik.
I'll telegraph the conclusion of the Renault peripeteia.

*371. Mayakovsky to Lili.
Telegram from Paris to Moscow, 19 November 1928.
Can't change. Car ready. Soon departs Moscow. Kiss you.
Your Schen

22.XI.28

My beloved Elsa and Volodik, why don't you write?

You swine! Not even to write with a detailed description of Renoshka! (I love her . . .)

Buy covers for the spare wheels.

Volosit! Please don't draw me the shape of the radiator! I know that anyway!! But write and tell me how long the car is, how wide, what colour and what decorations it's got — a clock, lamps, a mat and so on. Or else I'll die of impatience and uncertainty!

There was the first frost today.

I kiss your little muzzles.

Volosik, bring two foulard ties or else I've got nothing to wear with a jumper.

Stopped two days Berlin.[1] Eighth arrive Moscow. Kiss you love you.

Schen

Arrive Saturday.[2] Love you kiss you.

Your Schen

Money soon transferred.[2] Kiss you.

Your Kitty

State Publ. House promises soon transfer.[1] Kiss you.

Your Kitties

Categorically refused transfer hard currency. Love you kiss you.

Your Kitty

My own dear sweet beloved Lichik

I send you and Oska as big a greeting as I am able to.

I'm miserable.

It's wretched getting "letters" from you without a single word in them. Well all right then.

Tomorrow I'm off to Nice[1] — for as long as I can take. And I can clearly take only the smallest drop of it. During April — towards the end — I'll come back to Moscow.[2]

I'm of course travelling both to Nice and to Moscow in a state of prepossessing and pleasant independence.

Forgive me for confusing you about the money. So much the better — I'll leave earlier, but all the same it's a swinish trick.

I love and kiss my own Kitty.

Kiss Osik and Bulka.      Schen

Telegraph permission alter your grey coat. Kiss you.

Kitty

5.4.29

Dear Volodik, just in case I'm sending you Afanasev's[1] requests.

The things that are <u>absolutely essential</u> are marked with two little crosses, those with one little cross are <u>essential</u> and those without a cross are very necessary. Bulbs especially — big ones, send them with everyone who's coming here, because we're already driving around with one headlight. When the last bulb goes we'll stop driving. It's quite impossible to buy them here for our type of Renault.

I telegraphed you in Nice — the telegram was returned with gone away written on it.[2]

We're healthy.

Nothing sensational

I kiss you. Your

Arrive second May. Transfer Negoreloye poste restante hundred roubles. Kiss you love you.

Schen

My own dear Lichik

Drop me a line please telling me how you are and when you're thinking and if you're thinking of coming to Moscow.

I still haven't received any telegrams from Lavut and therefore I don't know anything about myself.[2]

I'm sending you moneys. I'm gradually paying my debts.

I have no more news than there is in the papers, and in the papers there's none.

I kiss you my own Kitty

your

Volodik!

I'm now "unwell". My shoes will be ready on the 4th (2 pairs). I want to leave on the 5th. Write or telegraph whether I'll catch you.[1]

If you can get hold of them, send 250 roubles before the 4th.

I embrace and kiss you and Bulka.

Your

Leaving about tenth.[1] Transfer money third. Kiss you.

Your Schen

Transferred telegraph twohundred fifty.[1] Kiss you.

Schen

Utterly miserable. Please please please telegraph Yalta poste restante.[2]
Kiss you.

Schen

Strenuous efforts Ref.[1] Waiting eagerly your material.[2] Healthy. Kiss
you.

Kitty Osya

Sending express letter[1] Yalta poste restante. Kiss you.

Kitty

31.VII.29

Volodik, please, please don't meet Katayev.[1] I have serious reasons for
this request. I met him at the Society of Dramatists and Composers, he's
off to the Crimea and he asked for your address. I ask you once again —
don't meet Katayev. On the ninth I'm off to Odessa for two weeks —
Osya will come and pick me up there.

I kiss you

Everything fine. Dealt with Borts.[1] Kitty Odessa Lustdorf[2] dacha
Folmer. I arrive twentieth morning Sevastopol. Kiss you warmly.

Osya

Volodya departs today Moscow Osya tomorrow Yalta Hotel Marino. Kiss you warmly love you.

Osya Volodya

Arrive Wednesday morning.[1] Kiss you.

Kiss you warmly.

Your Kitties

Puppy! Trip going very well. Of course you'll have received our telegram from Stolbtsy. We kiss you and Bulka.

Kiss warmly you all friends.

Your Kitties

We kiss you miss you.

Your Schen Bulka

My own dear sweet and beloved little Kitties

Thank you for the two little telegrams and the postcard. But what else? I very much want to receive more of various kinds of letters and telegrams from you — I'm very miserable that both of you have gone away together.

Valya and Yanya[1] came rushing up to the station when the train had already slunk off. Yanya was very sorry not to have managed either to say goodbye or to give you various errands and requests. He will send you a letter in Berlin <u>without fail</u>.

Of course I haven't accumulated any particular news yet. I handed in the pantomime to the circus, they liked it very much.[2]

They immediately signed a contract with me for a review for the Music-Hall.[3]

My exhibition is apparently going to Leningrad from the 5th to the 12th of March and I'm going as an exhibit.[4]

Kitty don't forget to write down in a notebook all the work you do and everything you see.[5]

Bulka is genuinely missing you a great deal. When I come home at night she not only jumps but in my opinion has even learnt to hang in the air until she has licked me on the face.

Many kisses to you both.

I love you and I'm waiting for you.

24/II 30

[Words in the drawings: Schen. Bulka.]

Kitty please send "150,000,000" from Malik Verlag — the translation.[6]

398. Lili and Osip to Mayakovsky.
Postcard from Berlin to Moscow, 25 February 1930.

Volodenka!

Our address is 57 Ansbacherstr., "Kurfürstenhotel", Berlin W 50.[1] Please write. We kiss you warmly.

Osya Lilya

399. Lili to Mayakovsky.
Express letter from Berlin to Moscow, 2 March 1930.
2.3.30

My beloved Puppy!

You can't write anything in a letter — we'll tell you everything when we arrive. We get masses of visitors. So far we're still wearing all our Moscow clothes, all we've bought is a coat and a hat for Oska.

I spoke by telephone to Mama and Elsa — it was great! They'll come to us — they probably won't give us an English visa.

The Bedbug isn't on in Frankfurt yet,[1] but when it's on I'll go for the première.

Osya has bought masses of "our" classics in antiquarian bookshops and is thrilled to bits with them.

Best of all here are the doggies! Yesterday in the Tiergarten I saw two white bulldog puppies on a single little leash, and the scotties are just impossibly sweet! Schneidt[2] comes to us for a biscuit, sits up and begs and gives us his little paw; he travels in the lift with us.

Write how things are with you in RAPP and with us in Ref.[3]

Stroke all Bulka's little places, and tell Motya[4] not to forget to wash her.

Malik sent you two copies of "150,000,000" yesterday.

You must tell Snob[5] that I left my address, but nobody's come to me and it's very bad.

I'll send you a parcel any day now. What are you doing? Who do you see?

Love me please.

I love you v. v. much and I miss you v. v. much.

I kiss you terribly hard

Dear Volodik!

I'm glad they liked the "melomime"; we're sorry you're going to write for the music-hall without me. It's very interesting here; there's a great deal that is instructive. A mass of material.

I kiss you warmly.

Osya

400. Lili and Osip to Mayakovsky.
Postcard from Berlin to Moscow, 4 March 1930.

Volosit! See how chic the Kurfürstenhotel is now![1] There's a little cross to mark my window, but Osya's looks out into the yard. We love you kiss you.

401. Lili and Osip to Mayakovsky.
Postcard from Berlin to Moscow, 7 March 1930.

7.3.30.

Puppies! We kiss you very hard. Why don't you write? We're healthy. We miss you very much.

Your

210

We miss you love you kiss you. Write more often.

Schen Bul

10.3.30

Puppies! This is the second day I've been walking around the Zoo —
huge numbers of puppies have been born! Lion pups, tiger pups,
elephant pups, kangaroo pups, monkey pups. I held a little lion cub in my
arms and he licked my face! He was impossibly sweet. We've received
your telegram. I kiss you love you.

Lilya

Send "The Bath-House" with power of attorney to Maryanov so that
you can receive royalties.[1]

13.3.30

Volosit! I've already written to tell you to send "The Bath-House" to
Maryanov with power of attorney, because things are dragging out with
"The Bedbug": three translations (according to Maryanov) in Germany,
three in France! The première is being held up and it's not clear what will
happen about the royalties.[2]

Why doesn't anyone write to us? It makes us very alarmed.

What's happened with my union?[3] What about the flat?[4] Did
Obolensky[5] give our greetings to you and Yanya?

How much I'd like a little lion cub like that one! You can't imagine what
soft little paws they have!

Please please write.

Schneidt asks you to give his photographs to Bulka and sends her his
heartfelt greetings.

Elsa and Aragon will arrive in a few days.[6]

I love you very much my Puppy. Do you love me?

I kiss you very warmly.

We kiss you love you writing miss you badly.

Schen Bul

17.3.30

Volodik! Comrade Turek[1] has gone to Moscow. Unfortunately we didn't have time to meet him, but Maria[2] gave him your address and please please be very very nice to him. Both the Germans and <u>our</u> Soviet people say he's completely one of us. He's written a book called "A Proletarian tells his tale" which is being published in Moscow now. I've received an English visa, but Osya hasn't. If Mama has even the slightest possibility of coming to me I shan't go to England.

I received your telegram: "we miss you, writing . . ." but I can't understand who you're writing to, certainly not to me. Though it would be good if you did write.

I kiss your little muzzles and your little paws and your little chests.

My own dear sweet and beloved Kit

Thank you for the photographs and the letter. Bulka looked at Schneidt with curiosity, but was offended by the other photographs. "Oh I see, Kitty now carries various fashionable lion cubs around in her arms and has forgotten about us." I persuaded her that you hadn't forgotten us, and that when you came back you would carry her around too. She calmed down a bit and promised to wait.

By the way what's the name of our lady dog-lover at the dacha with Bulka's husband, and where can I find her? Write to me.

Don't give Maryanov any plays or any powers of attorney. The Society of Dramatists and Composers is against it and as far as I know has replaced him.

As regards the union and flat news, I'm still pacing around, but relatively confidently.

I was very glad to see Obolensky and get all your greetings.

Kitty, if you get to my play, you must send me some photos. If you append to the photos some grey flannel trousers I shan't take offence.

The day before yesterday was the première of "The Bath-House",[1] I liked it with the exception of certain details. In my opinion it's my first proper production. Shtraukh[2] is excellent. It was funny how much the audience was divided — some said "we've never been so bored", others said "we've never had such fun". What else they're going to say and write I don't know.[3]

We have exactly the same people round. Not a single new face. We have lunch on the 5th and 20th, the 7th and the 12th[4] and we boast to one another about your postcards.

Everyone write to you and to the two of you and loves you both as always, and some of us (we) more than ever, because we miss you very badly. Apparently the Meyerholds[5] will be in Berlin at the beginning of April. They're not taking The Bedbug with them, but I'm not making much of a protest since my attitude is I'd rather they liked it in Saratov.[6]

Of the new faces (I almost forgot) I've had a couple of visits from Syoma and Klavka[7] — they (Lyova) wanted to introduce me to Aseyev — I didn't shy away, but I wasn't very keen either.[8]

But the young Refists are pining for Osya.

Write, my own ones, and come back as soon as possible. We kiss you, ever yours

Kiss Elsa and Aragon.   19/III

408. Lili to Mayakovsky.
Letter from Berlin to Moscow, 20 March 1930.
20.3.30

Volodik I'm quite amazed by your silence. Please write and say whether you had a visit from Obolensky.

Osya and I have received our English visas. Elsa and Aragon are arriving on the 23rd — we'll live with them for about ten days and then leave for London. We'll be in London for two weeks and from there, stopping for a day or two in Berlin — home. That means we'll see each other on the 22nd of April.

If you don't write to me immediately, I'll get angry!
I kiss you both.

Lilya

<u>22.3.30</u>

Volosit! I've just received your little letter. I'm rushing to reply: look for Bulka's husband in the telephone book under the name Anatoly Aleksandrovich Butler. The lady of the house is called Lidiya Aleksandrovna. Both Bulka and we need little puppies very badly. You absolutely must take the matter up.

Oska's giving a lecture on Tuesday: Die neueste Literatur im sozialistischen Aufbau der Sowjetunion in German.[1]

Elsa's arriving today. As regards the Frankfurt première, for some reason there's not a word. They're doing a play by Bill-Belotserkovsky there at the moment.[2]

Schneidt stands by me and spends all the time sitting up and begging — I'm afraid of him overeating, I shan't give him any more.

I kiss and squeeze you both with all my might,

(Lilya)

<u>26.3.30</u>

Volosit! We're going to London on the 30th. Write to me at this address: 35 Ashbourne Avenue, Golder's green, London NW 11, H. Kagan[1] (for Lili). Berlin has become beastly boring, but I must stay here for a few days with Elsa. Oska gave a brilliant lecture yesterday in German!! He even cracked jokes with great success!! The audience was from the Polytechnic museum. All the objections were rubbish.[2]

How's "The Bath-House" doing? Have you written a lot of the new long poem?[3]

Oska reads all the German newspapers and even cuts things out!

I really want to come back as soon as possible and tell you both about everything!

Don't forget Annushka and Vera Georgiyevna.[4] Make sure Bulka gets washed. See about the flat and the union.

Give Snob a kiss — I don't know his address.

Do you miss me? I kiss you very warmly. Stroke Bulka. I kiss you again

Lilya.

411. Mayakovsky to Lili and Osip.
Telegram from Moscow to Berlin, 28 March 1930.

We miss you we're glad you're coming soon. Waiting love you kiss you.

Schen Bul

412. Lili and Osip to Mayakovsky.
Postcard from Windsor to Moscow, 1 April 1930.[1]

—Volosik!

I don't have to tell you . . . . We kiss you both warmly.

LilyaOsya

413. Mayakovsky to Lili and Osip.
Telegram from Moscow to London, 3 April 1930.

We kiss you love you miss you waiting.

Puppies

414. Lili, Osip and others to Mayakovsky.
Postcard from London to Moscow, 5 April 1930.

Volosik, I kiss you right in the parliament.[1]
The session's about to begin.

Friendly greetings from D. Bogomolov.[2]
When are you going to come to London?

R. C. Wallhead[3]
W. P. Coates[4]

415. Lili and Osip to Mayakovsky.
Postcard from London to Moscow, 7 April 1930.

Sweet puppies, I'll send you trousers from here. All the Scotties send you their regards. Please think up a new text for the telegrams. We're fed up of this one.

We kiss you warmly.

LilyaOsya

Amsterdam 14.4.30

Volosik!

It's absolutely great the way the flowers grow here! Real carpets —
tulips, hyacinths and narcissi.[2]

We kiss your little muzzles.

LilyaOsya

Whatever you turn to, everything Dutch is terribly indecent!

NOTES TO THE CORRESPONDENCE

1. 1 The telegram is addressed to Mayakovsky at the Palais Royal Hotel on Pushkin Street, where the poet moved immediately after he met Lili Brik.
2. 1 In the second half of September, Mayakovsky left Petrograd for Moscow to give a reading. At the end of September or the beginning of October he returned to the capital.

    2 On the 24th of September (7th of October) Mayakovsky appeared at the Polytechnic museum, giving a lecture entitled "The Bolsheviks of Art" and reading his poetry. In the autobiography *I Myself* the poet mistakenly — or intentionally? — dates this lecture to the first days of the February Revolution.

    3 Abram Vasilevich Yevnin, an acquaintance of Mayakovsky, is mentioned in the long poem *Man (Chelovek)* (the "Mayakovsky in heaven" section), which the poet was finishing at the time.

    4 Elsa Kagan (1896-1970) was the younger sister of Lili Brik and a close friend of Mayakovsky; the poet met Elsa in the autumn of 1913, more than a year and a half before he met her sister. In 1918 Elsa left for Paris, where she married a French Officer, André Triolet. In France she started writing books, first in Russian, then in French. In 1928 she met Louis Aragon, with whom she spent the rest of her life.

    5 Lev Aleksandrovich Grinkrug (b. 1889), a friend of the Briks since 1914, first met Mayakovsky in the summer of 1915, on the same day as Lili Brik. "On one of her trips to Moscow . . . Lili and I went out to see her parents at their dacha in Malakhovka, where they were living with Lili's sister, the future writer Elsa Triolet. When we arrived it turned out that Mayakovsky was with them, having come to visit Elsa. When we got to the dacha, Mayakovsky and Elsa weren't at home. They'd gone out for a walk, and her mother was in a state of utter terror and despair that she'd let her daughter, a young girl, go off alone in the evening with such a man. At the time she didn't know Mayakovsky at all, but he had the reputation of being a wild man, capable of anything. And we ourselves had never seen him at such close quarters before, and to tell the truth we waited for them to come back with a certain nervousness. Imagine our amazement when they returned home a little while later and instead of this monster we saw a quiet, calm, tender and affectionate man. . . . Lili Yurevna spent the night at the dacha, but Mayakovsky and I returned to Moscow that same evening" (Grinkrug).

    Lev Grinkrug grew up in Smolensk, where his father was the director of the Smolensk branch of the Moscow International Bank. After completing his secondary education, Lev Grinkrug moved to Moscow, where he graduated from the law faculty of Moscow University in 1911. Until the revolution he worked as a bank clerk.

    The Grinkrugs were one of the few families of hereditary Jewish noblemen in the history of Russia. Lev Grinkrug's father, Aleksandr Mironovich, was a doctor by education (he became a banker after marrying Lev Grinkrug's mother, Anna Germanovna Shmelkina, the daughter of a Moscow banker), and during the Russo-Turkish war of 1877-78, in which he served as a military doctor, he was awarded the order of St Vladimir fourth class and hereditary nobility. This elicited newspaper discussion about whether a Jew should be awarded hereditary nobility, and the matter was taken up in the Senate, which confirmed that the rights to hereditary nobility extend to Jews who have been awarded this order.

219

Lev Grinkrug always remained a very close friend, almost a member of the Mayakovsky and Brik "family".

6 On this visit Mayakovsky lived with his mother and sisters at No. 44 Bolshaya Presnenskaya Street.

7 Arkady Averchenko (1881-1925), Russian writer and humorist. Known particularly, both before and after the revolution, for his short stories satirising petit bourgeois behaviour. Emigrated. Died in Prague.

8 Onisim (Nika) Grinkrug (1895-1978) was the younger brother of Lev Grinkrug.

9 Probably a reference to the poster for Mayakovsky's appearance at the Tenishev College in Petrograd, where he read the long poem *Man* on the 11th (24th) of October. The poster was printed in the capital.

10 *War and the World (Voyna i mir)* appeared in December 1917.

3. 1 Mayakovsky made a second move from Petrograd to Moscow after the 5th (18th) of December 1917 (see note 16 to this letter). The reasons for his move were Mayakovsky's disagreement with Bolshevik policy in the sphere of culture, and his polemic on this subject with Anatoly Lunacharsky. "Failing to reach agreement with the People's Commissar," Osip Brik later recalled, "and finding no other ways to propagandise 'Left' art, Mayakovsky left for Moscow, where together with David Burlyuk and Vasily Kamensky he attempted to converse with the people . . . from the stage of the 'Poets' Café' . . ." (O. Brik, 1940). Mayakovsky remained in Moscow till the summer of 1918.

2 Slightly altered lines from the romance "Where are you, answer me".

3 David Burlyuk (1882-1967).

4 Vasily Kamensky (1884-1961).

5 The Poets' Café (*Kafe poetov*), headed by Burlyuk and Kamensky, opened in the autumn of 1917, before the October Revolution. It was closed on the 14th of April 1918.

6 The Stray Dog (*Brodyachaya sobaka*), an artists' café in Petersburg, where Mayakovsky performed several times between 1912 and 1915.

7 The "Futurists' Christmas tree" was organised at the Polytechnic museum on the 30th of December (12th of January 1918): "Bacchanalia. Poetry. Speeches. Paradoxes. Discoveries. Possibilities. Oscillations. Prognostications. The ambushing of geniuses. Carnival. A shower of ideas. Laughter. Snarls. . . ."

8 This event, which took place on the evening of the 27th of February 1918, consisted of the "Election of the King of Poets". Igor Severyanin was elected king — according to Kamensky after "rigged" vote-counting.

9 The reading took place at the Polytechnic museum on the 2nd (15th) of February 1918. During the evening Andrey Bely "made a passionate speech about the strength of Mayakovsky's poetic gift and literary style . . . 'after the Symbolists. Mayakovsky is the greatest poet in Russia, because he speaks his own unexpected new word'."

10 Well-known Moscow businessmen.

11 Burlyuk's poem:

> He was terribly fond of flies,
> With plump backsides,
> And of this he often sang,
> Aloud with his friends at random, —

was one of those poetic works which Mayakovsky and Burlyuk called "wild songs of our native land", and which were sung in unison to the tune of "Many years, many years, Orthodox Russian Tsar".

12 Mayakovsky was putting away money for a trip south, giving it to Lev Grinkrug for safe-keeping. He wrote the sums down in a notebook, the so-called Southern fund.

13 In October-November 1917 the Briks moved from a two-roomed flat to a bigger, six-roomed one in the same house on Zhukovsky Street. Mayakovsky is in all probability speaking about the so-called dancing room, which Lili Brik was evidently furnishing at that time. See the Introduction.

14 Asis — The Association of Socialist Art (*Assotsiyatsiya sotsialisticheskogo iskusstva*); the imprint under which Mayakovsky published the long poem *Man* and the second edition of *A Cloud in Trousers* (*Oblako v shtanakh*) in the second half of February 1918. Asis was financed by Mayakovsky's friends.

15 The meetings of the Union of Art Workers (*Soyuz deyateley iskusstv*), in which Osip Brik took active part, took place at the Academy of Arts.

16 In Maksim Gorky's Social Democratic newspaper, *Novaya zhizn (New Life)*, on the 5th (18th) of December 1917 a "Letter to the Editor" from Osip Brik was printed under the heading "My position". The article was provoked by the fact that Brik was elected without his knowledge as a member of the Petrograd duma on the Russian Social Democratic and Labour Party (Bolshevik) list: "Nobody asked for my agreement, nor did I give it to anyone." Explaining that he was not a politician and not a member "of any party", Brik nevertheless declared that "the only correct path is to conduct one's cultural line unflinchingly, to be everywhere where culture is endangered, to defend it staunchly from any form of vandalism, including Bolshevik vandalism". He therefore did not renounce his "unexpected election", but at the same time he stressed "that I am not a member of the Bolshevik party, I do not submit to any party discipline, and I will not take part in any political meetings". At that time the Bolshevik party was actively supporting and subsidising the Proletkult, and that cultural programme was for Brik "totally unacceptable; it is precisely against this programme that I consider it essential to struggle particularly energetically". Brik ended his article with the words: "If my position does not suit the Bolsheviks, then I request them to erase my name from the list of members." To all appearances, Brik's position did not suit the Bolsheviks, since there is no information on his participation in the Petrograd city duma.

Mayakovsky's reaction to Brik's article is remarkable in that it reveals the dissatisfaction with Bolshevik cultural policy which forced the poet to leave for Moscow. Brik's letter and Mayakovsky's reaction to it are examined in detail in Jangfeldt 1979, pp. 121-37.

17 Aleksandra (Pasya) Dorinskaya (1896-1978) — ballerina, danced with Nijinsky in the Russian Ballet abroad. She returned on leave from London to St Petersburg in 1914, and when the First World War broke out in July she was unable to rejoin the company and remained in Russia. She met Mayakovsky and the Briks in the late autumn of 1915. There follows an extract from Dorinskaya's memoirs: "Then too I had the opportunity of taking a real look at Lili Yurevna Brik . . . of medium height, very slender, frail, she was the embodiment of femininity. With a sleek haircut, a middle parting, with a plait wound low on the

221

back of her head, shining with the natural gold of her fabled [in *The Backbone-Flute*, B.J.] 'red' hair. Her eyes really had 'been dug like the pits of two graves' [from the same poem], they were large, brown and kind; she had a fairly large mouth, which was beautifully shaped and brightly painted, and when she smiled she parted her pleasant,even lips. She had pale, narrow, typically feminine hands, adorned only by her wedding ring, and small, elegant feet, shod with taste and delicacy, a delicacy apparent in all her clothes, in her skilful marriage of the demands of fashion and an individual approach to it. The only blemish about Lili Yurevna's external appearance might have been considered her slightly large head and the heavyish lower half of her face, but perhaps this had its own particular charm in looks that were very distant from classical beauty" (Dorinskaya).

At that time Lili Brik had conceived an enthusiasm for amateur ballet, and Aleksandra Dorinskaya became her teacher. "From then on, Lili and I saw each other almost every day: first because ot the lessons, and secondly because our acquaintance turned very quickly, almost immediately into friendship (ibid.).

18 Aleksandr Izrailevich — acquaintance of the Briks and of Mayakovsky. From a rich merchant family, owners of enterprises in dachas and forestry. According to Lev Grinkrug, Izrailevich "graduated in car-maintenance at an English polytechnic, and worked in that profession all his life". (Letter to B.J., June 1980.)

19 Polya and Nyusha — domestic servants. Before Lili Brik's marriage, Polya worked for her parents.

4. 1 Osip Brik, like Mayakovsky, contributed to the newspaper *Novaya zhizn* (*New Life*) from the very beginning of its existence on the 1st of May 1917. Apparently, after Brik's attack upon the cultural programme of the Bolsheviks (see No. 3, note 16), he was offered a permanent position on the newspaper. After this "letter to the editor" Brik published several other articles in the paper directed against the measures taken by the Bolsheviks in the sphere of culture.

2 The artist Natan Altman (1889-1970).

3 A reference to the Yasny publishing family, who published several books by Mayakovsky. In the summer of 1917 Mayakovsky compiled a collection of his poetry from 1913 to 1917, *The Fop's Jacket* (*Kofta fata*), which he offered to Yasny. It was intended that the collection should be published in 1918, but it did not appear.

4 This reference is unclear.

5 Boris Kushner (1888-1937), writer, poet, member of the "left block" in the Union of Art Workers (*Soyuz deyateley iskusstv*). Author of several books of poetry. His experiment in "Futurist" prose, *The Meeting of the Palaces. Alliterated prose. (Miting dvortsov. Alliterovannaya proza)*, appeared in 1918. In the 1920s he was a contributor to *Lef* and *Novyy Lef*. Victim of the purges.

6 Sergey Bobrov (1889-1971), poet and theorist of poetry, leader of the Futurist group The Centrifuge (*Tsentrifuga*). It is possible that Lili Brik has in mind Mayakovsky's poem for the third Centrifuge Almanac, which had been planned as early as the end of 1916, but which did not appear.

7 On Brik's letter, see No. 3, note 16. The "Left reaction" to this letter appeared in *Izvestiya* (Petrograd, 13th December 1917), where the Proletkult activist Vasily Ignatov accused Brik of betraying his initially benevolent attitude to the

222

Proletkult position.

8   On the 17th (30th) of December there was a huge demonstration in Petrograd "in honour of a universal democratic peace". (Peace negotiations had begun in Brest-Litovsk a week earlier.) The newspaper *Nash vek* (*Our Age*) ironically rephrased the aim of the demonstration: "in honour of peace outside the country and internecine war within it" (19th of December).

Lili Brik's remark about Mayakovsky's couplet

> Eat your pineapples, chew your hazel-grouse,
> Your last day is coming, bourgeois —

is confirmed by a newspaper announcement: "To a dashing tune, borrowed from folk verse, various groups were singing at the tops of their voices: Eat your pineapples, chew your hazel-grouse/Your last day has come, bourgeois!" (*Den* (*Day*), Petrograd, No. 225, 19 December 1917).

Mayakovsky himself remembered it like this in 1927: ". . . during the first days of the revolution, the Petersburg newspapers wrote that sailors walked towards the Winter Palace singing some song: Eat your pineapples . . . etc." (XII, 152). The couplet was first published in the "journal of Proletarian satire" *Solovey* (*The Nightingale*) on the 24th of December 1917 (6th of January 1918), which casts some doubt upon the suggestion in Mayakovsky's memoirs that the lines were popular at the time of the storming of the Winter Palace.

5.   1   The Comedians' Halt (*Prival Komediantov*) was a cabaret-theatre that succeeded The Stray Dog. It opened in April 1916. After "a long break", The Comedians' Halt reopened on the 31st of December 1917. "The reopening has been timed to meet the New Year, in view of which the evening's programme will have a specially New Year character" (*Novaya zhizn*, Petrograd, No. 214 (208), 31 December 1917 (13 January 1918)). Mikhail Kuzmin (1875-1936) — poet, author of many plays and popular songs; constant visitor to the Briks' salon.

2   Artur Lurye (1892-1966) — avant-garde composer. In 1918 he composed music for Mayakovsky's poem "Our March (*Nash marsh*). Emigrated in 1922.

3   The trip to Japan did not take place.

6.   1   Aleksandr Kayransky (Koyransky) — well-known art critic.

2   On the 30th of Decmeber 1917 (12th of January 1918). See No. 3, note 7.

3   Vladimir Goltsshmidt, a "living futurist", one of the organisers of The Poets' Café. To demonstrate his philosophy of "health and sun", he broke planks on his head on the stage of the café. In the spring of 1918, Goltsshmidt had close links with the Moscow anarchists, whose headquarters was a stone's throw from The Poets' Café, on Malaya Dmitrovka Street, and for whom the café was a sort of "secret address".

4   Vladimir Khenkin (1883-1953), famous variety artist.

5   The reading took place on the 2nd (15th) of February. See No. 3, note 9.

6   The long poem *The Backbone-Flute* (*Fleyta-pozvonochnik*), Petrograd, 1916.

7   The long poem *Man* and the second, uncensored edition of *A Cloud in Trousers* appeared in the second half of February 1918. See No. 3, note 14.

7.   1   Starting with this letter, dates are given in the new style.

2   *Man* and *A Cloud in Trousers*. See No. 6, note 7.

3   The first issue of the "social-democratic newspaper" *Vechernyaya zvezda* (*Evening Star*) appeared in Petrograd on the 22nd of January 1918. This issue included Brik's article "Autonomous art", and several other articles by Brik appeared in

later issues. Many famous writers were published in *Vechernyaya zvezda*, including Mandelshtam, Yesenin, Zamyatin, Kushner, Larisa Reysner and Babel.

4 On the 3rd of March (18th of February) German aeroplanes dropped two bombs on Petrograd. The first bomb killed and wounded thirteen people.

8. 1 Judging by Mayakovsky's reaction, the pet name "little puppy" was first used by Lili Brik in letter No. 7. Afterwards the name puppy/Shchen, also Shchenyonok, Shchenik, Shchenyatik etc. became a staple part of domestic usage, and Mayakovsky began to sign his letters to Lili Brik Shchen etc. See the Introduction.

2 *Gazeta futuristov* (*The Futurists' Newspaper*), the organ of "The Flying Federation of Futurists" ("*Letuchaya Federatsiya Futuristov*"), i.e. Mayakovsky, Kamensky and Burlyuk, appeared on the 15th of March 1918. This first and only issue of the newspaper (consisting of one newspaper-sized sheet printed on both sides) was financed by Lev Grinkrug. The newspaper included poems by all three poets. It also contained three manifestoes, two collective ones ("The Manifesto of the Flying Federation of Futurists" and "Decree No. 1 on the Democratisation of Art"), and one signed by Mayakovsky ("An Open Letter to the Workers"). *Gazeta futuristov* was published when the attraction of the three Futurists to Anarchism was at its height, as is clear from the manifestoes. At the same time as the publication of the newspaper, the Futurists occupied part of the former Peterhof restaurant in Moscow, where they planned to create a "House of Free Art". On the 20th of March, however, they were "evicted". In the anarchist organ, *Revolyutsionnoye tvorchestvo* (*Revolutionary Creation*) (Moscow 1918: I/II), the "House of Free Art" was counted as one of the anarchist clubs, and *Gazeta futuristov* considered an anarchist organ. For more details on *Gazeta futuristov*, see Jangfeldt, 1975, 1976 and 1979.

3 A notebook received as a present from Lili Brik.

4 A landscape by David Burlyuk (a tree and a haystack).

5 "Our March" was published in *Gazeta futuristov*.

6 The printed dedication to the poem *Man*.

9. 1 Mama is Yelena Yurevna Kagan (1872-1942), the mother of Lili and Elsa.

2 In March 1918 Mayakovsky wrote a screenplay *Not born for money* (*Ne dlya deneg rodivshiysya*) from Jack London's novel *Martin Eden*, and himself played the main part, that of the poet Ivan Nov. David Burlyuk, Vasily Kamensky and Lev Grinkrug also took part in the film. Grinkrug recalls: "He also persuaded me to act in the film, but since there wasn't a suitable role for me in the novel, he made one up — the role of the brother of the girl the hero's in love with." Unfortunately, not a single copy of this film has yet turned up.

10. 1 Probably a reference to the film discussed in the previous letter, *Not born for money*. In April Mayakovsky was also at work on another film, *The Lady and the Hooligan* (*Baryshnya i Khuligan*), which was first screened in May, at almost the same time as the first film. *The Lady and the Hooligan* was filmed without a screenplay, directly from Edmondo de Amicis's story, *The teacher of workers* (*La Maestrina degli Operai*), which first appeared in the collection *Fra Scuola e Casa*, Milan 1892 (the fifth edition of the Russian translation appeared in spring 1918). Mayakovsky himself played the leading role. The film has survived.

2 Compare the letter from Mayakovsky to his mother and sisters in early

November 1917: "I'll be in Petrograd for two or three months. I'm going to work and have my teeth and nose seen to. Then I'll make a visit to Moscow, but after that I intend to go south to complete my repairs" (XIII, 28).

3   Jacques: Yakov Izrailevich, elder brother of Aleksandr Izrailevich. Later in 1918 Yakov Izrailevich paid spirited court to Lili Brik, even after she began to live with Mayakovsky, and despite the fact that the attraction was not reciprocated. Things got so bad that in the summer of 1918 he and the jealous Mayakovsky had a fight in the street.

11.   1   Yakov Izrailevich. See No. 10, note 3.

2   Mayakovsky gave Lili Brik a ring with her initials L.Yu.B. in a circle, so that they could be read uninterruptedly "lyublyulyublyulyublyu . . ." (I love you I love you I love you). On the inside of the ring was the word Volodya. On the ring which Lili Brik gave Mayakovsky the letters M/W are engraved in Latin script, and on the inside is the word Lilya.

12.   1   This letter is written on paper from the Pittoresk café (see note 6 to this letter).

2   The film *Not born for money* was completed at the end of April.

3   The actor Oleg Frelikh, a schoolfriend of Osip Brik's, was filming in the next studio; he was the same height as Mayakovsky.

4   This is the first allusion to the idea of writing the poem "*A good attitude towards horses*" ("*Khorosheye otnosheniye k loshadyam*"), which appeared in the Moscow edition of the newspaper *Novaya zhizn* on the 9th of June 1918.

5   In May Mayakovsky wrote the screenplay *Fettered by Film* (*Zakovannaya filmoy*), in which the main parts were played by Lili Brik and Mayakovsky himself. The film was completed at the beginning of June. A few damaged extracts from this film were found in the mid-1970s. In 1926, Mayakovsky returned to the subject of this film and wrote a new version of the screenplay (under the title *The heart of the Cinema* (*Serdtse kino*) or *The heart of the Screen* (Serdtse ekrana)) which was, however, never filmed.

6   The Pittoresk café on Moscow's Kuznetskiy most, had been decorated by Georgy Yakulov and other painters, and had the reputation of being more "elegant" than the Poets' Café.

13.   1   Konstantin Miklashevsky (1886-1944), author of several plays and specialist on the Commedia dell'arte. In 1917 he published the book *The Theatre of the Italian Comic Actors* (Teatr italyanskikh komediantov), (part I). At the time he was a member of the theatrical history section of the theatrical department of the Commissariat of Enlightenment (the TEO Narkomprosa). Miklashevsky emigrated in the 1920s.

2   According to Grinkrug, Liberman was the manager of a Moscow bank (letter to B.J., August 1980).

14.   1   A reference to the rehearsals for *Mystery-Bouffe* (*Misteriya Buff*) which were taking place in the Theatre of Musical Drama. The staging of "the first Soviet play" was accompanied by endless difficulties connected with the theatre, the actors and so on. What Mayakovsky has in mind in this note is obstructive behaviour on the part of the employees of the theatre. As he later recalled: "The theatre staff harassed us in every way possible and impossible. They locked the entrances and hid away the nails. They even stopped us displaying a printed copy of Mystery-Bouffe on their counter so redolent of art and tradition. They brought the posters only on the day the show was due to open, and then it was

225

just an unpainted outline. Then they announced that no one was allowed to stick it up. I myself painted the poster by hand" (XII, 155). The première took place on the first anniversary of the October Revolution. On the later fate of *Mystery-Bouffe* see No. 17, note 2.

15. 1 At the beginning of March 1919, Mayakovsky and the Briks moved from Petrograd to Moscow. This letter was written during one of Mayakovsky's trips to Petrograd on publishing business for IMO (*Iskusstvo molodykh*, Art of the Young). This publishing house was founded in 1918, headed by Mayakovsky and Brik, and subsidised by the Commissariat of Enlightenment (*Narkompros*). IMO existed until mid-1919, and during that time it published seven books, including *Mystery-Bouffe* (first and second editions), *War and the World* (second edition), and *Everything written by Vladimir Mayakovsky* (*Vsyo sochinyonnoye Vladimirom Mayakovskim*).

A curious document survives from one of Mayakovsky's trips to Petrograd, the "Diary for Lichika", written in a notebook. The trip lasted from the 7th to the 11th of March.

As is clear from the "Diary", the Moscow-Petrograd train took almost twenty-four hours, twice as long as normal. This was caused by difficulties on the railways connected with the Civil War. It was precisely in March and April of 1919 that the crisis on the railways worsened — the trains began to burn firewood, on some lines passenger traffic ceased altogether. Transport was in a state of "total disruption, bordering on total breakdown" (*Severnaya kommuna/ The Northern Commune*, Petrograd, 1919, No. 75, p. 1).

The "Diary for Lichika" is published from photocopies of the original (Lili Brik archive). Dates in italics are Mayakovsky's.

DIARY FOR LICHIKA

7

1.28 I think only of Lilik all the time I hear My eyes hurt* I love her terribly I miss her I'd go back with pleasure. Gukasov** is travelling he disgusts me. I sit down to Holmes.

3.09 Child I'm travelling I kiss you I love you. Ten times I wanted to return but for some reason it seemed stupid. If I didn't need to earn money nothing would have made me go away.

3.21 "My eyes hurt". My sweet.

3.50 I drink tea and I love you.

4.30 I pine for Lichika.

5.40 I think only of Kitty.

6.30 Kitty I love you.

6.30 Lilyok I love you I love you tenderly I think of you all the time but I write only when my yearning for you is terrifying I write so that if if you wanted to you'd be convinced that even in your absence I have nothing except you my beloved.

7.05 Child I pine for you.

7.25 It's dark I'm afraid I shan't be able to write I think only of Kitty.

9.45 I love Lika in the lamplight Goodnight I'm asleep.

226

8

7.45 Good morning I love Kitty. I've opened my eyes.

9.06 I think only of Kitty.

9.40 I love my Child Lika.

10.40 Dear Kitty.

11.45 Lilyok I think only of you and I love you terribly.

12.00 Lisik.

12.30 I'm arriving pining for Kitty I rush to you puppy that loves Kitty.

1.10 In the cab too I love only Kitty

3.00 I love Kitty in the department***

4.50 In the dining room too only Kitty

5.45 After lunch on the sweet also Kitty

6.30 Came home miserable it's terrible without Kitty

8.05 Sit at home and want to go to Kitty.

10.15 At Stanya's**** thinking about Kitty

11.30 Going to bed Goodnight little child

9

9.30 Good morning Liska

10.35 I love Kitty before tea

12.00 I love Lisik

12.45 I love Kitty at Shklovik's*****

2.00 I love Kitty at St Isaac's Square

6.30 Kitty

7.15 My eyes hurt

7.17 I play billiards to win Kitty chicolads

9.35 I love Kitty

10.30 I love

12.20 I love

10

8.10 Good morning Beloved child

10.45 I love Lika in the Lit. society

1.00 I love Kitty in the Commis

I love Kitty at 3.45.

8.00 I'm coming to you terribly glad my child

10.00 Soon Kitty

11

7.35 Kitty

9.35 The train is approaching Kitty or as my travelling-companion puts it Moscow

* "My eyes hurt": an allusion to hunger which affected Lili Brik's eyes. See in the long poem *Good!* (*Khorosho!*): "The swelling of hunger pressed the brown eyes".

** Pavel Gukasov, major industrialist, member of the State Council; emigrated to Paris in 1919 or 1920.

*** The department of Fine Arts in the Commissariat of Enlightenment (*IZO Narkomprosa*).

227

****Stanislav Gurvits-Gursky — engineer, artist and friend of Mayakovsky and the Briks. On the 2nd of May he read a paper on industrial terminology at the Moscow Linguistic Circle. Mayakovsky was among those present.

***** Viktor Shklovsky (1893-1984), eminent literary scholar and Formalist critic, close friend of Mayakovsky and the Briks. In the 1920s a member of Lef. Author of the book *Mayakovsky and his circle*, London 1974. The Briks had given him their flat in Zhukovsky Street when they left Petrograd a week earlier. Shklovsky was the representative of IMO in Petrograd.

16. 1 A reference to his work on the "Satire Windows" posters at Rosta (the Russian Telegraph Agency), where Mayakovsky started working in October 1919.

    2 A dining-room in a private flat, where Mayakovsky had lunch.

    3 Lev Grinkrug also worked at Rosta.

17. 1 A state institution which took charge of the distribution of literature.

    2 A reference to the "comradely disciplinary court" where the case of the payment of royalties to Mayakovsky from the edition of *Mystery-Bouffe* was being examined. In December 1920 Mayakovsky had finished a second, re-worked version of the play. Rehearsals began in the First RSFSR Theatre at the beginning of January 1921, under the direction of Vsevolod Meyerhold. Nevertheless, just as in 1918 (see No. 14, note 1), there was serious opposition to the staging of the play, and only after several interventions in support of the *Mystery* were Mayakovsky and Meyerhold able to arrange a première on the 1st of May 1921. (At the discussion "Should 'Mystery-Bouffe' be staged?" (30 January 1921), Mayakovsky complained: "This three year Calvary has got me down terribly" (XII, 259). A similar story occurred with respect to the publication of the second version of the play. The State Publishing House refused to publish it, and the journal *Vestnik teatra* (*Theatre Herald*) printed the play as a supplement to its issue No. 91/92 of the 15th of June 1921. Royalties for materials published in this journal were paid by the State Publishing House. Despite this, on the 15th of July the management of the State Publishing House refused to pay any fee for *Mystery-Bouffe*. Mayakovsky went to court, and on the 25th of August the court ordered the State Publishing House to pay the money. Then the management of the publishing house deposited a document at the court announcing that they would re-examine the case, and it was only after this re-examination, on the 8th of September 1921, that Mayakovsky received his royalties and "carried home the equivalent of the lines in flour, groats and sugar" (XII, 157).

      The journalist Lev Sosnovsky, defending the management of the State Publishing House, reacted to the court's decision in the following words: "I think that this episode must be seen as the last straw. We are good-natured and patient fellows. But we will not allow our gates to be daubed with tar. . . . We shall try to stop your [the Futurists'] inappropriate jokes which cost the republic too dear. Let us hope that Mayakovskyism will soon be sitting in the defendant's chair. . . . Give us art which is accessible to the simple eye and to simple common sense. — Enough of Mayakovskyism . . ." ("Enough of 'Mayakovskyism'", *Pravda*, Moscow, 8 September 1921).

    3 A slang term for money introduced during the Provisional Government under Aleksandr Kerensky.

18. 1 Since this letter begins without addressing Mayakovsky by name, it is probable

that what is published here is the continuation of a letter the beginning of which is lost. At the beginning of October 1921 Lili Brik left for Riga, where she tried to get an English visa so as to visit her mother who was working in the Soviet trade delegation in London. She remained in Riga until the beginning of February, when she returned to Moscow. She did not receive an English visa.

2 Vera Geltser, the sister of the famous ballerina Yekaterina Geltser (1876-1962), a close friend of Lili Brik. Vera Geltser was a famous dressmaker. After the revolution she and her husband left for Riga, and from there moved to Berlin (verbal communication from Lev Grinkrug).

3 Mikhail Levidov (1891-1942), writer and journalist, He was working at the time in the press bureau of the Soviet trade delegation in London. During the 1920s he was a member of Lef. Victim of the purges.

4 Lev Alseksandri — counsellor at the Soviet Legation in Riga.

5 See No. 20.

19. 1 See No. 18, note 2.

2 Elsa Hirschberg, Lili Brik's aunt. Lili's mother's family came from Riga.

3 Mayakovsky's acquaintance Maksim Benediktov, laureate of the Prague Conservatoire. Mayakovsky often played cards with him.

4 Clearly, Mayakovsky had asked Lili Brik to buy a rubber basin in Riga. Mayakovsky kept such a bath-basin in his room in Lubyanskiy Passage (see No. 53, note 3), and he took it with him on his trips (see his story *How I made her laugh* (*Kak ya yeyo rassmeshil*). Mayakovsky's cleanliness was a reaction to the death of his father in 1906 from blood poisoning. The words of Lev Grinkrug, a man who knew the poet in his daily life, are worthy of note: "Mayakovsky was morbidly anxious about his health, obsessed with cleanliness and morbidly fastidious. . . . He was afraid of the slightest scratch, of getting dirt into it . . . he would never drink from someone else's glass or eat from someone else's plate, in other people's houses and in hotels he would always try not to touch the door handles, as far as possible he avoided public transport, preferring to walk right across town if it meant avoiding touching someone else's hands; he washed his hands dozens of times a day and always had eau de cologne on him for this purpose.

Always neatly and cleanly dressed, always in an immaculately 'freshly-washed' shirt and a pressed suit, always clean shaven, Mayakovsky would never let himself go in any circumstances, either at home or, even more so, outside the home, and he allowed himself no licence in his outward appearance." (Grinkrug)

20. 1 Adolf Menshoy (Gay), a journalist who was working at the time as secretary to the Deputy People's Commissar for Foreign Affairs. He was evidently making a speech somewhere on the day in question. Victim of the purges.

2 Grigory Vinokur (1896-1947), famous linguist and literary critic, at the time in charge of the press bureau at the RSFSR Legation in Riga.

3 Mikhail Krichevsky, journalist. Worked with Vinokur in the press bureau.

4 "In a letter from Riga Lili Brik compared Riga to Moscow" (*Literaturnoye nasledstvo* 65, p. 112). We did not have access to this letter — possibly a reference to the beginning of letter 18 (see No. 18, note 1).

21. 1 The letter is dated by Lili Brik. All three versions of the letter mentioned by Lili reached their addressee and have been preserved.

2   Anatoly Lunacharsky (1875-1933), People's Commissar of Enlightenment.

22.   1   Tatyana Shchepkina-Kupernik (1874-1952), writer and translator.

23.   1   See No. 20, note 1.

2   A reference to the "Satire Windows".

3   A performance of theatrical parodies by the studio of the director Nikolay Foregger.

4   A reference to Levidov, Vinokur and Krichevsky, who had arrived from Riga. See No. 20.

5   Lunacharsky's secretary Aleksandr Flakserman and his wife.

6   Emmanuil German (1892-1963), satirical poet, often published under the name Emil Krotkiy (Meek Emil).

7   Pegasus' Stall (*Stoylo Pegasa*), a literary café organised by the Imaginists on Tver Street.

8   The first reference to work on the long poem "The Fourth International" (*IV Internatsional*). The poem was later called "The Fifth International". Only two of the planned eight parts were finished and published (in 1922). See No. 53, note 3.

9   Boris Arvatov (1896-1940), critic and theorist of literature, the author of a number of articles and books, including *Sociological Poetics* (*Sotsiologicheskaya poetika*), Moscow 1928 (with a preface by Osip Brik). Member of Lef. One of the chief theoreticians of production art. See No. 117, note 3.

24.   1   After his visit to Moscow, Vinokur returned to Riga.

2   See No. 25.

25.   1   Addendum to No. 24.

2   A slip of the pen. In No. 24, dated 26-27 October, Mayakovsky writes that "Today I've just received your 'trip' letter".

3   The Union of Art Workers (*Rabotniki iskusstva: Rabis*).

4   Leonid Krasin (1870-1926), important Soviet diplomat, at the time head of the Soviet trade delegation in London.

5   Pavel Yuzbashev, chief Soviet trade representative in Riga.

6   Shvets: evidently a worker at the London trade delegation.

27.   1   Zinovy Grzhebin (1869-1929), publisher. His business was founded in Petrograd in 1919. Lili Brik's question was provoked by Grzhebin's decision to transfer his publishing activities to Berlin. On the 3rd of October 1921 the politbureau of the Central Committee of the Russian Communist Party gave him permission to go abroad with his family. On the 16th of October he left with Maksim Gorky for Helsingfors (Helsinki), and from there he continued via Stockholm to Berlin.

2   Mayakovsky's long poem *The Backbone-Flute* (first edition, Petrograd 1916).

28.   1   Mikhail Grinkrug (1887-1959), a barrister, was the elder brother of Lev Grinkrug. From 1920 onwards he lived in Berlin.

29.   1   On the 30th of October, Lunacharsky gave a lecture entitled "Heroism and Philistinism" in the Polytechnic museum.

30.   1   A variant of the letter, sent to Lev Grinkrug, also arrived. In it Lili Brik adds: "Send them with someone *absolutely trustworthy!* I've received the letter about the trip on official business. I've answered in detail."

2   The first Soviet postage stamps had appeared only in 1921, which explains the interest of the Rigan collector in full sets.

3 Mayakovsky, like the Briks and Lev Grinkrug, was a compulsive gambler. Grinkrug recalls: "The four of us would play together, and always with the same teams: Osip and Lili Brik, Mayakovsky and I. . . . But his compulsive gambling was evident not only in his card-playing. He could play, and loved to play, all sorts of games: home roulette, and odd and even, which he played on anything you like, in the street on the numbers of cars and trams, at home on any pieces of paper with figures on them." (Grinkrug)

31. 1 Innokenty Zhukov (1875-1948), sculptor, worked for a time in the Far Eastern Republic.

2 Nikolay Nasimovich-Chuzhak (1876-1937), journalist and old bolshevik, lived in the Far East, in Vladivostok and Chita. Around him and the avant-garde poets and artists who had gathered there (David Burlyuk, who had left Moscow in April 1918, Nikolay Aseyev, who left Russia as a deserter in 1917, Sergey Tretyakov and others) was formed in 1920 the "Tvorchestvo" ("Creative Work") group, which published a journal of the same name. The collection of Chuzhak's articles to which Mayakovsky refers in this letter, *Towards a dialectics of art* (*K dialektike iskusstva*), appeared in 1921. Chuzhak was an ardent propagandist and defender of Futurism, in particular of the work of Mayakovsky, and he achieved the proclamation of Futurism as the "art of the proletariat" in the Far Eastern Bolshevik party organisation. He attacked the bureaucrats of the State Publishing House, and his article "The Danger of Arakcheyevism" was the subject of a special public speech by Mayakovsky. In the spring of 1921 Mayakovsky sent the long poem *150,000,000* and *Mystery-Bouffe*, which for a long time the State Publishing House would not publish, to Chuzhak for publication. Chuzhak commented on the procrastination on the part of the State Publishing House, which was caused by their evident hostility towards Mayakovsky's poetry, in the following words: "The story of Mayakovsky's 'Mystery-Bouffe', and particularly *the story of his new long poem* . . . for the publication of which, after a year of preposterous delays, now with the State Publishing House, now with the Proletkult, the greatest of modern poets was forced to send his manuscript to Chita, this story *will with time be entered as a page of shame in the history of the manners of revolutionary Russia"* (*Tvorchestvo*, 1921, No. 7, p. 136). Mayakovsky himself reacted extremely sharply to the dilatoriness of the State Publishing House, and in a letter to Chuzhak he wrote: ". . . I'm sending my latest work. . . . The Arakcheyevs have multiplied. There's exchange of fire along the entire front. Print it . . . the Arakcheyevs have been holding me up for a year. Let's get organised. Step across . . . into permanent relations . . ." (the cuts in this letter were made by Chuzhak, who quoted it in the article mentioned above). On the "Tvorchestvo" group and Mayakovsky's contacts with it, see Jangfeldt, 1975a and 1976.

3 Chuzhak's response to the article written by Sosnovsky in connection with the trial of Mayakovsky (see No. 17, note 2), appeared in the newspaper *Dalnevostochnyy telegraf* (*The Far-Eastern Telegraph*), of which Chuzhak was himself the editor, on the 9th of October 1921.

4 Seven issues of *Tvorchestvo* included extracts from the long poems of Mayakovsky, who also sent them other materials.

5 Rita Rayt (b. 1898), a close friend of Mayakovsky and the Briks, translated *Mystery-Bouffe* into German for the third congress of the Komintern in the

summer of 1921. She met Mayakovsky and Lili Brik in 1920.

6 As is evident from the later correspondence, Mayakovsky's trip to Kharkov was postponed several times. He finally set off on the 11th of December. His readings took place on the 12th, 14th and 15th, and he returned to Moscow on the 18th.

7 Anna (Annushka) Gubanova (1869-1957), the Briks' domestic servant. There is an allusion to her in the long poem *About This* (*Pro eto*).

32. 1 Onisim Grinkrug, like his elder brother Mikhail, lived in Berlin from 1920 onwards.

33. 1 See No. 22.

2 This letter has not survived. Osip Volk was a childhood friend of Lili Brik.

3 André Triolet, Elsa's husband.

4 According to Lev Grinkrug, at one time the Briks kept a piglet as a pet. In a letter to Lili Brik of the 27th of November, Osip Brik reported that the piglet had fallen from a first-floor window and "we ate him".

5 Boris Arvatov.

6 According to Vasily Katanyan, a reference to the wife of Mikhail Krichevsky.

7 After Lili Brik's departure, Mayakovsky lived for a time with Osip Brik in the flat in Vodopyanyy Lane. The he returned to his room in Lubyanskiy Passage, which he held on to right up until his death. He had occupied this room since 1919 when Roman Jakobson, to comply with the measures taken to limit individual living space after the revolution, had needed more tenants. One floor lower, in the flat which had belonged to Jakobson's parents, who had left Russia in 1918, were the premises of the Moscow Linguistic Circle.

34. 1 A play upon the name of Osip Volk (Volk is Russian for wolf).

2 The letter sent with Grigory Vinokur (No. 24).

3 As is clear from No. 29, Mayakovsky numbered his letters to Lili Brik.

4 The fourth anniversary of the revolution.

5 Mariya (Mukkha) Natanson, the secretary of Kom-fut. See No. 36, note 1.

6 In Russian a play on the closeness of the phrases tvoy ves — all yours, and tvoy bes — your devil.

35. 1 Possibly sent at the same time as No. 34 (cf.: "Along with this letter I'm sending you another full one" at the end of this letter).

36. 1 Lili Brik calls the dog by the same name as a character in Nikolay Gogol's story *Saint John's Eve* (*Vecher nakanune Ivana Kupala*) (first published 1830), a mysterious figure suspected by villagers of being the devil in human form.

2 Kom-fut, Communism-Futurism — the Kom-fut collective was founded in Petrograd in January 1919 by Brik, Kushner and several workers from the Vyborg district Russian Communist Party (Bolshevik). (Since it had to be a party collective, Mayakovsky, who was not in the party, could not formally become a member; he did, however, take an active part in the propagandising of Kom-fut ideas.) The Kom-futs asserted that Bolshevik cultural policies lacked revolutionary character, that the cultural revolution was lagging behind the revolution in politics and economics "by more than a year", and that it would therefore be necessary to subordinate "Soviet organs of culture and enlightenment to the leadership of the new . . . cultural communist ideology" (*Iskusstvo kommuny/Art of the Commune/*, Petrograd, 1919, No. 8). The Kom-fut organisation was supposed to work within the party as a party collective. But it

was not accepted into the party, and moreover the refusal was motivated by the fact that "our party statutes do not allow for the existence of collectives of this kind" and that "by the ratification of such a collective we might create an undesirable precedent" (*Iskusstvo kommuny*, 1919, No. 9). With this decision, in the elaboration of which Lunacharsky clearly participated, the story of the first Kom-fut was inaugurated. This time the foundation of a Kom-fut organisation was motivated chiefly by the difficulties which Mayakovsky was experiencing in connection with the second production of *Mystery-Bouffe*. Although Kom-fut as an organisation had no influence and lasted only a short time, the name "Kom-futs" became a popular designation of those Futurists who were close to Communism. In 1920 Boris Arvatov, speaking about Kom-fut before the Moscow Proletkult, announced: "Communist Futurism is a leap across earlier Futurism." In 1923 Osip Brik explained: "At the present . . . time, the name Communist-Futurists is essential, since it distinguishes us from the Communist-Passéists, of who, unfortunately, there are still a very great number."

37. 1 Lili Brik has in mind the poet B. Livshits, mentioned in No. 40.

2 *Everything written by Vladimir Mayakovsky*, Petrograd 1919.

3 The dining-hall at the Arbeiterheim on Derpt Street —see No. 40, note 1.

4 On the journal *Tvorchestvo* and Chuzhak's articles see No. 31, note 2.

5 Pasternak's verse collection *My Sister Life* (*Sestra moya zhizn*) appeared only in 1922. Lili Brik has in mind the manuscript copy of the collection, which had been given to her by Pasternak. Photographs of the title page and title poem of this manuscript copy appeared in *Russian Literature Triquarterly*, 12, 1975, pp. 163-64.

6 The newspaper *Novyy put* (*New Path*) was published by the press bureau of the R.S.F.S.R. (Russian Soviet Federal Socialist Republic) Legation in Riga.

7 Osip Brik worked for a time in the Cheka, probably as a legal expert. Judging from a document of the political department of the Moscow GPU, he served in the organisation from the 8th of June 1920 until the 1st of January 1924. (Lili Brik archive.)

38. 1 This letter is sent to celebrate Lili Brik's birthday on the 11th of November.

39. 1 This letter was erroneously dated October by Mayakovsky.

2 The dining-room in the flat of Nadezhda Robertovna Adelgeym on Bolshaya Dmitrovka Street.

3 Probably a reference to the prologue of "The Fourth International".

40. 1 The Arbeiterheim was a Jewish educational organisation which had links with the Latvian Communist Party. The organisation had its own printing-works and its own book co-operative, which in May 1922 published Mayakovsky's long poem *I Love* (*Lyublyu*). For further details see No. 77, note 1. Which Jewish Futurists are being referred to (with the exception of B. Livshits, see below, note 2) is not clear.

2 B. Livshits, secretary of the Arbeiterheim, author of short stories and articles in the Rigan and Polish press.

3 This reference is unclear. The most famous "Left" poet, Alexander Čaks, returned to Riga from Russia only in the spring of 1922.

4 The "Satire Windows".

5 Probably a reference to the collection *A Bomb* (*Bomba*), Vladivostok, 1921.

6 A weekly publication of the Fine Arts Department of the Commissariat of

Enlightenment, it was edited by Brik, Natan Altman and Nikolay Punin, and appeared from December 1918 until the middle of April 1919 (19 issues). The newspaper was closed down after several protests from the Proletkult, from party organs and from "academics". Mayakovsky spoke later of the "baiting of left art, which reached its brilliant apogee in the closing of *Iskusstvo kommuny*" (XII, 42). Brik published several articles devoted to questions of proletarian art in the newspaper, and Mayakovsky published his poems on art in the new society as editorials. See Jangfeldt 1976, pp. 30-71.

7 A worker in the Commissariat for External Trade.

8 Alter, an acquaintance of Lili Brik, worked at the Commissariat of Foreign Affairs. Clearly he had links at the time with the newspaper *Novyy put* in Riga.

9 A photograph from one of Mayakovsky's films.

42. 1 Given Mayakovsky's contacts with Left Socialist Revolutionaries like Yury Sablin (see No. 45, note 6) and Boris Malkin (see No. 45, note 6 and No. 59, note 1), it is quite feasible that this is a reference to Vladimir Aleksandrovich Karelin (1891-1938). One of the leaders of the Left Socialist Revolutionary Party, he was commissar "without portfolio" in the first Soviet government (the Sovnarkom), formed in December 1917. He was condemned in his absence to three years' forced labour in the trial of the left SRs in November 1918 in which Sablin was also sentenced. He was arrested in February 1919, but soon released. In 1938 he was executed together with other Left SRs.

2 "The Fourth International".

44. 1 i.e. the work on the "Satire windows".

2 A book of this title, *"Iskusstvo kommuny". A collection of articles on questions of the building of Communist culture,* is listed among publications planned by the IMO publishing house. The book was never published, however, since IMO ceased to exist in 1919.

3 Olga Vladimirovna Mayakovskaya (1890-1949), Mayakovsky's younger sister, worked at the main post office in Moscow.

4 This reference is unclear. After the closure of the newspaper *Iskusstvo kommuny* in April 1919, the Futurists were deprived of the opportunity of propagandising their ideas in their own publications or in ones sympathetic to them. An attempt to create a publication of this kind may be seen in the reference to an "illustrated art journal" in the list of proposed publications by MAF (The Moscow Association of Futurists) (see No. 47). This project came to fruition with the publication of the first issue of *Lef* in 1923.

5 Regina Glaz, Lili Brik's cousin.

6 Nadezhda Lamanova (1861-1941), famous dress designer, who after the revolution created some interesting designs for "everyday wear". From the second half of 1921 Lamanova worked in the Fine Arts Department of the Commissariat of Enlightenment as an instructor in artistic manufacturing. Lili Brik had a high opinion of Lamanova's work, wore her clothes and even modelled them.

7 According to Lev Grinkrug, Lili Brik's dressmaker lived on Furmannyy Lane (verbal communication).

45. 1 Mayakovsky erroneously dated this letter October.

2 Bas(s)ias — diplomatic courier.

3 The play *Yesterday's valiant deed (What we did with the seeds we took from the peasants)*

/Vcherashniy podvig. (Chto sdelano nami s otobrannymi u krestyan semenami)/.

4   Nothing is known about the staging of this agit-play.

5   See Lili Brik's letter of the end of October (No. 28): "Write some poetry *for me.*" Mayakovsky then began to write the long poem *I Love* (*Lyublyu*), which was finished in the first half of February, in time for Lili Brik's arrival. Mayakovsky then made her a gift of a manuscript copy of the poem, with the subheading: "To sweet Kitties in place of explanations and letters." The poem was published by the MAF publishing house at the end of March 1922, with the dedication *L.Yu.B.*

6   After the delay with *150,000,000* and the play *Mystery-Bouffe*, relations between Mayakovsky and the State Publishing House were spoilt. In a jocular verse letter to Boris Malkin, the former head of Central Press, who had moved to Yekaterinburg in August, Mayakovsky wrote:

> . . . In a word,
> take me in Yekaterinburg,
> if I have to run from crazy Gosizdat.   (XIII, 49-50)
> [Gosizdat — the State Publishing House]

On Malkin, see No. 59, note 1.

Yury Sablin (1897-1937) was an officer and a leading member of the Left Socialist Revolutionary Party. He collaborated closely with the Bolsheviks after October 1917. In November 1918 he was sentenced to a year's imprisonment for participating in the revolt of the Left SRs against the Bolsheviks in July of that year. He was amnestied immediately after sentence. He joined the Russian Communist Party (Bolshevik) in 1919 and was made commander of a division of the Red Army and a member of the All-Russian Central Executive Committee (VTsIK). In 1937 Sablin was arrested and executed. Mayakovsky probably knew Sablin through Boris Malkin (see No. 59, note 1), another prominent member of the Left SRs, with whom Mayakovsky was in close contact.

46.   1   No. 43.

47.   1   This letter was sent in two copies, one with the courier and the copy, apparently, by post. This and the next two letters (Nos. 48 and 49) bear the same date. They were taken to Riga by the journalist Mikhail Koltsov.

2   Nikolay Meshcheryakov (1865-1942) was at the time chairman of the board at the State Publishing House.

3   A copy of this "Memorandum" was appended to the copy of the letter:

> To the People's Commissar of Enlightenment, comrade A.V. Lunacharsky from V.V. Mayakovsky and O.M. Brik.

MEMORANDUM

We are organising a publishing house for left art, "MAF" (the Moscow — in the future, International [*Mezhdunarodnaya*] — Association of Futurists).

The aim of the publishing house is to publish a journal, collections, monographs, collected works, textbooks etc. devoted to the propagandising of a basis for the future communist art, and to the demonstration of what has been achieved on the path towards it.

In view of the succession of difficulties we have encountered in connection with our attempts to publish our books in Russia, we shall publish abroad, and then import and disseminate our books in the RSFSR.

The funding for the publishing house will come from private sources.

We request you to assist us in organising the "MAF" publishing house as quickly as possible, and in receiving permission to import our publications into the RSFSR.

4   Nadezhda Konstantinovna Krupskaya (1869-1939) was a member of the board of the Commissariat of Enlightenment and chairman of its principal Political Enlightenment Committee. Mayakovsky's lack of confidence in a successful outcome to a conversation with Krupskaya was caused in part by the extremely negative assessment of Futurist activity which Krupskaya gave in *Pravda* in February 1921. In her article she described the Futurists as expressing "the worst elements of the old art . . . sensations . . . that are extremely abnormal and perverted" (*Pravda*, 13 February 1921).

48.   1   Mayakovsky was working on the "Satire Windows" for the Political Enlightenment Committee.

50.   1   This letter was sent in three copies.

     2   Mikhail Kolstov (1898-1942), journalist and writer. He was working at the time in the press department of the People's Commissariat for Foreign Affairs. Victim of the purges. See No. 47, note 1.

     3   K. Krayevich's *Textbook of Physics* and A. Malinin's arithmetic textbook(s).

     4   See No. 37, note 6.

     5   Evidently the copy of No. 47 sent by post with the memorandum attached to it had not yet reached Lili Brik.

51.   1   Mistakenly given the number 11 by Mayakovsky (see No. 49).

52.   1   The Kharkov première of *Mystery-Bouffe* took place on the 7th of November.

     2   Mayakovsky left for Kharkov on the 11th of December.

53.   1   Lili Brik mistakenly dated this letter to November.

     2   Dubinsky is a pseudonym of Moysha Lifshits, a Left poet who worked in the Komintern.

     3   A reference to Leo Matthias's book *Genie und Wahnsinn in Russland. Geistige Elemente des Aufbaus und Gefahrelemente des Zusammenbruchs*, published in Berlin in 1921. The German writer Leo Matthias (b. 1893) visited Moscow in 1920 and met Lunacharsky, David Shterenberg (the head of the Fine Arts Department of the Commissariat of Enlightenment), Mayakovsky and others. He recalls his meeting with Mayakovsky in his room in Lubyanskiy Passage in the following words: "He lives in a Moscow lodging-house, in a small room, between a rubber bath-tub, a pile of books and an enormous quantity of photographs.

He himself seems equally unsentimental: a big fellow, with a bony, roughly chiselled face, uncouth in speech, but refreshing, with a fixed gaze, lumbering movements and a loud voice.

/. . ./ He spoke of his drama 'Mystery-Bouffe', the performance of which had been demanded at a public gathering of proletarians, whereas all the lecturers had rejected it for proletarian art as being 'bourgeois'. He also said that almost all the poets of Proletkult were copying him /. . ./ 'I will certainly find the forms of expression appropriate for the one hundred and fifty million!' he proclaimed to me.

236

What he is seeking is a more outward-looking art, art for the masses, which is what art is. He is now writing a new play, in which the principal characters will be Lenin, Einstein and a third person whose name he did not want to give away. In addition God appears in it, and he even lets him sing folksongs, and even well known operatic arias."

The "drama" mentioned by Matthias is the poem "The Fifth International", which was indeed, as far as can be judged, originally planned as a play.

4   For Mayakovsky's answer see No. 56. Before that Osip Brik replied to Lili's letter in a letter of the 14th of December: "I'm sending you "Satire Windows"; I can't find Aseyev and "My Sister Life", someone must have borrowed them to read or I've lost them. I'll send some fat cigarettes if I can get hold of them before Dubinsky leaves . . . it's ghastly here in Moscow. . . . The hacks and profiteers are flourishing. People with 'ideas' are swelling up from starvation.

The publishing house is a splendid thing. And of course it will come off. Volodya and I are terribly respected. By the way the idea of production art is winning along the entire front: the Proletkultists passed a resolution at their congress* 'primarily to teach production art in their studios, and to retain fine arts only in the form of posters and cartoons'. A similar resolution has been passed by the art education departments of the Commissariat of Enlightenment. The Institute of Artistic Culture/Inkhuk/ is flourishing. Lunacharsky is already saying in his speeches that production art is the art of the future.

I'm constantly being invited to give lectures and write articles and books about production art.

A certain German gave a very successful talk at Inkhuk about art in Russia and Germany; he said that art in Germany is degenerating and dying out, whereas in Russia it is experiencing a renaissance through Constructivism and production art.**. . .

In general the left is winning all along the line, but since everyone is so preoccupied with getting hold of food and firewood it's very difficult to derive any benefit from this victory. Nobody wants to do anything without getting paid for it, and since the people with the money are still far from vanquished, there's nowhere to get any money from. — It's an old story!"

*The Second All-Russian Congress of the Proletkult, 17th-21st of November 1921.

**On the 8th of December the Hungarian critic Alfréd Kemény (who was living in Germany) gave a lecture at Inkhuk in German: "The most recent trends in modern German and Russian art." He gave a second lecture on the 26th of December entitled "Construction works by the Society of Young Artists / Obmokhu/".

54.   1   The legation of the RSFSR was on Albert Street. Apparently Lili Brik moved there.

55.   1   An Englishman working on the Nansen mission (see No. 60).

56.   1   This letter either did not arrive or has been lost.

2   The three readings took place on the 12th, 14th and 15th of December.

3   David Petrovich Shterenberg (1881-1948), an artist summoned by Lunacharsky from Paris, where they had met before the revolution, to take part in the elaboration of Bolshevik cultural policies. In 1918 he became the head of the Fine Arts department at the Commissariat of Enlightenment, where he worked with

Mayakovsky and Brik.

4 Vasily Yevtushevsky was the author of several books and textbooks on arithmetic.

58. 1 In his letter of the 14th of December (see No. 53, note 4) Osip Brik wrote that "I sent you a detailed letter yesterday".

59. 1 Boris Malkin (1890-1942) leading member of the Left Socialist Revolutionary Party and of the All-Russian Central Executive Committee (VTsIK). Former head of the Central Agency of the All-Russian Central Executive Committee for the Dissemination of the Press (Tsentropechat). He was working at Yekaterinburg at the time and had come to Moscow for the Ninth All-Russian Congress of Soviets. See No. 45, note 6.

2 Levky Zheverzheyev (1881-1942) was ex-president of the society of artists called the "Union of Youth" (Soyuz molodyozhi). After the revolution he worked in the Fine Arts department of the Commissariat of Enlightenment. Zheverzheyev recalls his meetings with Mayakovsky in November-December 1921 in the following words: "Mayakovsky kept trying to tempt me to go to the newly-opened restaurant No. 1, and once, when he'd got really involved in his work, he missed the train for Kharkov, where he was supposed to be appearing. He reproduced all these 'events' in cartoon sketches in my album, which parodied his "Rosta Windows" style, without the slightest element of self-flattery."

63. 1 David Shterenberg and his wife lived in the same flat as the Briks in Poluektov Lane in 1919-1920. In 1920 the Briks moved to Vodopyanyy Lane.

2 Galina Flakserman (1888-1958) was an acquaintance of Mayakovsky from the days of the journal *Letopis* (*Chronicle*), which appeared from 1915 until 1917, and where she had worked as secretary.

3 Velimir Khlebnikov had returned from his trip to the Caucasus and Persia. On the 14th of January 1922 he wrote to his mother and sister: "I travelled to Moscow in my shirtsleeves: the south had stripped me to the final thread, but the Muscovites dressed me in a fur coat and a grey suit." Apparently Mayakovsky included with his letter a note from Khlebnikov to Lili Brik in which he told her: "This postscript is proof that I have arrived in Moscow and come to see my dear friends on Myasnitskaya Street". Khlebnikov stayed with the Briks more than once, and they helped him in all sorts of ways.

64. 1 On the 8th of January Mayakovsky appeared at "The First Real Satire Evening" at the Polytechnic museum.

2 The "Purge of modern poetry" took place at the Polytechnic museum on the 17th of February.

65. 1 The Ginzburg sisters, Zinaida, Roza and Sofya, were childhood friends of Lev Grinkrug. The youngest of them was Zinaida.

66. 1 Boba — Roman Grinberg (1897-1969) the Briks' neighbour in the communal flat in Vodopyanyy Lane (a flat which the Grinberg family had occupied before the implementation of the measures to limit living space). He emigrated to Paris in the 1920s, and from there to New York, where in the 1960s he published the *Vozdushnyye puti* (*Aerial Paths*) almanacs.

2 Tsetsiliya Yakovlevna Tsipkina, a dentist.

67 1 Mistakenly given the number 20 by Mayakovsky (see No. 64).

2 Lev Elbert (1900-1946) was an acquaintance of Mayakovsky, who when he was working in the chief political directorate of the People's Commissariat for

238

Communications (Glavpolitput) in 1920, ordered propaganda posters from the poet for the Rail Committee of the Union of Rail Transport Workers (Dorprofsoyuz). Vasily Katanyan reports that: "In the autumn of 1921, when he was seeing Lili Yurevna off to Riga, Mayakovsky ran into Elbert at the station and discovered that he had started working for the People's Commissariat for Foreign Affairs and was leaving for Riga by the same train.

. . . this melancholy man, sluggish and impassive, whom Mayakovsky had christened 'Snob' more by contrast than by similarity, for his way of speaking through his teeth, was a fearless undercover agent who sailed across the Mediterranean in the funnel of a steamer. We used to hear rumours about his adventures and exploits, and maybe Mikhail Koltsov, who was a close friend of his, knew a little more. . . . From time to time Snob would disappear for a year, or two, or three — then he would turn up again, ring up and call round.

Mayakovsky was amicably disposed towards him for all the ten years that they knew each other, and would meet him both abroad and at home in Moscow up until the very end" (Katanyan, 1974). Elbert lived with Mayakovsky for a few days in March 1930 — see No. 399.

68. 1 No. 65.
2 No. 66.
71. 1 Zivs, the Rigan publisher and book-dealer with whom Lili Brik was negotiating.
2 See No. 66.
3 See No. 23, note 8.
4 Apparently a reference to Bronislava Matveyevna Runt, writer and sister-in-law of Valery Bryusov.
5 In November 1921 Lili Brik had sent Mayakovsky and Brik the music of the song "Mon Homme", by Maurice Yvain, which was popular at the time. It was first sung by Mistinguett at the revue *Paris qui jazz* (1920).
72. 1 Dubinsky's second "introduction" (see No. 53) is probably because Mayakovsky was on a trip to Kharkov during his previous visit (see No. 58) and did not manage to see him. Sharik was his pet name.
2 Apparently Lili Brik had also sent a letter to Kharkov to be sent on from Moscow.
75. 1 The March tour did not take place. A little later, on the 2nd of May, Mayakovsky left for Riga, where Lili Brik was once again (see No. 77, note 1).
76. 1 Lili Brik returned to Moscow at the beginning of February 1922.
77. 1 In April 1922 Lili Brik again went to Riga, apparently with the same aim as on her first trip, to obtain German and English visas. Judging from this letter, the publishing plans had not yet been definitively buried.

On the 2nd of May Mayakovsky left for Riga, where he stayed for nine days; he returned to Moscow on the 13th of May. The visit to Riga was the poet's first trip abroad. In Riga he stayed at the Hotel Bellevue, where Lili was living. The two appearances which Lili had arranged for him in Riga (see No. 74) were banned by the police, but Mayakovsky managed to read *150,000,000* at the Arbeiterheim. The Arbeiterheim publishing house also published the poem *I Love* in an edition of 10,000 copies, but it was confiscated by the police. See Mayakovsky's poem "How a democratic republic works" ("Kak rabotayet respublika demokraticheskaya"):

I published "I love" —
love lyrics.

239

Try to find something more harmless in the entire world!
But the police — they'll grab at anything.
They're sluggish with their repressions.
They just managed to arrest it three days later.

2 Soon after this Alter set off for the sanatorium at St Blasien in southern Germany.

78. 1 In the summer of 1922 Mayakovsky and the Briks lived at a dacha in Pushkino, outside Moscow. In August Lili Brik left for Berlin, and from there she went on to visit her mother in London (see the next letter).

2 Aleksandr Mikhailovich Krasnoshchokov (1880-1937) was an important Bolshevik, an economist and lawyer. He was born in the Chernobyl stedtl, in the province of Kiev, in the family of a Jewish shop-assistant. In 1896 he joined an underground social-democratic circle: several times he was arrested, imprisoned and exiled. In November 1902 Krasnoshchokov avoided another period of exile by escaping to Berlin, from where, in March 1903, he left for America. When he arrived in New York, Krasnoshchokov got work as a tailor and painter. In 1912 he graduated from Chicago University in law and economics, and from 1915 onwards he worked as a defence lawyer in trade union cases, the rector of a workers' university and a lecturer on legal and economic questions. When a left-wing faction of the American Socialist Party was founded in 1904, Krasnoshchokov became a member, and he remained so until he left for Russia in 1917. He was a member of the American Federation of Labour and of the Industrial Workers of the World (the IWW), he knew Joe Hill, and he contributed to the English, Hebrew and Russian party and trade union press.

Krasnoshchokov describes his return to Russia in his autobiography: "I arrived at Vladivostok at the end of July 1917, and immediately joined the Bolshevik faction, was elected to the Soviet in August, and in September was elected a member of the town duma in Nikolsko-Ussuriysk and President of the Soviet of workers' and soldiers' deputies to represent the Bolsheviks; I was a member of the Nikolsko-Ussuriysk party conference to elect candidates to the Constituent Assembly, chairman of the Nikolsko-Ussuriysk party committee, deputy president of the First Far Eastern Congress of trade unions in October, then president of the Far Eastern Soviet of People's Commissars throughout its existence from December 1917 until September 1918, being re-elected by three congresses (nos. III, IV and V).

In September 1918 I went off into the taiga, and, making my way to Soviet Russia, I was arrested on the 1st of May 1919 as I crossed the front near Samara (Kinel-Cherkassy). After the 'death train' across the whole of Siberia, via Ufa, Tomsk and Krasnoyarsk, I was thrown into Irkutsk prison in September 1919. Along with other Bolsheviks, I was liberated on the 28th of December 1919 by a rebellion among the workers of Irkutsk.

After I crossed the Czech front and joined the headquarters staff of the fifth army, I was nominated by the Siberian bureau and by the Central Committee of the All-Union Communist Party (Bolshevik) as a member of the Far Eastern Bureau of the Central Committee of the All-Union Communist Party (Bolshevik) on the 3rd of March 1920, and I remained a member of the Bureau through all its staff changes until my departure from the Far East in July 1921.

240

Throughout this entire period I held the posts of President of Government of the Far Eastern Republic and Minister of Foreign Affairs.

In 1920 while on an official trip, I was a member of the delegation of the All-Union Communist Party (Bolshevik) at the second congress of the Komintern.

In Moscow in 1921 I went through the purge of the Moscow Committee. My party card was marked: 'member of the All-Union Communist Party (Bolshevik) since 1917, in the revolutionary social-democratic movement since 1897'.

On the Soviet side I occupied the following posts after my return from the Far East in November 1921: Deputy People's Commissar for Finance, Member of the Presidium of the Supreme Soviet of People's Economy and President of the Industrial Bank.

I was arrested on the 19th of September 1923, released in November 1924, and returned to work after a long illness in June 1926." (Krasnoshchokov 1934).

On Krasnoshchokov's arrest, see No. 122, note 4.

Krasnoshchokov is the author of the book *The modern American bank (Sovremennyy amerikanskiy bank)*, Moscow 1926, the appearance of which was delayed by his imprisonment.

Krasnoshchokov met Mayakovsky in Moscow in the summer of 1921.

3 At the time Mayakovsky was taking German lessons from Rita Rayt. This is possibly why Lili Brik sent him Busch's book.

4 Oswald Spengler published two parts of his fundamental work *Untergang des Abendlandes* between 1918 and 1922. It is not impossible, however, that the book Lili sent Osip was *Preussentum und Sozialismus* (1920).

5 That summer, Rita Rayt lived with Mayakovsky and the Briks. She recalls: "We behaved badly in Lili Yurevna's absence. When she was there, only our very closest friends came to visit us on our days off, about seven or eight people, rarely more. While she was away we began to be descended upon not only by our friends, but by mere acquaintances, who would bring their own acquaintances along with them. . . . Lilya Yurevna sent us all presents from Germany: wonderful ties and shirts for Vladimir Vladimirovich and Osip Maksimovich, and a dark blue suede hat for me" (Rayt, 1963).

79. 1 On the 18th of August Lili Brik left Berlin for London.

2 Elsa Triolet had separated from her husband and moved to London, where she worked for an English architect (in 1918, before leaving Russia, she had passed her examination in the architecture and building section of the Moscow Women's Building Courses).

3 Mayakovsky and Brik did not leave for Berlin until the beginning of October 1922. There they met Lili Brik and Elsa Triolet, who had arrived from London. Mayakovsky made several appearances in Berlin, which at the time was a major centre of Russian culture.

80. 1 The letter is postmarked Kilburn.

81. 1 This letter and the following thirty-two letters and notes (Nos. 81-113) are connected with the two-month separation between Mayakovsky and Lili Brik, which lasted from the 28th of December 1922 until the 28th of February 1923, during which time Mayakovsky lived in his room on Lubyanskiy Passage and Lili in her flat on Vodopyanyy Lane. The decision to part was evidently taken on the 27th of December. In these two months the intention was that they should think through their relationship, and they decided neither to see each other nor

241

to correspond. Nevertheless they did exchange letters and notes through intermediaries. "I was angry with him and with myself that we were not keeping to the conditions, but I did not have the strength not to answer, I loved him very greatly, and at times we were almost conducting a 'correspondence'" (Lili Brik 1956). Compare also in the poem *About This*, written during those two months: ". . . a giant/will stand for a second/and collapse,/burying itself under the ripple of notes".

In fact, Mayakovsky and Lili Brik "corresponded" almost every day. More than fifty letters and notes have survived, the majority of them undated. All the letters and notes which represent any kind of "plot" interest are published here; not included are the "plotless" notes along the lines of "I kiss my little kitten", "To the little kittens and the little birdies" and so on. The majority of the letters and notes are dated tentatively on the basis of their content.

For more details on the circumstances of the parting, see the Introduction.

2 "I do not remember what this was" (Lili Brik 1956), Lyuda: Lyudmila Mayakovskaya (1884-1972), Mayakovsky's elder sister.

3 Mayakovsky's telephone number in Lubyanskiy Passage.

82. 1 This word was burnt by the seal.

83. 1 Nikolay (Kolya) Aseyev had brought Mayakovsky a note from Lili.

2 According to Lili Brik (1956) this letter was an answer "to my answer that I loved him". The following note has survived: "My beloved little Puppy, you don't know how much I love you! Don't be jealous! There's no one to be jealous of! I'm expecting you on the 28th. Your Lilya." Possibly this letter from Mayakovsky is an answer to this note.

3 Compare Lili Brik (1956): "Sometimes, unable to restrain himself, Volodya would telephone me, and once I told him that it would be better if he wrote to me when he very much needed to." The following note has also survived: "Puppy, I don't want to be *obliged* to answer, but when you need to, write."

4 The fact that during their two-month separation Lili Brik, unlike him, saw her friends and led a more or less normal life, was reinterpreted by Mayakovsky in the poem *About This* (*Pro eto*) in the following manner:

And the raven guests?!

          The door's wing

Has been slammed against the corridor's sides a hundred times.

Bawlers bawling,

          Yellers yelling,

Wove dead drunk towards me.

. . .

Yes

    their voices.

          Familiar cries.

I froze in recognition,

               ivying myself silently against the wall,

I cut out phrases from the pattern of their cries.

Yes —

    it's them —

          they're talking about me.

. . .

And once again
> slamming of doors and cawing,
And once again dancing, floor-shuffled.
And once again
> the scorching steppes of the walls
Resound below my ear and pant in the two-step.

Compare, in Lili Brik's memoirs: "More than once during those two months I tormented myself over the fact that Volodya was suffering in solitude, whereas I was living my ordinary life, seeing people, going out." (Lili Brik, 1956.)

84. 1 A reference to chance meetings in the street, at editorial offices etc.

2 At the beginning of January Mayakovsky had sent Lili Brik some birds in a cage to remind her of him. This note has been preserved: "To Kitty. Only don't you gobble them up. Puppy. Give them hempseed and water."

86. 1 Mayakovsky names his "place of imprisonment" after Oscar Wilde's *Ballad of Reading Gaol*, written while Wilde was in prison. It was published in 1898, and Valery Bryusov's Russian translation appeared in 1915. Mayakovsky also gave this title to the first part of his long poem *About This*.

2 A note bearing the words: "Thank you, Volosik!" has survived.

3 Byron's *The Prisoner of Chillon* was written in 1816.

4 One word is burnt by the seal.

5 I.e. One of the birds which Mayakovsky had sent Lili Brik.

91. 1 Verse inscription on the first volume of Mayakovsky's collection *Thirteen Years of Work* (*13 let raboty*), which had just appeared.

92. 1 Lili Brik translated Karl Wittfogel's tragedy "The Fugitive" for the first issue of *Lef*, which appeared in March 1923.

94. 1 Mayakovsky and Lili met by chance at the State Publishing House, "where I think I was taking some work I'd done (for Lef?)" (Lili Brik, 1956). Thus the "kitty worker". Compare No. 92, note 1.

97. 1 In addition to purely literary disagreements there were conflicts of another kind between Mayakovsky and Korney Chukovsky, and Lili Brik's sour remark about Chukovsky here has a more personal motivation. It apparently stems from events in early 1918, when Chukovsky "learnt" from a certain doctor that Mayakovsky had become infected with syphilis and had himself infected a certain woman with the disease (this was not in fact true). For some reason Chukovsky decided to "inform" Gorky about this matter, and he in turn "warned" Lunacharsky. I was told this story by Lili Brik; it is also mentioned in the memoirs of Sofya Shamardina ("Sonka", one of the heroines of *A Cloud in Trousers*; she was the woman Chukovsky's "information" referred to); and by Viktor Shklovsky: "And then we learnt that someone had told Gorky that Volodya had wronged a woman.

Lili Brik and I want to see Aleksey Maksimovich.

Of course, Gorky found the conversation unpleasant, he drummed his finger on the table and said: 'I don't know, I don't know, I was told by a very serious comrade. I'll find out his address for you.'

. . . [Gorky] wrote a few words on the back of Lili Brik's letter to him . . ." (Shklovsky 1974, p. 78).

Here is Lili Brik's letter to Gorky (Lili Brik archive):

Aleksey Maksimovich,

I earnestly request that you tell me the address of the person in Moscow from whom you wanted to find out the doctor's address. I am leaving for Moscow today in order to clarify definitively all the circumstances of the case. I consider it to be impossible to postpone matters.

L. Brik

Gorky wrote the following answer on the back of Lili Brik's letter:

So far I haven't been able to ascertain either the name or the address of the doctor, since the person who might have been able to tell me them has gone to the Ukraine on official business.

A.P[eshkov].

This episode left its mark not only upon Mayakovsky's relationship with Chukovsky, but also upon his relationship with Gorky.

98. 1 This sentence went into *About This* almost word for word:

> She's in bed.
> > She's lying there.
>
> . . .
>
> She's ill!
> > She's lying there!

101. 1 The autograph copy of the poem "On 'fiascos', 'apogees' and other unknown things" ("*O 'fiaskakh', 'apogeyakh' i drugikh nevedomykh veshchakh*"), which was published in *Izvestiya* on the 21st of February. On the back of the manuscript Mayakovsky had written: "The Izvestiya drivel".

102. 1 A reference to the collection *Lyrics* (*Lirika*), which appeared in the first half of February. Lili Brik (1956) recalls: "The book has been lost, but I remember the inscription on it:

> Forgive me, Lilinka, my sweet,
> For the poverty of my verbal world,
> The book should be called 'Lilinka',
> But it's called 'Lirika'."

The cover was designed by Anton Lavinsky. On the table of contents see No. 103, note 1.

103. 1 The *Lyrics* collection has a printed dedication: *To Lilya*. It brings together all the long love poems connected with Lili Brik: *The Backbone-Flute*, *I Love* and *Man*. The table of contents, which Lili thought "lousy", does indeed look strange: the titles of individual sections of the poems *I Love* and *Man* are set in the same type as the titles of the poems, and since the page number of each section is also given, the impression is that the book consists not of three long poems but of a large number of separate short poems.

104. 1 Kseniya (Oksana) Aseyeva (1900-1985), the wife of Nikolay Aseyev.

2 This reference is unclear. Perhaps Mayakovsky had sent Lili Brik an orange, just as he had sent her flowers and other gifts.

107. 1 The Grinbergs were the Briks' neighbours in the flat in Vodopyanyy Lane. See No. 66, note 1.

109. 1 'The separation was due to end at 3 o'clock on the 28th of February, but the Petrograd train did not leave until 8.00. Compare in No. 113: "Just think, after travelling for two months, to spend two weeks driving up to the house and then to wait another half a day for the signal to change!"

2   Clearly Lili Brik planned to move in with Mayakovsky in Lubyanskiy Passage, or simply to register as living there. There were practical reasons for such a scheme: Mayakovsky, who was often abroad, wanted to make sure he held on to his room in Lubyanskiy Passage. Lili Brik's archive contains copies of two letters from Lunacharsky to the housing department of the Supreme Soviet of People's Economy, in which he asked them to "preserve in the name of comrade Mayakovsky his room in house No. 3 flat 12 on Lubyanskiy Passage" (letters of the 23rd of October 1924 and the 4th of April 1926). Compare later in Mayakovsky's letter: "I'll still have to change or let the room if I leave Moscow."

3   Appended to the letter is a note to Tomchin, who worked in the administrative department of Moscow City Council:

Respected comrade,

Please see Lili Yurevna Brik and arrange her "exchange" without particular delay.

I spoke to you about this and made this request the last time we met.

Please don't mislay the passport (or my work-book) because it has a visa in it. England is a long way away, and you can't get another one in a hurry!

I shake your hand

With comradely greetings

Vlad. Mayakovsky
23/2 23

111.   1   Rita Rayt, who accompanied Lili Brik to the station, recalls the meeting between Lili and Mayakovsky in the following words: "We were in a cab, it was cold and windy, but Lilya suddenly took her hat off; I said to her: 'Kitty, you'll catch a cold', and she pulled it down over her eyes again, and it was clear how agitated she was. We went on to the platform, the train came in, and we walked along until suddenly at the far end we saw Vladimir Vladimirovich standing in a carriage doorway. Lilya gave me a hurried kiss and said: 'Right, run along now! There's Volodya.' As I left I turned round and saw Lilya walking up to the carriage and Mayakovsky standing motionless, petrified, in the doorway . . ." (Rayt 1967, p. 121). Lili Brik (1956) adds: "As soon as the train started moving, standing there, leaning against the door, Volodya read me the poem 'About This'. He finished it and burst into tears of relief."

112.   1   Words from the revolutionary song the *Warszawianka*.

113.   1   This letter is written on the same large-size paper as the poem *About This*. It is published here in the version which Lili Brik herself prepared for publication (Lili Brik 1956).

    The diary-letter was never sent, and Lili Brik discovered it only after Mayakovsky's suicide: "After Volodya's death I found in a drawer of his desk in Gendrikov Lane a bundle of my letters to him and several photographs of me. The whole lot was wrapped up in a letter to me which had gone yellow with age and which shed light on 'About This'. Volodya had never spoken to me of it" (Lili Brik 1956).

    2   No. 97.

    3   A meeting of *Lef* was arranged for, and took place on, the 5th of March.

    4   See No. 109, note 1.

114.   1   A reference to the cover of the second issue of the journal *Lef*, which was to be published on the 1st of May 1923.

2 The "announcement-advertisement" included the cover of the issue, the editorial (written by Mayakovsky) and May Day poems by Aseyev, Kamensky, Kruchonykh, Mayakovsky, Pasternak and others (all included in the second issue).

3 Aleksandr Rodchenko's cover is a photomontage with two green lines through it.

4 Mayakovsky was responsible editor of *Lef*.

115. 1 From its content this letter can be linked with Nos. 87 and 109, but it is unlikely that it was written during the two-month separation.

2 On the 3rd of July 1923, Mayakovsky and the Briks left for Germany. In August Lili Brik wrote to Rita Rayt: "We're coming home in a month. Volodya has got an engagement in America and will apparently go there in about three weeks (if it doesn't fall through at the last moment). They suggested I go too, but I declined (!!). I want him to go on his own." On the 15th of September, Mayakovsky wrote to David Burlyuk from Berlin: "If you send me a visa, I'll be in New York in about two or three months." Mayakovsky did not get to America until 1925.

116. 1 Written on the Berlin-Moscow train. Mayakovsky and the Briks spent the summer of 1923 in Germany, at the resort of Bad Flinsberg on the island of Norderney, and in Berlin. On the 15th or 16th of September, Mayakovsky returned to Moscow by train, but Lili and Osip Brik stayed on in Berlin for a few days longer.

2 It is not clear which screenplay Mayakovsky is referring to. Possibly he has in mind the unfinished screenplay "Benz No. 22", which he wrote under the impression of his first trip to Germany in the autumn of 1922. Clearly Dubinsky played some part in work on the screenplay.

117. 1 No. 116.

2 See in Lili Brik's memoirs: "In 1920 Mayakovsky saw a boy with a tiny squirrel in his arms on Kuznetskiy most. The boy wanted three roubles for the squirrel. Mayakovsky turned out to have no money on him at all. He took the boy to the 'Mayak' /'Lighthouse'/ bookshop on the Petrovka, borrowed the three roubles there and brought the little squirrel home" (Lili Brik 1941).

3 In the summer of 1923 Boris Arvatov had an attack of the serious nervous illness from which he suffered throughout his life.

4 Aleksey Babichev (1887-1963), artist, sculptor, art theorist. He was invited to the Institute of Artistic Culture soon after it was organised and became a member of its presidium, deputy chairman, head of the organisational section and a member of the board.

5 It was precisely at this time, in September 1923, that Lev Trotsky's article "Futurism", which Mayakovsky described as "wise", appeared in *Pravda*. (It is also included in Trotsky's book *Literature and Revolution (Literatura i revolyutsiya)*, Moscow 1923.) Mayakovsky wrote Trotsky a letter in connection with the People's Commissar's work on his article (the "Letter about Futurism", printed in the USSR without any indication of the addressee), and they even met. (Trotsky also met Pasternak on the same subject.)

Trotsky is mentioned a number of times in Mayakovsky's poetry, including a reference at the beginning of section 6 of the poem *150,000,000*:

Not to Trotsky
Not to Lenin is my verse tender.
In battle
I glorify the millions
I see the millions
I sing the millions.

    Quoted from the first edition, Moscow 1921; in Mayakovsky's "Collected Works" the first line is missing. Since the 1930s Trotsky has been completely "removed" from Mayakovsky's works.

119.   1   On the 10th or 11th of January 1924, Mayakovsky set off on a lecture tour to Kiev and Kharkov. He returned to Moscow on the 18th or 19th of January.

    2   This reference is unclear. Possibly Mayakovsky wanted to offer his books to a publishing house in Kiev or Kharkov.

120.   1   At the beginning of February 1924 Lili Brik left for Paris, where, judging from this telegram, she arrived on the 13th. After spending two months in Paris, she went to visit her mother in London. (See No. 126.)

121.   1   On the 14th of February 1924, Mayakovsky set off on a lecture tour of Gomel, Vinnitsa, Odessa and Kiev.

    2   Lili Brik's letter was sent from Berlin, where she had stopped for a few days on the way to Paris; it has not been found.

    3   A letter from "Sharik" Dubinsky.

    4   Aristophanes' *Lysistrata*, staged in the music studio of the Moscow Arts Theatre, provoked an extremely negative reaction in Mayakovsky.

122.   1   Mayakovsky never abandoned the idea of making a trip to America, and when he was in Paris in the autumn of 1924 he made another attempt to get an American visa. (See No. 135.)

    2   Lev Gertsman worked for the All-Russian Co-operative Society Ltd. in London. Lili Brik had met him in London in 1922. He was a very good dancer.

    3   A diplomat.

    4   Aleksandr Krasnoshchokov was arrested on the 19th of September 1923. "In the light of the various rumours circulating in the town about the reasons for the arrest of the President of the Industrial Bank A. M. Krasnoshchokov", Kuybyshev, the People's Commissar of Workers' and Peasants' Inspection, considered it necessary to place an official announcement in the newspapers which stated that "incontrovertible facts have been established concerning Krashnoshchokov's criminal use of funds from the economic department for personal ends, his use of these funds to pay for disgraceful drunken sprees, the use of the bank's administrative funds to enrich his relatives and so on", and that "Krasnoshchokov has criminally betrayed the trust which was placed in him and must endure the stern punishment of the courts" (*Pravda* and *Izvestiya*, Moscow, 3rd October 1923). This was the first trial of a major Communist figure in Soviet Russia. Krasnoshchokov was held in Lefortovo prison until November 1924, when he was transferred to the prison hospital (he suffered from hereditary bronchiectasia). The baselessness of the charges brought against him is confirmed by the fact that when his treatment was over he was not returned to prison, but simply released, despite having been sentenced to six years in solitary confinement. During his imprisonment Krasnoshchokov translated Walt Whitman.

The Krasnoshchokov case provided the starting-point for Boris Romashov's play *Meringue* (*Vozdushnyy pirog*) (premièred in February 1925) about the bank director Koromyslov and his lover, the actress and ballerina Rita Kern. In Romashov's treatment Koromyslov, who is surrounded by rogues and swindlers, is most likely a victim of circumstance. After his arrest he says: "Koromyslov is not a scoundrel. . . . I may have been the victim of commercial illusions, I may not have understood what was going on around me, but I did not betray the interests of the workers."

Krasnoshchokov was shot in 1937.

125. 1 In all probability this letter was sent to Berlin. Mayakovsky left for Berlin on the 15th or 16th of April, and arrived on the 19th.

2 Apparently Lili Brik had made an attempt to go to England without a visa. Mayakovsky's poem *"Curzon"* (*"Kerzon"*) was published in 1923. The English newspaper *The Morning Post* demanded that the Soviet government hold the journal *Krasnaya nov* (*Red Virgin Soil*), which had printed it, equally responsible for this "slanderous" poem. It is possible that the refusal to let Lili Brik into England was connected with this matter.

3 Basavryuk. See No. 36, note 1.

127. 1 Lili Brik and Mayakovsky met in Berlin, and on the 9th of May they left Berlin for Moscow together.

2 Lili Brik acquired a Scotch Terrier in England. See letter 125: ". . . everyone advises me to buy one in England, because that's where they come from . . . and there's a good choice. So expect us both!" The dog which Lili Brik brought back to Moscow was given the name Scot or Scotik. In this telegram, however, Lili calls it Shchen (Puppy), which in telegrams sent from abroad was sometimes transcribed as Schen.

129. 1 Mayakovsky had left to make appearances in Leningrad on the 17th of May 1924. He returned on about the 24th of May.

2 Mayakovsky appeared at the Philharmonia Hall on the 19th, 20th and 22nd of May.

3 The twelfth congress of the Russian Communist Party opened in Moscow on the 23rd of May.

4 At this time Mayakovsky was preparing for publication issue No. 1 of *Lef* for 1924 (No. 5 by continuous numeration). The bulk of the issue was devoted to "Lenin's language". There is the following note in the diary of the critic Boris Eykhenbaum: "21 May: with Mayakovsky in the Hotel Yevropeyskaya, room 26. There were Jakubinsky, Tynyanov, N. S. Tikhonov, Punin, Vinokur and I. We spoke about Lef." (Katanyan 1961, p. 464.)

5 The word "soul-strings" also occurs in the notes to the talk Mayakovsky gave that same day.

130. 1 Sent in connection with Mayakovsky's birthday (old style).

131. 1 This note and the next one date from the summer of 1924, when Mayakovsky was living partly in Moscow and partly in the dacha at Pushkino.

2 The critic Iuda Grossman-Roshchin (1883-1934). The reference is to a game of cards.

132. 1 Mayakovsky prepared several advertising posters in the summer of 1924 for the State Publishing House (*Gosizdat*), the Moscow Society of Agricultural Produce Processing Enterprises (*Mosselprom*) and the Press Agency.

248

133.	1	On about the 20th of August 1924, Mayakovsky set off on a lecture tour of Sevastopol, Yalta, Novocherkassk, Vladikavkaz and Tiflis. He arrived in Tiflis on the 28th of August.
134.	1	An inscription in a notebook. Dated by Lili Brik. The book was later thrown away, but the sheet with the inscription has been preserved. The greeting is connected with Mayakovsky's departure abroad, to Paris, and, he hoped, to America. He left on the next day, the 24th of October.
135.	1	Mayakovsky arrived in Paris on the 2nd of November, and stayed there for a month and a half.
	2	His first attempt to get to America had been made in the autumn of 1923 (see No. 115, note 2). Mayakovsky made a second attempt in the spring of 1924 (see No. 122, note 1), when in his own words he was in Berlin "en route for America". The third attempt also ended in failure.
	3	Elsa Triolet was living in this hotel, and when Mayakovsky was in Paris he always stayed there too. As Elsa Triolet recalls: "The Istria Hotel, where Mayakovsky used to stay, looked like a tower from the outside; it had a narrow stairwell and narrow stairs, with five landings and no corridors; around each landing were five panelled doors, behind each of which was a small room. All the rooms had harshly striped wallpaper that looked like mattresses, and each of them contained a double bed, a bedside table, a little table by the window, two chairs, a mirrored wardrobe, a wash-stand with hot water, and on the floor a worn yellow flowered rug. Among the famous people who lived there at the time were the Dadaist painter Picabia and his wife, the artist Marcel Duchamp, the American surrealist photographer Man Ray, with a girl who was famous in Paris, an ex-model by the name of Kiki, and so on." (Triolet 1975, pp. 41-42.)

We find a poetic parallel to this description in Mayakovsky's poem *"Verlaine and Cezanne"* (*"Verlen i Sezan"*) (1925):

> I bump against
> > the table,
> > > the sharp edge of the wardrobe —
> Measure the four metres every day.
> I'm cramped here
> > in the Hotel Istria —
> On the dumpy
> > rue Campagne Première.

| | 4 | Before going abroad, Mayakovsky had signed two contracts with the State Publishing House, for the long poem *Vladimir Ilich Lenin* and the collection *Poems of 1924* (*Stikhi 1924 goda*) (which appeared under the title *Only the new/Tolko novoye*). He had also entered into negotiations with the State Publishing House about the publication of his collected works. While he was in Paris the third edition of the poem *War and the World* and other books appeared. Before his trip, Mayakovsky had also agreed with the Red Virgin Soil publishing house to a new edition of *150,000,000*, the first edition of which had been published by the State Publishing House in 1921. A copy of the poem in Lili Brik's hand has survived, with the publishing house's decision to publish and pay for it. The edition did not, however, appear. *150,000,000*, which had been harshly criticised by Lenin in 1921, was not reissued in a separate edition until 1937. |
| | 5 | Mayakovsky contributed to the satirical journal *Krasnyy perets* (*Red Pepper*). |

249

6 Mayakovsky had met Fernand Léger on his first trip to Paris in 1922.

7 The painter Mikhail Larionov (1881-1964) had left Russia in 1915. He spent several years with the Ballet russes in Switzerland, Spain and Italy before settling in France with his wife, the painter Natalya Goncharova (1881-1962). From 1919 onwards they lived in Paris, where they worked regularly for Diaghilev's Ballets russes.

8 Tamara Beglyarova, an acquaintance of Elsa Triolet.

9 The artist Valentina Khodasevich (1894-1970) and her husband, the artist Andrey Diderikhs (1884-1942).

10 The brilliant poet Vladislav Khodasevich (1886-1939), uncle of Valentina Khodasevich, and, unlike her, an emigré. His famed wit was often directed at Soviet targets, which would in part explain the unlikelihood of a meeting between him and Mayakovsky. He was later to write negatively of Mayakovsky himself.

11 Ilya Zdanevich (1894-1975), Futurist poet, composer of transrational (*zaum*) poems, theorist of avant-garde art. In addition to his poetic experiments, Zdanevich had published, under the pseudonym Eli Eganbyuri, *Natalya Goncharova. Mikhail Larionov.* He had emigrated to Paris in 1920, and there, under the pseudonym Iliazd, he continued his creative work right up until his death.

12 Osip Brik was working at the time in the advertising department of Mosselprom.

13 Mayakovsky does not use the Russian word *stikhi* here, but his own "German" invention *fyorzy*.

14 Kseniya Aseyeva.

15 The artist Aleksey ("John") Levin, with whom Mayakovsky and the Briks often played cards.

138. 1 France had just established diplomatic relations with the USSR.

139. 1 Aleksandr Krasnoshchokov was transferred from Lefertovo prison to the prison hospital in November 1924.

2 At about this time the Briks and Mayakovsky had moved to Sokolniki (see the Introduction). When they were in town they spent the night either in Mayakovsky's room in Lubyanskiy Passage or in the flat in Vodopyanyy Lane.

3 Osip Beskin (1892-1969), critic and worker in a publishing house.

4 Osip Brik was working in Mosselprom (see No. 135, note 12).

5 Otto Shmidt (1891-1956) was head of the State Publishing House from 1921 until November 1924.

6 Ilya Ionov (1887-1942), poet, head of the Petrograd section of the State Publishing House since 1919. Did not replace Shmidt as head of the State Publishing House.

7 Lili Brik's enthusiasm for Malkin can be put down to the latter's personal closeness to Mayakovsky and the Futurists. See No. 45, note 6. Malkin turned down the job at the State Publishing House (see No. 145).

143. 1 A reference to the first part of the long poem *Vladimir Ilich Lenin*, which was due to be published in *Lef* No. 3 (7), 1924. The issue did not appear until after Mayakovsky had returned from Paris, at the end of January 1925. See No. 145.

2 Lengiz (the Leningrad branch of the State Publishing House) was due to publish the third edition of *War and the World* (which appeared in December 1924) and

Vladimir Ilich Lenin (which appeared in February 1925).

3 Extracts from *Vladimir Ilich Lenin* appeared in a number of newspapers and journals before the publication of the first edition.

4 The threat of closure was hanging over the *Lef* journal at the time. See No. 145.

5 A reference to work on the poems later collected under the general title "Paris" (*"Parizh"*).

6 While Mayakovsky was in Paris, France recognised the government of the USSR, and on the 4th of December the first Soviet ambassador, Leonid Krasin, who had been working until then in London, moved to Paris.

7 Boris Kushner.

145. 1 Aleksey Kruchonykh was living on the seventh floor of a house in the courtyard at 21 Myasnitskaya Street.

146. 1 Mayakovsky left for Berlin about the 20th of December.

148. 1 That same day, Mayakovsky left Berlin for Riga. He returned to Moscow on the 27th of December.

149. 1 This note and the next one date from the winter of 1924-1925, when Mayakovsky and the Briks were living in Sokolniki.

       2 Lili Brik's mother, who had come to Moscow on a visit.

150. 1 Mayakovsky and the Briks had lived in Levashovo, outside Moscow, in the summer of 1918.

151. 1 Written in an exercise book before Mayakovsky left to go abroad that same day.

       2 On the 26th of March, Mayakovsky had signed a contract with the State Publishing House for a collected edition of his work in four volumes. The first volume was to be handed in on the 1st of June, the second on the 1st of July, the third on the 1st of August and the fourth on the 15th of August.

       3 Mayakovsky's sister Olga Vladimirovna worked for a time as secretary of the journal *Lef*. No further issues of the journal appeared after Mayakovsky's departure abroad.

       4 On the 20th of May, Mayakovsky had signed a contract with the Surf (*Priboy*) publishing house for two tales for children: *What is good and what is bad* (*Chto takoye khorosho i chto takoye plokho*), and *For every Petya and every Vasya a tale about the working class* (*Kazhdomu Pete i kazhdomu Vase rasskaz o rabochem klasse*). Mayakovsky was to hand in the first of these by the 22nd of May (and had apparently done so); the second was due by the 15th of June. Mayakovsky apparently wanted to finish it on his trip abroad — see request No. 8 in this letter.

       5 The first edition of *The tale of the fat child Petya, and of Sima who was thin* (*Skazka o Pete, tolstom rebyonke, i o Sime, kotoryy tonkiy*) appeared in May 1925. See No. 169.

       6 Apparently the cycle of poems collected as "Paris" (see No. 143, note 5) was handed in to the Moscow Worker (*Moskovskiy rabochiy*) publishing house a few days before Mayakovsky's departure.

       7 The long poem *The Flying Proletarian* (*Letayushchiy proletariy*) was finished at the beginning of April. It was published in September 1925.

152. 1 On the 25th of May, Mayakovsky flew to Königsberg, and from there he went on to Paris via Berlin. This was Mayakovsky's longest trip abroad: he also visited Mexico and the United States of America and remained abroad for six months.

153. 1 Mayakovsky arrived in Paris on the 28th of May.

154. 1 On this occasion Mayakovsky apparently did not want to wait for an American visa in Paris and decided to get in Mexico.

2 A reference to the *Parizhskiy vestnik* (*Parisian Herald*), a newspaper published by the Soviet Embassy in Paris. On the 3rd of June it printed four poems by Mayakovsky under the general title "From the poem *Paris*".

3 Elsa Triolet was preparing to go to Moscow.

4 The Exposition Internationale des Arts Décoratifs et Industriels Modernes. The Soviet pavilion opened on the 4th of June. Mayakovsky had himself taken an active part in the meetings of the Organisation Committee of the Soviet Pavilion in January and February 1925. (See also No. 155.)

5 The artist Arseny Urechin.

6 The rest of this letter is written in pencil.

7 Nikolay Shebanov (1899-1952) was a famous pilot.

8 The Moscow-Königsberg flight had been inaugurated by a joint Soviet-German company, Deruluft.

9 Lili Brik had a benign tumour. In a letter to Rita Rayt of the 23rd of February 1925 she writes: "I really have been lying in bed for over a fortnight! It turns out I have a large tumour and the foul creature has swollen up . . .

I lie here in Sokolniki. Volodya looks after me like a nurse (it makes you weep! . . .)"

Isaak Braude was a gynaecologist.

155. 1 Elsa Triolet describes the visit of the French writer Paul Morand to Moscow, where he stayed with Mayakovsky and the Briks at Sokolniki, in the following words: "They were extremely hospitable to him, they fed him pies, they sent him back to Paris laden with presents. Soon after his return, Morand published a book of short stories, in one of which, under the title 'I burn Moscow', he described an evening spent with Mayakovsky and everyone who was present. It was an utterly malicious lampoon, scarcely disguised by its invented names. I remember Mayakovsky, much later, in Paris, shrugging his shoulders in bewilderment at the affair; and that he kept meaning to publish a book in which every page of Morand's text would be printed opposite an account of what really happened." (Triolet 1975, pp. 60-61.)

The story "Je brûle Moscou" forms part of Morand's book *L'Europe galante* (Paris 1925). He writes in fictionalised form about Mayakovsky and the Briks, who are easily recognisable under the names Mardochée Goldvasser, Vasilissa Abramovna and Ben Moïsevitch. The mood of Morand's book is hostile to the USSR and his assessment of Mayakovsky and the Briks is extremely negative. It was hardly surprising that the story, steeped as it is in anti-semitism, struck its subjects as a "lampoon". Later Bruno Jasieński replied to this book with his *Je brûle Paris* (Paris 1929).

2 The Bois de Boulogne.

3 Gustave Welter, a French teacher at the Valitskaya secondary school in Moscow, which Lili Brik and Elsa Triolet had attended.

156. 1 On the 10th of June, Mayakovsky was robbed in his hotel. He lost the entire 25,000 francs which he had put aside for his trip to Mexico and the United States. The telegram in which Mayakovsky reported that he had been robbed has not survived. This telegram, obviously the second, was sent that same evening. Mayakovsky describes the robbery in No. 161.

After the theft, Mayakovsky turned for help to the Soviet Embassy in Paris,

252

and that same day the following telegram was sent to the State Publishing House. "Mayakovsky in Paris departing Mexico robbed. Steamer leaves nineteenth ticket bought. Trade delegation learning his contract State Publishing House Collected Works agrees pay Mayakovsky now two thousand roubles so that you November December hold back two thousand roubles due him those months which transfer us not later end December this year. Telegraph agreement immediately. We shall pay on receipt Mayakovsky's official signature which shall send you. Deputy Trade Representative Lomovsky. Mayakovsky agrees."

As Elsa Triolet recalls: "I went to the bank with him in the afternoon, he took out all the money that had been transferred to him, and we were obviously followed from the bank by a professional thief; the thief rented the room next to Volodya's at the Istria, and when next morning Volodya left the room for a minute in his pyjamas, without locking the door, he managed to steal into his room, take his wallet from his jacket pocket, and disappear. . . . I remember clearly that when Mayakovsky reported the theft to Leonid Krasin, the ambassador, Krasin not only showed no sign of sympathy, or willingness to help, but even replied, caustically and almost joyfully: 'Even a wise man stumbles!'" (Triolet 1975.)

157.	1	On the 15th of June the Trade Delegation gave Mayakovsky 2,000 roubles as an advance against his Collected Works. According to the contract signed on the 25th of March 1925, Mayakovsky's royalty of 12,000 roubles was to be paid in monthly sums of 1,000 roubles from the 1st of May 1925 until the 1st of May 1926.
160.	1	For the Collected Works. See Nos. 151, 154 and 155.
	2	A visa to visit Moscow.
161.	1	See No. 156, note 1 and No. 157, note 1.
	2	On the Surf publishing house see No. 151 (request No. 8). "A sheet with a text" — apparently the text of the children's book *We go for a walk* (*Gulyayem*), written instead of the promised *For every Petya and every Vasya a tale about the working class*.
	3	Lev Grinkrug spent six months in Paris and Juan-les-Pins in 1925. Because of Mayakovsky's trip to America they did not meet in France.
	4	Lili Brik was going to the Volga for a rest. See No. 169.
163.	1	One of these letters did not arrive.
	2	Mayakovsky is mixing up his Tropics.
	3	The poem "Christopher Columbus" ("*Khristofor Kolumb*") was finished on the 7th of July. On the "diminutive" of Christopher see the variant "Christy Columbus and other libertines" ("*Kolumb Khristya i drugiye zabuldygi*"). "Odessans" could be useful to Mayakovsky because in some people's opinion Columbus was a Jew.
	4	On the steamer Mayakovsky also wrote the poems "Spain" ("*Ispaniya*"), "Six nuns" ("*6 monakhin*"), "The Atlantic Ocean" ("*Atlanticheskiy okean*"), "Shallow philosophy in deep places" ("*Melkaya filosofiya na glubokikh mestakh*") and "Black and White ("*Blek end uayt*").
	5	Mayakovsky had crossed out the word Columbus.
165.	1	Mayakovsky arrived at the port of Vera Cruz on the 8th of July, and in Mexico City the next day.

167.   1   This telegram was sent to mark Mayakovsky's birthday.
168.   1   Viktor Yakovlevich Volynsky — second secretary of the Soviet Embassy in Mexico City.

       2   Sic. Correctly "excusado".

       3   Mayakovsky telegraphed the Soviet trade organisation in New York, Amtorg, about an American visa. The secretary of the Embassy, Lev Khaykis, recalls that "Mayakovsky managed to get a visa for the United States of America by persuading the consulate that he was simply an advertising worker for Mosselprom and Rezinotrest [The RubberTrust]. In New York Mayakovsky was looked after by David Burlyuk, and on the 15th of July a letter was sent to Mayakovsky in Mexico City from the Willy Pogany Artists' Studio: "Your friends have informed us of your desire to visit the USA and to arrange an exhibition here of your posters and other advertising material. Our studio will be pleased to offer you the possibility of doing so, and will also be ready to afford any necessary help. We are writing to the State Department about it." This letter did not help, however, and Mayakovsky was already on the point of returning to France. Finally permission arrived, and on the 27th of July Mayakovsky entered the USA through Laredo.

       4   This trip did not take place.

       5   Lili Brik intended to go to Italy for a health cure. See the later correspondence.

       6   Mayakovsky's constant anxiety about his Collected Works was caused by the fact that according to the contract all four volumes were supposed to appear within a year of the signing of the agreement on the 25th of March 1925.

       7   "The Discovery of America" ("Christopher Columbus") could not appear in *Lef*, since by now the journal had ceased to appear. It appeared in print only after Mayakovsky's return to Moscow. The poems "Six nuns" and "The Atlantic Ocean" were puiblished in August; "Spain" did not appear in print, but was broadcast on Radio Rosta (as was "Six nuns").

       8   Yakov Galitsky was head of the literary department at Radio Rosta.

       9   Lili Brik's mother and Elsa Triolet were living in Sokolniki at the time.

169.   1   Mayakovsky left Mexico City before this letter arrived, and it was sent on to him in New York. (See No. 174.)

       2   Like other members of Lef, Osip Brik had begun to take a serious interest in photography and cinematography. His first essay on photography as the art of modern times appeared in 1924: "We need facts, so as to know life, so as to study it, so as to affect it. And in this enterprise the artist is not a help to us but a hindrance. Here we need photography, precise and guileless. It cannot be replaced by drawing. . . . The artists of Lef, production artists, are artists who have given up painting pictures and correctly evaluated the enormous significance of photography; they have created a new art, the art of photomontage."

       3   See No. 151.

       4   See No. 151.

       5   See No. 151.

       6   See No. 151.

       7   *What is good and what is bad* was published by the Surf publishing house in November 1925, with drawings by Nikolay Denisovsky.

       8   The collection *Paris* appeared in October 1925, with a cover designed by

Aleksandr Rodchenko.

9 See No. 151.

10 See No. 161, note 3.

11 See the Introduction and No. 213, note 1.

12 Mayakovsky always dreamt of making a trip around the world. When he set off for Berlin and Paris in the autumn of 1924 he intended to continue his trip further (with the approximate itinerary: America, the Pacific Ocean, Japan, Moscow), but the American authorities refused him a visa and the plan could not be put into practice. He made a third attempt in 1928.

13 Mayakovsky had announced his intention of writing a novel as early as 1923. In December 1924 the newspaper *Vechernyaya Moskva* (*Evening Moscow*) reported that the poet had, while in Paris, "begun a novel (in prose)". David Burlyuk also writes about Mayakovsky's novel which he even "managed to eavesdrop on".

On the 5th of December 1925, after his return from the United States of America, Mayakovsky signed a contract with the State Publishing House for a 300-page novel. It was to be delivered no later than the 15th of April 1926. In the winter and spring of 1926, references to Mayakovsky's novel appeared in the press: "Vladimir Mayakovsky is writing a novel, having signed a contract with the State Publishing House. The novel is set in St Petersburg and Moscow, and covers the period from 1914 to the present day. At the centre of the novel is a description of literary life and manners, the struggles between opposing schools and so on." Mayakovsky mentions his work on the novel in his autobiography: "I'm writing . . . my literary biography" (I, 29). The novel was never finished.

14 Madeleine Vionnet was the owner of a famous Parisian fashion house. Lili Brik used to buy dresses from her.

171. 1 Mayakovsky arrived in New York on the 30th of July. He stayed with the chairman of the board of Amtorg, Isay Khurgin, at No. 3 Park Avenue.

David Burlyuk wrote at the time about his first meeting with Mayakovsky since 1918 in the following words: "I heard his sonorous, masculine basso profundo down the telephone with particular emotion.

"I recognised him immediately from his voice — it was the same! It hadn't changed!

"I rushed down to the subway and tore along Fifth Avenue, where Vladimir Mayakovsky was staying.

"From some distance away I saw this big 'Russian' leg, striding across the threshold, and a pair of bulky cases stuck in the doorway . . .

"Aha, I thought, he hasn't abandoned his proletarian Russian habits even here — he's carrying his cases himself! . . .

"I guessed immediately from the leg that it could not belong to anyone except Mayakovsky. . . ."

174. 1 See No. 169, note 1.

2 Lili Brik writes of Mayakovsky's complex relationship with his family in the following terms: "Every visit from his sisters, despite his love, and, above all, his pity for them, was a torment for him. If, to his good fortune, I happened to be at home, he would leave them to me and shut himself away in his room on the pretext that he had some urgent work to do. . . . When I remembered that Vladimir Vladimirovich had not visited his mother or given her any money for some time, and reminded him of this, he would always try to persuade me to go

with him, and if I was busy he would ask Aseyev or someone else, because he found visiting them on his own too boring. And he would set off weighed down with presents so as to postpone the next visit for as long as possible. . . . When at home, at our home, Mayakovsky read a new work for the first time, he would always invite 20 or 30 people, but he never asked his sisters." (Lili Brik 1951.)

In her diary entry for the 23rd of January 1930, Lili Brik writes: "How his relatives irritate Volodya — he's actually trembling, even though Lyuda only visits us once every three months. I even went into his room and said 'You must at least talk to Lyuda for half an hour, or even open the door — she won't come in'. But he replied: 'I can-not, she ir-ri-tates me!!!' and he became completely contorted. It was terribly embarrassing for me."

3   Platon Kerzhentsev (1881-1940), famous writer and party worker, whom Mayakovsky and the Briks had met in 1919 when he had been head of Rosta. During the 1920s he occupied important diplomatic posts: he was Soviet Ambassador to Sweden from 1921 until 1923, and to Italy from 1925 until 1926.

4   Sergey Tretyakov (1892-1939), poet and prose writer, Mayakovsky's colleague in Lef. He had just returned from China, where he had spent a year and a half as a teacher of Russian literature at Peking University. Victim of the purges.

176.   1   An American visa for Lili Brik.

180.   1   Isay Khurgin, with whom Mayakovsky was staying, drowned in a lake near New York on the 27th of August.

2   Mayakovsky appeared at the Central Opera House on the 10th of September, and in Coney Island on the 12th of September. The lecture tour of towns on the American East Coast did not begin until the end of the month.

184.   1   Archival materials show that during Mayakovsky's absence abroad the State Publishing House reconsidered the question of publishing his collected works several times. On the 20th of July, the Trade Section of the State Publishing House declared that it was making a "categorical protest against the publication of the Collected Works of Mayakovsky in view of the absence of demand for such a publication and the large remaining stocks of previous editions of this author's works". On the 31st of August the matter was discussed at a plenary meeting of the Editorial Planning Commission of the State Publishing House. The commission decided "not to proceed with the edition", and entrusted the literary-artistic department with the task of negotiating with other publishing houses for the transfer of the project "with Mayakovsky's agreement". Two weeks later, on the 15th of September, the board of the State Publishing House announced that it was not in agreement with the decision taken by the Trade Section and the Editorial Planning Commission, but it did propose altering the conditions of the contract: "Author's royalties should be paid out to Mayakovsky on condition that the Legal Bureau concludes an additional agreement with comrade Mayakovsky for the extension of the period of the contract to five years, and of the period during which the first volume will appear to three years."

A "memorandum" sent to Broydo, the head of the publishing house, dates from this same period. It makes it clear that all the publishing houses that had been approached with regard to the transfer of Mayakovsky's collected works had categorically refused to take over the project. "Bearing in mind that on Mayakovsky's part the contract has not been broken, and taking into consideration . . . the great cultural significance of Mayakovsky's work . . . the Legal Bureau is at present awaiting Mayakovsky's return in order to propose to him the renegotiation of the contract and the extension of our rights to publish the edition.

The Department might state, in addition to this formal side of affairs, that the contract with V. V. Mayakovsky was drawn up on the categorical insistence of the Chairman of the Editorial Planning Commission, P. M. Kerzhentsev; negotiations about the same contract had been taking place since October 1924, and at that time the Department had refused to sign such a contract. Under pressure from the Department, Mayakovsky has made a very large number of concessions with regard to his royalty (200 roubles per printer's sheet, or twelve copecks per line of poetry — that is how it works out according to the contract — this is unprecedentedly low in the practice of the State Publishing House and in publishing practice in general). Thanks to this relatively low remuneration, and to the fact that the only editions of Mayakovsky on the market are odd individual works, and that these exist, moreover, in limited quantities, the Department continues to consider the contract to be advantageous to the State Publishing House and completely acceptable. As regards the refusal of the Trade Section, in the opinion of the Department this is based on a misunderstanding, and on an underestimation of the significance of Mayakovsky as the founder of a major school in poetry. In the first place, the unsold stocks of Mayakovsky's works are relatively insignificant, in the second place, they are technically editions of extremely poor quality, for the most part bought in from other publishing houses, and besides, they comprise only two or three titles, which include less than ⅛ of the material we have acquired for this edition. . . . Can it really be that these remaining stocks (which are unavoidable in publishing) can have an influence upon the dissemination of the *first full collected edition of the most talented poet of a significant school*? The Department considers the repudiation of such an edition to be a decision that is diametrically at odds with our ideological mission and will not enhance the prestige of the State Publishing House."

On his return from America, Mayakovsky made a partial concession to the State Publishing House on the 4th of December: ". . . the three-year length of the contract was established as lasting from the day the volumes were delivered, and not the day the contract was agreed. The time in which the edition should be concluded was extended to two years. . . ."

Yet this was not the end of the "Mayakovsky case" — as it is referred to in State Publishing House documents — and we shall return to this question later.

185. 1 See No. 168.

187. 1 Mayakovsky appeared in Cleveland on the 29th of September, and in Detroit on the 30th. He arrived in Chicago on the 2nd of October, and appeared there that same day. On the 4th of October he returned to New York.

196. 1 This telegram is addressed to Lili Brik in Moscow, despite the fact that in the previous telegram she had given her address in Italy.

197. 1 Apparently Lili Brik had arrived at Salsomaggiore that day. A telegram of the 23rd of October has survived in which "Elsa, Osya, Lyova" congratulate her on her arrival. In a letter of the 25th of October, addressed to Elsa Triolet, Osip Brik, Lev Grinkrug, Llewella Krasnoshchokova and Osip Beskin, Lili Brik describes

her journey to Italy and gives her initial impressions: "... I travelled through wonderful picture postcard scenery from Berlin to Munich.... I only managed to spend about an hour and a half strolling round the town in Verona — I liked it very much!

Salso is a foul little town.... And I'm going to have to sit here an entire month.... Two days ago I went to Parma (it's an hour by car) to take a look at Mussolini — he was passing through.... Today I got a telegram from Volodya [No. 199]. He's leaving America on the 28th of October and wants to arrange himself an Italian visa in Paris. I'll write and tell him it's senseless to hang around in Paris for that."

199.	1	Mayakovsky left New York for Le Havre on the 28th of October on the steamer Rochambeau.
204.	1	On the 5th of November Mayakovsky arrived in Le Havre and immediately set off by train for Paris.
206.	1	On the 14th of November Mayakovsky arrived in Berlin, where he met Lili Brik. On the 18th of November they set off via Riga for Moscow, where they arrived on the 22nd of November.
209.	1	On the 24th of January 1926 Mayakovsky set off on a lecture tour of towns in the Ukraine, the northern Caucasus, Azerbaidzhan and Georgia. On the 25th of January he gave a lecture in Kharkov.
212.	1	Mayakovsky arrived in Kiev on the 27th of January. He lectured there on the 28th and 31st of January and the 1st of February.
213.	1	At the end of 1925, Mayakovsky and the Briks received a four-roomed flat in Gendrikov Lane in the Taganka area of Moscow. Since the flat was in need of major repairs, they could not move in until the end of April 1926 (see the Introduction).
214.	1	For a time Lili Brik lived in the flat of Osip Beskin, to whose address Mayakovsky sent telegrams Nos. 209, 210, 212 and 213. As is clear from this telegram, she then moved to Mayakovsky's room in Lubyanskiy Passage.
215.	1	On the 4th of February Mayakovsky arrived in Rostov-on-Don, where he lectured three times — on the 6th, 7th and 10th of February.
216.	1	Mayakovsky left for Krasnodar on the 11th of February. His appearances in Krasnodar took place on the 14th of February.
219.	1	On the 15th or 16th of February Mayakovsky left for Baku, where he appeared seven times on the 19th, 21st, 22nd, 23rd and 24th of February.
220.	1	Although Lili Brik had informed Mayakovsky of her change of address in telegram No. 214, he continued to send telegrams to Beskin's address. After this reminder, however, all Mayakovsky's telegrams were addressed to Lubyanskiy Passage.
221.	1	The poem "Krasnodar" was published under the title "The Back of Beyond" ("Sobachya glush").
	2	Regina Fyodorovna Glaz, a cousin of Lili Brik.
	3	Osip Brik took part in a discussion in The Hall of Columns in the House of Unions on the subject of "Literary Russia".
	4	The article "The Latest Thing" ("Posledniy krik") in the journal Sovetskiy ekran (Soviet Screen), 1926 No. 7.
	5	"It's enormous star-ticked ear" is the last line of A Cloud in Trousers. The third edition of the poem had appeared in May 1925 with a print-run of 20,000 copies.

223.	1	There is a gap in the copy of the telegram.
224.	1	On the 24th of February Mayakovsky left Baku for Tiflis, where he appeared twice, on the 26th of February and the 1st of March.
227.	1	Sent off en route for Moscow from Mineralnyye vody railway station.
	2	Judging from this telegram, Mayakovsky arrived in Moscow on the 5th of March.
228.	1	In the first half of May Lili Brik went for a holiday on the Black Sea, in Sochi, Gagry and Batum.
229.	1	This letter has been dated by Lili Brik. It was addressed to Osip Brik and Mayakovsky.
	2	Buster Keaton's film "Our Hospitality" (1923) tells the story of the difficult first journey of the first American steam locomotive.
	3	The Riviera Hotel in Sochi, in which Lili Brik was staying.
230.	1	On the 16th of May Mayakovsky left to give readings in Leningrad, from where he returned on the 23rd or 24th of May. In a telegram to Lili Brik of the 18th of May, Osip Brik reported: "Volodya Leningrad. Sent on telegrams."
231.	1	Judging from this telegram, Lili Brik had just returned to Moscow.
232.	1	On the 19th of June, Mayakovsky left for Odessa and then the Crimea, where he stayed until the middle of August. His first appearance in Odessa was on the 23rd of June, the other three on the 25th, 26th and 27th of June.
	2	On the 28th of June Mayakovsky went to Yalta on the steamer Hawk.
234.	1	Mayakovsky remained in the Crimea for a month and a half.
236.	1	On his birthday (the 7th of July old style).
237.	1	Mayakovsky read in Simferopol on the 7th of July.
	2	A reading by Mayakovsky in Sevastopol was arranged for the 6th of July, but it was wrecked through the fault of the organisers. Pavel Lavut, the organiser of Mayakovsky's lecture tour, recalls: "The Crimean performances were due to start in Sevastopol, in the Lieutenant Shmidt Sailors' Club.

The local committee of MOPR (The International Organisation for the Assistance of Fighters for the Revolution) took on itself the material expenditure on the lecture. (Takings from the evening were to go to MOPR funds.) The MOPR official who signed the contract behaved irresponsibly and prepared the evening badly. Few people turned up. Then he decided to cancel Mayakovsky's appearance and slandered him, accusing him of being self-seeking and of other sins. He persuaded his bosses to share his opinions, and the local leaders of MOPR formed a false idea about Mayakovsky.

When he found out about this, Vladimir Vladimirovich refused to accept his fee, and was ready to make up all the losses at his own expense. He said: "Tell them to give the public their money back and I'll appear free." But the rumour discrediting Mayakovsky had already reached the public. And it was not possible to avert a scandal.

About a hundred or a hundred and twenty people had gathered in the hall. When Mayakovsky appeared on stage they would not let him speak: they whistled and stamped their feet. The audience made a show of rushing out into the foyer.

Insulted and indignant, Mayakovsky clambered on to a table in the foyer and, nervously waving a stick, attempted to shout them down.

Vladimir Vladimirovich spent an extremely difficult night. Then in the morning he wrote a letter and addressed it to two newspapers, *Mayak kommuny/ The Commune Lighthouse* and *Krasnyy chernomorets/Red Black Sea Dweller.* After that he went to the regional party committee and insisted that they punish the guilty ones. The regional party committee took his side in the dispute.

Mayakovsky's letter was published on the 8th of July:

"I offer my profound apologies to those who came to hear my lecture on the 6th of July. The cause of the failure of the lecture to take place was the incompetence of the organisers, and their unwillingness not only to fulfil the contract they had signed, but even to enter into any discussion of the matter." (Lavut 1969, pp. 9-10.)

238. 1 On the 8th of July, Mayakovsky arrived in Yevpatoriya, where he appeared that same day and the next day.

2 Mayakovsky could not leave for Yalta on the 12th of July because he fell ill with flu. See No. 241.

239. 1 Lili Brik dated this letter to the 2nd of July, which is clearly mistaken, since it is a reply to Mayakovsky's letter of the 8th of July. It was apparently written on the 12th of July.

2 Tikhon Churilin (1892-1944), writer and poet close to the Futurists, author of several collections of poetry and experimental works in prose.

3 Viktor Pertsov (1898-1980) was close to the Lef group at this time. He is the author of a semi-official three-volume study of Mayakovsky's life and works which has gone through several editions.

4 Lili Brik jokingly describes Lev Grinkrug as being part of "financial Moscow" because of his "banking" past. (See No. 2, note 5.)

5 Yevgeniya Zhemchuzhnaya (née Sokolova) (1900-1982) was the wife of the film director Vitaly Zhemchuzhny and a close friend of Osip Brik. As she relates in her manuscript memoirs: "I met Osip Maksimovich Brik in March 1925. My friendship with him lasts from that time. At the beginning of 1927 it developed into a closer relationship which lasted right up until his death, that is to say eighteen years.

I was working in a children's library . . .

At the time Osip Maksimovich was working on Turgenev. He told me a lot about that time and tried to persuade me to work with him as his secretary.

We met often. In my spare time I went around second-hand bookshops with him. We spent a long time rummaging through the books. He bought so-called 'literature of fact' — memoirs, correspondence, collections of articles." (Sokolova)

6 There were Jewish landworking colonies near Yevpatoriya.

7 Abram Roóm (1894-1976), film director (*Bed and Sofa*, 1927, etc.). See note 8.

8 Lili Brik was taking part in the making of the silent film *The Jews on the Land.* The script was written by Viktor Shklovsky, the director was Abram Roóm. As Shklovsky recalls: "This film, for which Mayakovsky wrote the intertitles, tells of an attempt to create Jewish landworking colonies in the region of Yevpatoriya. It's a dry steppe area, they get water from deep wells, using two horses which go round and round in circles turning a drum. . . .

The Jews are urban people. They'd come to this place in the steppe and had to deal with oxen. The oxen did something to calm the town-dwellers' nerves. New villages were constructed out of Yevpatoriyan sandstone, which they sawed through with an ordinary saw." (Shklovsky, 1965.)

Lili Brik remembers: "On his arrival in Moscow, Mayakovsky helped OZET [The Society of Jewish Worker Farmers] to arrange an enormous writers' evening in the House of Unions, all the takings from which went to the Jewish colonies. He wrote the poem 'The Jew' ('*Yevrey*') for this evening and read it with enormous success. He wore the OZET badge he was given for several days, and he dedicated his poem 'The Jew' to his 'comrades from OZET'." (Lili Brik 1941.)

The poem "The Jew" is not included in Mayakovsky's latest Collected Works (1978).

9 Osip Beskin.

10 The delay over the publication of Mayakovsky's Collected Works was continuing. On the 6th of March 1926 the presidium of the Editorial Planning Commission of the State Publishing House resolved "in view of the refusal of the Trade Section to place an order for the edition, to hand over a decision on the question to the Board of the Publishing House". On the 30th of May, Mayakovsky sent the State Publishing House a letter proposing to add a fifth volume to the Collected Works, and to issue a second edition of the poem *Vladimir Ilich Lenin*. On the 7th of June the Editorial Planning Commission reiterated its decision "in view of the disagreements which have arisen to hand over a decision on issuing the works of Mayakovsky to a meeting of the board". The contract for the fifth volume was not signed until the 6th of September 1926.

11 Mayakovsky's mother and sisters lived together in the Krasnaya Presnya area of Moscow.

12 On the 5th of December 1925, at the same time as signing a contract for a novel, Mayakovsky had signed with the State Publishing House a contract for a three-act "drama", which was to be delivered not later than the 15th of January 1926. But the "drama" (the "Comedy with a murder"/"*Komediya s ubiystvom*") was never finished, although in the spring of 1926 Mayakovsky committed himself to giving it to the Meyerhold theatre. Only drafts of individual scenes have survived.

241. 1 See No. 235. Isaak Drapkin was a famous pre-revolutionary industrialist.

2 The lecture announced for the 13th of July in Sevastopol took place on the 17th. There is no information about the other two lectures.

3 At the beginning of August Mayakovsky and Lili Brik spent about two weeks together at the Pension Chaïr near Khoreiz.

243. 1 Friday and Saturday the 23rd and 24th of July. Only one lecture by Mayakovsky in Yalta at this time is known of, and that took place on the 25th of July.

245. 1 Apparently Mayakovsky collaborated with Shklovsky at the beginning of work on the film script.

2 Viktor Shklovsky.

3 The film director Aleksandr Solovyov (1898-1973)(?).

247. 1 This telegram was sent at 1.40 a.m. on the 28th of July. Shklovsky and the cameraman left on Tuesday the 27th of July.

248. 1 Monday the 2nd of August.

251. 1 Tuesday the 3rd of August. On the 8th of August Lili Brik telegraphed Osip Brik in Moscow to tell him that she and Mayakovsky were staying at the Pension Chaïr, and that she would return a fortnight later. She and Mayakovsky returned to Moscow on the 20th of August.

252.	1	On the 10th of October, Mayakovsky left for Kharkov and Kiev. He appeared four times in Kiev, on the 18th, 19th, 20th and 21st of October. On Saturday the 23rd of October he returned to Moscow.
	2	Bulka was a French bulldog owned by Mayakovsky and the Briks.
253.	1	On the 21st of November Mayakovsky left for a lecture tour of Voronezh, Rostov, Taganrog, Novocherkassk and Krasnodar. On the 24th, 26th and 28th of November he lectured in Rostov (five times).
	2	Mayakovsky apparently left for Krasnodar on Sunday the 28th of November.
254.	1	Mayakovsky read in Voronezh on the 22nd of November, in Taganrog on the 25th, and in Novocherkassk on the 27th. For the readings in Rostov, see No. 253, note 1.
	2	Mayakovsky always carried a special travelling glass around with him, so as not to have to drink out of other people's glasses.
	3	In Elsa Triolet's story *Strawberries* (*Zemlyanichka*) (Moscow 1926), there is a chapter entitled "The Danger of Life".
	4	On the 30th of November, Mayakovsky left Krasnodar for Kiev, in connection with his work on a filmscript for the All Ukrainian Board of Photography and Cinematography (VUFKU). VUFKU had commissioned two scripts from him on the 17th of August, while he was on holiday in the Crimea. The first was called *Electrification* (*Elektrifikatsiya*), and nothing is known of it. The second, *Fettered by Film*, was a heavily reworked version of the filmscript of 1918. Towards the end of 1926 Mayakovsky renamed it *The Heart of Cinema* (*Serdtse kino*). The film was never made, either by VUFKU or by the Moscow production company with which Mayakovsky had talks later on.
	5	At the end of August or the beginning of September Mayakovsky had written an application to the Press Department of the Central Committee of the All Union Communist Party (Bolshevik) to publish a journal by the name of *Novyy Lef* (*New Lef*). On the 11th of September the State Publishing House resolved "to publish a trial issue in November and twelve issues a year, No. 1 in December". In fact the first issue appeared in January 1927.
255.	1	Sunday the 5th of December.
256.	1	Nizhniy Novgorod was the first stop on Mayakovsky's lecture tour, which included Kazan, Penza, Samara and Saratov. Mayakovsky left Moscow on the 16th of January, at the same time as Lili Brik set off for Vienna, where she met Elsa Triolet. This and the next telegram from Osip Brik were sent on the same day and are printed here in the order in which they were sent. That same day Osip Brik also sent a telegram to Lili Brik:

"Kiss you warmly beloved Kitty,"

Mayakovsky appeared three times in Nizhniy Novgorod on the 17th and 18th of January.

258.	1	Mayakovsky appeared four times in Kazan on the 20th, 21st and 22nd of January.
260.	1	Mayakovsky appeared four times in Samara on the 26th and 27th of January.
	2	A reference to the second issue of *Novyy Lef*, which appeared in February.
	3	FOSP, the Federation of Soviet Writers' Organisations, was founded on the 27th of December 1926. It brought together three groups: VAPP, the All Russian Association of Proletarian Writers; VOKP, the All Russian Association of Peasant Writers; and VSP, the All Russian Union of Writers. At the beginning of

January 1927, the members of Lef, who had not been invited to participate in discussions about the founding of the Federation, produced a statement which read: "We consider it to be a lamentable misunderstanding that Lef was not brought in at the very beginning of efforts to organise a Federation, since Lef's work has been well known to all literary workers since the first days of the revolution." (XIII, 212.) Soon after this, on the 9th of February, Lef was accepted into FOSP, and Mayakovsky joined the federation's Executive Bureau. Nikolay Chuzhak, however, spoke out against Lef's entry into FOSP until "the Averbakhs" "change their tone of corporals' arrogance and really want to work together amicably". Aleksandr Voronsky, the representative of the Pereval (The Pass) group, which entered the federation at the same time as Lef, has also described the strained atmosphere which was created in the federation by the representatives of VAPP: "The necessary collaboration does not yet exist in the Federation, there is still a lack of the essential mutual trust."

4   Mayakovsky went to Saratov not on Thursday the 27th of January, but on Friday the 28th.

262.   1   Mayakovsky appeared twice in Saratov, on the 29th and 30th of January. On the 2nd of February he returned to Moscow.

268.   1   Apparently Lili Brik had in mind the same Sunday (the 13th of February) on which she sent the telegram.

269.   1   On the 18th of February Mayakovsky left on a lecture tour of Tula, Kursk, Kharkov and Kiev. He appeared twice in Kharkov, on the 22nd and 23rd of February, and then twice more, after his visit to Kiev, on the 28th of February.

270.   1   Mayakovsky appeared in Kiev three times, on the 24th, 26th and 27th of February. He returned to Moscow on the 1st or 2nd of March.

271.   1   On the 15th of April 1927 Mayakovsky went abroad, visiting Poland, Czechoslovakia, Germany and France. On the way to Prague he spent a day in Warsaw. He arrived in Prague on the 19th of April and spent a week there. On the 27th of April he left for Paris via Berlin.

2   Roman Jakobson (1896-1982), major linguist, philologist, verse theorist and literary critic, an old friend of Mayakovsky, a childhood friend of Elsa Triolet and Lili Brik. Jakobson had been living in Prague since 1920, having come there as a translator with a Red Cross mission. He was working at the time in the Soviet Embassy.

274.   1   Lili Brik mistakenly dated this letter to March. Mayakovsky arrived in Paris on the 29th of April.

2   Nikolay Aseyev's Colected Poems in three volumes appeared in 1928. The introductory article was not, however, written by Osip Brik, but by I. Dukor. A fourth, supplementary volume appeared in 1930.

3   A reference to the so-called Lef Tuesdays in the flat in Gendrikov Lane, at which the work of Lef was discussed and new works were read. See Osip Brik's postscript at the end of this letter.

4   The actress Aleksandra Khokhlova (1897-1985), wife of film director Lev Kuleshov.

5   The fourth issue of Novyy Lef included poems and other materials by Mayakovsky.

6   Pavel Lavut (1898-1979), the organiser of Mayakovsky's lecture tours around the Soviet Union between 1926 and 1930. Mentioned in the long poem Good!:

I was

told

by the quiet Jew

Pavel Ilich Lavut . . .

       7 The fifth issue of *Novyy Lef* included Mayakovsky's poem "The Venus de Milo and Vyacheslav Polonsky" (*"Venera Milosskaya i Vyacheslav Polonsky"*) and the essay "This is how I travelled" (*"Yezdil ya tak"*).

276.   1 Mayakovsky left Paris not on the 8th of May but on the 9th. On the 8th of May he attended a dinner arranged in his honour by some French writers. See No. 279.

279.   1 This letter was not finished and was not sent.

       2 Letter 274.

       3 Mayakovsky appeared at the Café Voltaire at an evening organised by the "Union of Soviet Students in France".

       4 Yury Flakserman was working at the time in the Central Institute of Aero- and Hydrodynamics.

       5 On the 10th of May, the "Society for Soviet-German Rapprochement" arranged a "tea" in Mayakovsky's honour.

       6 Mayakovsky received a Polish visa, and arrived in Warsaw, where he stayed ten days, on the 12th of May.

       7 A reference to Mayakovsky's appearance at a "People's House" in Prague.

280.   1 Mayakovsky left for Berlin on the 9th of May.

281.   1 Mayakovsky arrived in Warsaw on the 12th of May.

283.   1 Saturday the 21st of May. Mayakovsky arrived in Moscow on the 22nd of May.

285.   1 At the beginning of July, Lili Brik left for Tiflis, where she joined the film director Lev Kuleshov (1899-1970), with whom she then spent a week in Batum (see No. 287). Prokhladnaya is a railway junction on the Rostov-Baku line. The telegram was sent to mark Mayakovsky's birthday on the 7th of July (old style). For congratulations on his 'new style' birthday (the 19th of July) see No. 288.

287.   1 Lili Brik and Lev Kuleshov left for a week's holiday in Batum.

288.   1 On his birthday (see No. 285).

291.   1 See No. 285, note 1.

       2 Mayakovsky was about to leave on a lecture tour of towns in the Ukraine, the Crimea and the Caucasus. Friday — the 22nd of July. See No. 293.

293.   1 Mayakovsky left for Kharkov on the 24th of July. On the 25th and 31st of July he appeared at the Summer Theatre there. Lili Brik was passing through Kharkov on her way back to Moscow (see No. 291). She recalls (1956): "On the 20th of July 1927, just as I was about to leave the Caucasus for Moscow, I received a telegram from Mayakovsky [No. 293]. We had not seen each other for almost a month, and when that night in Kharkov I saw him on the platform, and he said to me: 'Why are you going to Moscow? Stay in Kharkov for a day and I'll read you my new poems,' I just had time to drag my case through the carriage window before the train started and I stayed there. Mayakovsky was terribly glad. There was nothing he liked more than sudden manifestations of feeling.

         I remember the traditional decanter and glass of water on the little table we sat at in the hotel room; and there and then, in the middle of the night, he read me the thirteenth and fourteenth chapters of *Good!*, which he had just finished."

295.   1 Lozovaya is a railway junction south of Kharkov.

296.	1	Mayakovsky had arrived in Yalta that same day.
298.	1	The sixth issue of *Novyy Lef* appeared in August, and included the tenth chapter of *Good!*, and a note by Mayakovsky in the "Lef Notebook".
	2	See No. 300.
300.	1	Mayakovsky read in Lugansk on the 27th and 28th of July, in Stalino on the 29th of July, in Simferopol on the 4th of August, in Sevastopol on the 5th of August and in Alushta on the 8th of August.
	2	Valery Gorozhanin (1889-1941) worked for the Ukrainian GPU. While Mayakovsky was in Yalta they wrote a screenplay, *D'Arcy the Engineer* (*Inzhener d'Arsi*) together, but it was never filmed.
	3	Mayakovsky read in Gurzuf on the 12th of August, in Alupka on the 16th, in Yalta on the 17th, in Yevpatoriya on the 19th and in Simferopol on the 20th. Before the end of the month he gave another seven readings.
	4	Chapters 9-19 of *Good!* were published in the October and November issues of *Molodaya gvardiya* (*Young Guard*).
	5, 6, 7, 8	See Lili Brik's reply (No. 302). Osip Beskin was at the time the head of the literature and fine arts department of the State Publishing House.
	9	With this letter Mayakovsky sent the nineteenth chapter of *Good!* for inclusion in the seventh issue of *Novyy Lef*.
302.	1	Vladimir Yermilov (1904-1965), critic, at the time editor of the journal *Molodaya gvardiya*. Later a member of RAPP (the Russian Association of Proletarian Writers) and a literary opponent of Mayakovsky.
	2	The contract for the sixth volume of the Collected Works was signed on the 19th of September 1927. The volume did not appear until the end of January 1930.
	3	The contract with the State Publishing House for the long poem "The 25th of October 1917" ("*25 Oktyabrya 1917*") was signed on the 6th of July 1927. (It did not receive the title *Good!* until later; see No. 303.) The poem appeared in the middle of October 1927.
	4	A reference to the second edition of the poem *Vladimir Ilich Lenin*, which appeared at the same time as *Good!* (see above).
	5	The Tiflisites — Vasily Katanyan (1902-1980) and his wife Galina (b. 1904), who moved to Moscow from Tiflis in 1927.
	6	The poet and member of Lef, Semyon Kirsanov (1906-1972).
	7	Aleksandr Rodchenko (1891-1956), famous constructivist artist, designer of the book *About This* (1923), and of covers for *Novyy Lef*, and his wife, the artist Varvara Stepanova (1894-1958).
	8	A reference to Nikolay Nekrasov's story "*The newly invented privileged paint of Dirling Brothers and Co.*" ("*Novoizbretyonnaya privilegirovannaya kraska bratev Dirling i K°*") (1850). The screenplay was written in collaboration with Lev Kuleshov. The film was never made.
	9	The first edition of Elsa Triolet's book had been published by the Ateney (Athenaeum) publishing house in 1925. The second eidtion did not appear. See No. 368, note 7.
	10	See above, note 7.
	11	See in the memoirs of Vasily Katanyan: "Lili Yurevna's mother brought the Chinese game mah-jong to Moscow in 1925. . . . The first mah players were Mayakovsky, Aseyev, Osip Maksimovich, Lilya. Then the Rodchenkos, Levidov, Zhemchuzhny, John Levin and Kirsanov learnt to play, and even

Tretyakov, who never played any games." And Lev Kuleshov and his wife, Aleksandra Khokhlova recall: "One day Kuleshov brought ping-pong, which was becoming fashionable at the time, to the dacha. Mayakovsky asked him to teach him to play. At first he couldn't get the hang of it, but Vladimir Vladimirovich was stubborn and indefatigable. The game lasted almost twenty four hours. . . ."

12 See Nos. 303 and 304.

13 The whole of this paragraph refers to the love affair between Mayakovsky and the young journalist Natalya Aleksandrovna Bryukhanenko (b. 1905), whom he had met in 1926. They were holidaying in the Crimea at the time. On the 2nd of August, Mayakovsky sent her a telegram: "Waiting eagerly. Leave thirteenth. Will meet Sevastopol." Two days later he sent a second telegram: "Come soon possible. Hope spend together all your leave. Confirm miss you." On the 13th of August, Natalya Bryukhanenko left Moscow for Sevastopol, where Mayakovsky met her at the station. On the 15th of September, they returned to Moscow together.

303. 1 In this telegram Mayakovsky announces for the first time the definitive title of a poem which in contracts and in extracts published in the press was variously called "October" ("Oktyabr"), "October Poem" ("Oktyabrskaya poema") and "The 25th of October 1917" ("25 Oktyabrya 1917"). Three days later, Mayakovsky sent the State Publishing House a letter with the final changes in content and title.

2 Mayakovsky had sent the State Publishing House the last two chapters of the poem on the 5th of August. In that version the eighteenth chapter (of the definitive variant) came after the nineteenth.

304. 1 It is possible that 'Sven' is a slip of the telegraphist's pen, but Mayakovsky had once before signed himself with the name of Sven Hedin, the famous Swedish voyager and discoverer (No. 119).

306. 1 As is clear from telegrams 303 and 304, Mayakovsky left Yalta for Kislovodsk on the 3rd of September. He was due to lecture in Kislovodsk on the 8th of September, but because of his illness the lecture was postponed until the 13th.

308. 1 On the 25th of October, Mayakovsky left for Leningrad, where he attended several rehearsals of the theatrical show "The Twenty Fifth" ("Dvadtsat pyatoye") which had been adapted from his poem Good! He also read the poem in public. He returned to Moscow on the 4th of November.

309. 1 On the 20th of November, Mayakovsky left on a lecture tour of towns in the Ukraine, the Northern Caucasus and Transcaucasia. On the 21st and 22nd of November he appeared in Kharkov.

2 Along with this note he sent the article "The broadening of the verbal base" ("Rasshireniye slovesnoy bazy") for Novyy Lef No. 10 (1927), and a brief notice of his readings in Leningrad, Moscow and Kharkov between the 26th of October and the 22nd of November.

3 A reference to the tenth issue of Novyy Lef, which appeared in December.

310. 1 This telegram was sent to Rostov, where Mayakovsky appeared on the 23rd of November. On the 25th of November he was already in Taganrog.

311. 1 Mayakovsky appeared seven times in Baku on the 4th, 5th, 6th and 7th of December.

314. 1 Mayakovsky arrived in Tiflis on the 8th or 9th of December. He appeared on the 9th, 10th, 11th, 12th and 13th of December. He returned to Moscow on the 17th

of December.

2 Apparently Mayakovsky telephoned Lili Brik from Tiflis.

315. 1 On the 21st of January 1928, Mayakovsky left on a lecture tour of Kazan, Sverdlovsk, Perm and Vyatka. He arrived in Sverdlovsk on the 26th of January, and lectured there five times on the 26th, 28th and 29th.

318. 1 Mayakovsky arrived in Perm on the 30th of January. He lectured there twice, on the 31st of January and the 1st of February.

319. 1 Mayakovsky arrived in Vyatka on the 2nd of February, and lectured there three times on the 2nd and 3rd. On the 5th of February he returned to Moscow.

320. 1 On the 25th of February, Mayakovsky left on another lecture tour of Dnepropetrovsk, Zaporozhe, Berdichev, Zhitomir and Kiev. On the 27th of February he arrived in Dnepropetrovsk, where he gave three or four lectures, that same day and on the 5th of March.

321. 1 It has not been possible to establish where Lili Brik had visited.

322. 1 On the 5th or 6th of March, Mayakovsky went to Berdichev and gave a lecture.

323. 1 Mayakovsky appeared in Zhitomir on the 7th of March. This telegram was sent from Zhitomir railway station. On the 8th of March, Mayakovsky left for Kiev, where he appeared that same day.

2 Mayakovsky's appearance in Odessa was cancelled because of the poet's ill health. On the 10th of March he returned to Moscow.

324. 1 On the 18th of March, Mayakovsky left on a lecture tour of Kiev, Vinnitsa and Odessa. He appeared in Kiev on the 19th of March.

2 Mayakovsky appeared in Vinnitsa that same day, the 20th of March.

3 A reference to a flat which Mayakovsky and Osip Brik were due to receive in a co-operative housing development. See below, No. 404, note 4.

325. 1 Vapnyarka is a railway junction on the Kiev-Odessa line, not far from Vinnitsa.

326. 1 Mayakovsky appeared in Odessa three times, on the 23rd and 24th of March.

327. 1 Mayakovsky appeared twice in Kiev, on the 26th(?) and 27th of March. On the 29th of March he returned to Moscow.

328. 1 On the 14th-15th of April, Lili Brik left for Berlin, where she stayed at the Kurfürstenhotel.

329. 1 Mayakovsky, who was supposed to join Lili Brik in Berlin, contracted flu and was unable to go abroad. See the later correspondence.

332. 1 Lili Brik was supposed to buy sections of foreign newsreel for the film *The Glass Eye* (*Steklyannyy glaz*), which she was making with the director Vitaly Zhemchuzhny (1898-1966). The film was released by Mezhrabpomfilm (The International Workers' Aid Film Company), in which Osip Brik was head of the literary department. See below, Nos. 360 and 363.

2 Erwin Piscator (1893-1966), famous German theatrical director. Mayakovsky attempted to make contact with him in the autumn of 1928. See No. 363. Probably a reference to Leo Lania's play *Konjunktur* which had its première on the 10th of April.

3 Malik Verlag was a "left-wing" publishing house in Berlin, run by Wieland Herzfelde, the brother of the famous Dadaist John Heartfield. Malik had published a German translation of *150,000,000* by Johannes Becher in 1924.

4 Felix Gasbarra (b. 1898), German writer and playwright, member of the German Communist Party. Along with Piscator, Gasbarra had staged a number of revolutionary shows, including *Revue Roter Rummel* (1924) and *Trotz Alledem!*

(1925). In the application sent to the Propaganda Department of the Central Committee of the Russian Communist Party (Bolshevik) at the end of 1922 concerning the publication of the journal *Lef*, Gasbarra was named as one of Lef's representatives abroad. (XIII, 405)

5 Walther Ruttmann (1887-1941), German film director, close to the avant-garde film-makers in Berlin in the early 1920s. In 1926-1927 he made a film about twenty four hours in the life of the capital, *Berlin der Sinfonie einer Grosstadt*. This film was shown in the Soviet Union and was a great success. The Lef group particularly admired it, and included in the September 1928 issue of *Novyy Lef* an article by Ruttmann called "Absolute Film" (*"Absolyutnyy film"*), written especially for the journal. Possibly Lili Brik wanted to talk to Ruttmann in connection with this article, her own "cinema business" (see No. 363, note 5) and Osip Brik's scenario *Cleopatra* (see Nos. 335, 339 and 340).

6 Francesco Misiano (1884-1936), Italian communist, activist in the international workers' movement. In the 1920s he emigrated first to Germany and then to the Soviet Union.

334. 1 Raisa Kushner, the wife of Boris Kushner.

335. 1 A reference to Osip Brik's scenario *Cleopatra*, written in 1927 for Kuleshov and Khokhlova. The action takes place in one of the "bourgeois capitals". Presumably Lili Brik was to talk to German film-makers about this scenario. See below Nos. 339 and 340.

337. 1 Yefim Yurevich Segalov, a doctor.

342. 1 A reference to I. A. Adamovich, President of the Soviet of People's Commissars of Byelorussia, and husband of Mayakovsky's friend Sofya Shamardina.

343. 1 Lili Brik left that day for Paris, where she stayed for about a week.

345. 1 On the 21st of May, Elsa Triolet sent a telegram to Lili Brik, who was in Berlin en route for Moscow, to tell her that she had "received Volodya's money".

346. 1 Addressed to Paris, which Lili Brik had already left for Berlin. On the morning of the 21st of May, Elsa Triolet sent a telegram to Moscow: "Lili left Berlin", after receiving which Mayakovsky and Osip Brik sent another telegram (No. 347) to Lili Brik in Berlin.

347. 1 See No. 346, note 1.

348. 1 This telegram was received on the 31st of July. On the 23rd of July Mayakovsky had set off on a tour of the Crimea. He read in Yevpatoriya on the 1st of August.

349. 1 This telegram was sent by Mayakovsky before he received the previous one, and therefore there is no mention of the robbery at the dacha. See the next telegram.

     2 For the first half of the summer, before his departure for the Crimea, Mayakovsky had been living in the dacha in Pushkino.

350. 1 Mayakovsky had several revolvers: an American Bayard, given to him by workers in Chicago in 1925, a Mauser 6,35 and the Browning alluded to in this telegram. Many people owned and carried revolvers at the time.

352. 1 As far as is known, Mayakovsky did not read in Yalta during his first few days there.

     2 Mayakovsky appeared in Gurzuf on the 5th of August.

     3 Mayakovsky actually did appear in Yalta on the 8th of August. The reading on the 15th could not take place, since Mayakovsky returned to Moscow on the 11th (see No. 355), probably because of illness. (See the letter of the 11th of August from Lili Brik to Osip Brik quoted in No. 355, note 1.)

353.	1	Mayakovsky appeared in Simferopol on the 9th of August.
355.	1	On the day of Mayakovsky's arrival, Lili Brik wrote to Osip Brik: "Volodya has arrived, and has made a firm decision to build a house and bring a car from abroad. He had an abominable time in the Crimea — he was ill again there. . . . Volodya dreams of a journal like 'Ogonyok' ('Light') with a print-run of a hundred thousand!"

In a letter of the same day to Rita Rayt, Lili Brik told her of Mayakovsky's plans: "In a month and a half he's going to America via Japan. Or maybe not to America but to Europe, but he's definitely going to Japan."

356.	1	On the 28th of September Mayakovsky left to make appearances in Leningrad. He returned to Moscow on the 5th of October.
357.	1	Three days after he returned from Leningrad, on the 8th of October, Mayakovsky set off for Paris (stopping in Berlin on the way). This telegram was garbled by the telegraph company. See Nos. 360 and 363.
359.	1	Mayakovsky arrived in Paris on the 15th of October.
	2	Lev Kahykis, an employee of the People's Commissariat for Foreign Affairs who had been First Secretary of the Soviet Embassy in Mexico City at the time of Mayakovsky's visit in 1925.
	3	The new "lightning" zips were known as "dr", because of the sound they made.
	4	Yakov Magalif was an employee of the Soviet Embassy in Berlin
360.	1	A reference to the film *The Glass Eye*, on which work had started at the beginning of August. As Lili Brik recalled (1975): "This film was a parody of the commercial films which were flooding the screen at the time, and a propaganda defence of the film newsreel. I made it with the director Vitaly Zhemchuzhny, from a screenplay we had written together, at the Mezhrabpomfilm studio." The film was released in January 1929.
	2	This was the garbled form in which telegram No. 357 had arrived.
	3	On this evening, which took place on the 1st of November, see No. 368.
363.	1	The aim of Mayakovsky's trip to Nice was a meeting with his American friend Elly Jones (née Yelizaveta Petrovna Alekseyeva) whom the poet met in New York in 1925. In the summer of 1926, Elly Jones gave birth to a daughter, who was named Elly after her mother. Mother and daughter were spending the autumn of 1928 in Nice. Mayakovsky was in Nice for only a few days (he returned to Paris on the 25th of October), but judging from Elly Jones's letters to him, he intended to visit Nice a second time: "But I asked you to telegraph! Didn't you have time? Have you forgotten both Ellies at once? . . . to listen so attentively and to get so nervous every time there are footsteps in the corridor, every time there's a knock at the door — it's even terrifying." (Letter of the 8th of November 1928.) This trip did not, however, take place.

Four letters and two Christmas cards from Elly Jones to Mayakovsky dating from the period between the 20th of July 1926 and the 12th of April 1929 have survived. There are also two empty envelopes (the second of them stamped Moscow 22.10.29) and several photographs of the "two Ellies" taken on the beach at Nice.

Lili Brik knew that Mayakovsky had had a child by Elly Jones.

	2	Mayakovsky evidently wanted to offer Piscator the play *The Bedbug* (*Klop*) (see note 3), but the Piscator-Bühne theatre, which the German director had organised in 1927, suffered a financial collapse in 1928.

3 On the 30th of November 1928 Malik Verlag publishing house offered
   Mayakovsky a contract, by the terms of which it would receive exclusive rights
   to the German editions of all the unpublished works of Mayakovsky except
   those in verse. On the 20th of February 1929, en route for Paris, Mayakovsky
   signed a contract with Malik Verlag for the German editions of his plays and
   prose. The play which is being referred to in this letter is *The Bedbug*, on which
   Mayakovsky finished work in the second half of December 1928.
4 Wieland Herzfelde (see No. 332, note 3).
5 Yefrem Shalyto, member of the board of Mezhrabpomfilm. The reference is to
   newsreel for the film *The Glass Eye*. Whole sections of Ruttmann's film *Berlin der
   Sinfonie einer Grosstadt* did indeed go into the final film.
6 See Nos. 357 and 360.

364. 1 Sent at 15.58 on the 25th of October. That very same evening Mayakovsky met
         Tatyana Alekseyevna Yakovleva (b. 1906). See No. 370, note 6, and the
         Introduction.

365. 1 A reference to the third volume of the Collected Works, which appeared in
         January 1929, or the fourth volume, which appeared in March or April 1929. The
         first and second volumes appeared in November 1928.
      2 Vasily Katanyan. See No. 302, note 5.

367. 1 The outline, in French, of a filmscript, *L'idéal et la couverture* (in Russian *Ideal i
         odeyalo*) has survived. Evidently this was the screenplay that Mayakovsky
         discussed with René Clair (1898-1981).

368. 1 The evening "What the devil do we need poetry for?" took place at the
         Polytechnic museum on the 1st of November. Brik announced that he, Kirsanov
         and Aseyev were leaving Lef. (Mayakovsky's departure from the group he had
         founded had been known of as early as August.) Brik explained that all literary
         organisations had degenerated and begun to squabble among themselves:
         ". . . What definitively amazed the administrator of the Polytechnic museum, a
         man who in his day had seen everything under the sun, was Brik's
         announcement that the Lef group were renouncing the literary scandal as a
         method. When the Constructivists tried to demand that the 'Open letter to V. V.
         Mayakovsky' be made public, Osip Brik gave them a withering look and replied
         devastatingly: 'You're taking over from Lef the methods that Lef has
         discarded' . . ." (*Vechernyaya Moskva*, 2 November 1928).
      2 Grigory Arustanov (1898-1943), cinema worker, screenwriter. At the time he
         was working for Goskinprom (the Georgian State Film Industry Joint-Stock
         Company). In 1929-30 he was a member of the board of Mezhrabpomfilm.
      3 Probably a reference to Lili Brik's screenplay *Love and Duty* (*Lyubov i dolg*), which
         was not, however, filmed.
      4 The film director Vitaly Zhemchuzhny.
      5 A reference to Elsa Triolet's Parisian friend Anna (Nyuta) Simon.
      6 The film director Vsevolod Pudovkin (1893-1953) and his wife.
      7 Elsa Triolet's novel *Khaki* (*Zashchitnyy tsvet*) was published in November 1928 by
         the Federatsiya (Federation) publishing house.
      8 Aleksandr Tikhonov (pseudonym Serebrov) (1880-1956), publisher and
         journalist. Mayakovsky and the Briks had known him since before the
         revolution. After the revolution Tikhonov headed a number of publishing
         houses; at the time he was working for Federatsiya.

370. 1 The car arrived in Moscow in January 1929.

2 The play is *The Bedbug*, the screenplay *L'idéal et la couverture*.

3 i.e. the film *The Glass Eye*.

4 Anna Shatova, the wife of V. S. Shatov, who worked for the People's Commissariat of Communications.

5 Taras Kostrov (pseudonym of Aleksandr Martynovsky, 1901-1930), editor of the newspaper *Komsomolskaya pravda* (1927-1928) and the journal *Molodaya gvardiya* (1929). The poems alluded to by Mayakovsky are "A poem about sold veal" (*"Stikhotvoreniye o prodannoy telyatine"*), "Verses about the beauties of architecture" (*"Stikhi o krasotakh arkhitektury"*), and "A letter to comrade Kostrov from Paris about the essence of love" (*"Pismo tovarishchu Kostrovu iz Parizha o sushchnosti lyubvi"*). The last of these was published in the first, January, issue of *Molodaya gvardiya* for 1929.

6 The sister of Tatyana Yakovleva. This is the first indirect hint of Mayakovsky's new friendship (see No. 364, note 1). On the 24th of December 1928, Tatyana Yakovleva wrote to her mother in Penza: "This is how we met. Here in Montparnasse (where I am often), the Erenburgs and other acquaintances were endlessly telling me about him, and he used to send me his regards even before he'd set eyes on me. Then we were specially invited to a certain house to be introduced. That was the 25th of October. And until the 2nd of November (the day of his departure) I saw him every day and became very friendly with him." [This is clearly a slip of the pen: Mayakovsky left Paris on the 2nd or 3rd of December — B.J.] (Vorontsov/Koloskov, 1968.) On the 28th of December she wrote to Elsa Triolet in London: "Volodya keeps me on a constant diet of telegrams. The last one was 'See each other March-April'. I get letters from Moscow saying he goes around my acquaintances giving them my regards (which I didn't ask him to do). He tracked down my sister the very day he got back."

7 The fourth volume of the Collected Works contained sections called "Poster-slogans" and "Advertisements".

8 Mayakovsky returned to Moscow on the 8th of December.

373. 1 Mayakovsky spent three days in Berlin on the way home.

374. 1 Negoreloye was the border post, on the Soviet side of the then border with Poland.

2 That is to say the 8th of December.

375. 1 On the 14th of February 1929, Mayakovsky left for Prague. On the 15th of February he telegraphed Tatyana Yakovleva from Negoreloye: "Leaving today stay Prague Berlin few days." In Prague he stayed for a day with Roman Jakobson, who has recalled "the poet rushing westwards". On the 20th of February, in Berlin, Mayakovsky signed a contract with Malik Verlag (see No. 363, note 3), after which he set off for Paris.

2 See the following telegrams.

376. 1 On the 1st of February, Mayakovsky signed a contract with the State Publishing House for the publication "of all works, both published and unpublished, and of those works which will be created by the author during the period of this contract (four years)". This contract was suggested by Mayakovsky himself in a letter to the publishing house of the 9th of January 1929: "I consider that if the State Publishing House signed a general contract with me and paid me out about

1,000 roubles a month, it might be possible by planned publication considerably to increase the print-run, and to give me the opportunity of working unhurriedly and without wasting time on all sorts of red tape to do with contracts." (XIII, 127.) It is probably this money that is being referred to in the telegram.

378.   1   Tatyana Yakovleva stated in conversation with me that Mayakovsky did not go to Nice. Nevertheless memoirs of this trip exist: Elsa Triolet (1975): "I saw Mayakovsky for the last time in 1929, in spring . . . I remember he made a trip to Nice." In Nice he also had a chance meeting with the artist Yury Annenkov, who recalls: "Mayakovsky told me he was on the way back from Monte Carlo, where he had lost everything down to the last centime at the casino. . . . I gave him 200 francs, and we dropped in at an agreeable little restaurant near the beach. . . . During our conversation Mayakovsky asked when I would finally return to Moscow. I answered that I no longer considered doing so, since I wished to remain an artist. Mayakovsky slapped me on the shoulder and then, suddenly becoming gloomy, added in a hoarse voice:

'But I am going back . . . since I've already stopped being a poet.'

Then there was a truly dramatic scene: Mayakovsky burst into sobs and whispered, scarcely audibly:

'Now I'm a . . . functionary . . .'" (Annenkov, 1966).

See also telegram No. 379, sent to Mayakovsky in Nice.

Judging from Elly Jones's letter of the 12th of April to Mayakovsky in Moscow, they did not meet in Nice this time. At the end of February Elly Jones and her daughter went to Milan (her Milan address is written in Mayakovsky's notebook No. 66), and judging from her letters to Mayakovsky, they did not return to Nice until the first half of April, by which time Mayakovsky was already back in Paris.

    2   Mayakovsky returned to Moscow on the 2nd of May (see No. 381).

379.   1   This telegram is addressed to Mayakovsky at the Hôtel Royal, Nice. It has a note on it to the effect that that very day, the 30th of March, Mayakovsky had left for Paris, where the telegram was sent on to him by post. The sender in Moscow was sent a telegram with the following information: "Trente Mayakowsky Royal Hotel parti re-expeditions poste". This telegram was received in Moscow on the morning of the 31st of March, and that same day Lili Brik sent a second telegram about the grey coat to Mayakovsky in Paris. See No. 380.

380.   1   Afanasev was the chauffeur. The requests are connected with the car owned by Mayakovsky and the Briks.

    2   See No. 379, note 1.

382.   1   At the end of June Lili Brik drove in her Renault to Leningrad, where she stayed with Rita Rayt. Judging from a telegram from Osip Brik to Lili Brik, he too went to Leningrad, on the 27th of June, and returned to Moscow on the next day, the 28th of June. Presumably both this note and the next one (Lili's reply) were sent with him.

    2   Mayakovsky was preparing to go on a lecture tour of Sochi, Gagry, Khosta and the Crimea. As ever, it was organised by Pavel Lavut.

383.   1   A reference to the lecture tour mentioned above.

384.   1   Mayakovsky did not leave for Sochi until the 15th of July.

385.   1   The amount that Lili Brik had asked for in No. 383.

386.   1   Mayakovsky appeared in Sochi four times, on the 21st, 22nd, 27th and 28th of

July.

| | 2 | Mayakovsky left for Yalta on the 2nd of August. |

387. 1 In May and June 1929 the Ref (Revolutionary Front of Art) group, headed by Mayakovsky, brought together those writers who had left Lef. On the 14th of June, Ref sent to the State Publishing House an application, signed by Mayakovsky and Osip Brik, to publish periodical almanacs under the name of *Ref*, "aimed at activists among Soviet and worker-peasant youth" (XIII, 214). Three days later, on the 17th of June, the State Publishing House in a letter to Mayakovsky agreed to *Ref*'s requests: "The Literary and Fine Arts Department of the State Publishing House will take for publication two Ref collections, each 10-12 printer's sheets in size. (The publication of the second collection will be conditional upon the literary interest and the sales of the first collection.)" Despite the agreement of the State Publishing House, neither the first nor the second Ref collection appeared. On the 2nd of October Mayakovsky requested that the date for delivery of the manuscript be postponed to the 1st of December, "in view of the necessity of the resolution of complex theoretical questions", and on the 27th of December he made "a firm request" for a postponement until the 20th of January 1930. On the 3rd of February 1930 Mayakovsky made an application to be accepted into RAPP, and Ref collapsed.

2 According to his letter to the State Publishing House of the 25th of June, Mayakovsky wanted to include *The Bath-House*, poetry and prose in the *Ref* collection (XIII, 215).

388. 1 See the next letter.

389. 1 The writer Valentin Katayev (b. 1897). It has not been possible to establish the reason for this request.

390. 1 Iosif Borts was legal consultant of Modpik (the Moscow Society of Dramatic Writers and Composers). Possibly a reference to *The Bedbug*.

2 As is clear from No. 389, Lili Brik left for two weeks in Odessa on the 9th of August. Lustdorf is a famous beach in Odessa.

391. 1 On the 20th of August, Mayakovsky and Osip Brik met in Sevastopol. Mayakovsky was on his way back to Moscow. Osip Brik (together with Yevgeniya Zhemchuznaya) left for Yalta on the next day, and on the 23rd of August they went to Odessa to join Lili Brik. On the 26th Of August, all three of them set off for Moscow, where they arrived on the 28th. Yevgeniya Zhemchuznaya (Sokolova) recalls that they "bumped into Vladimir Vladimirovich on Sevastopol station. He had stayed on in the Crimea to see Brik."

392. 1 i.e. the 28th of August.

393. 1 This telegram was sent from Stolbtsy, the border post on the Polish side. On the 18th of February 1930, the Briks set off on a trip abroad. The journey had two aims: to familiarise themselves with the cultural life of Germany, and to visit Lili Brik's mother in London.

The Briks' depaprture was preceded by newspaper discussion as to the advisability of their "official trip". On the 10th of January, *Komsomolskaya pravda*, under the general headline "Save foreign currency. Stop official trips abroad by people who are not with us" published an article with the title: "Husband and wife take trip abroad at state's expense": "Osip Brik and his wife Lili Brik are off on an official trip abroad. They are both being sent by the same organisation

273

[clearly Glaviskustvo (The Supreme Art Board) — B.J.]. Both Osip Brik's and Lili Brik's trips have the same aim.

Why not, the question arises, send just one of the two Briks? And if it is essential to have a second worker, why must this function be carried out precisely by Lili Brik, and not by one of the other specialists on the questions which are the subject of this official trip?"

Mayakovsky replied to this article on the 14th of January in the same newspaper with a letter to the editor, in which he stressed that "no 'state funds' and no 'foreign currency' have been asked for by comrades Brik in connection with their trip" and that "in such circumstances any conversations whatsoever about their being 'husband and wife' lose their significance". Mayakovsky went on to enumerate Osip Brik's services "to left revolutionary art" and also the work of Lili Brik — "co-director of the film 'The Glass Eye', designer of posters for the 'Rosta Windows', first translator of theoretical works by Grosz and Wittfogel, regular participant in all manifestations of revolutionary art connected with REF" (XIII, 134-35).

In fact, the Briks had wanted to go to England as early as the autumn of 1929. See Lili Brik's diary entry for the 10th of October: "We've been refused visas for England." Two weeks after the appearance of the article by Mayakovsky quoted above, Lili Brik wrote in her diary: "Volodya went to see Kaganovich today about our trip. It'll probably be decided tomorrow" (27 January 1930). On the 3rd of February she wrote: "Volodya has told me that our passports are a matter not even of days but of hours", and on the 6th of February: "We've got our passports". On the difficulties over getting visas see the Introduction.

397. 1 Valentina Agranova and her husband Yakov Agranov. Since 1919 Agranov had been a member of the Cheka and secretary of the Sovnarkom (Council of People's Commissars). In the 1920s and especially the 1930s Agranov occupied important posts in the GPU (State Political Directorate). In 1938 he was himself a victim of the purges. Agranov (and his wife) first "appeared at the dacha of Mayakovsky and the Briks in Pushkino in the summer of 1928 . . . perhaps they were introduced by V. M. Gorozhanin, whom Mayakovsky had met earlier, in 1926 and 1927 in Kharkov, where Gorozhanin was working. . . . An Old Bolshevik, he worked after the October Revolution in Lenin's secretariat, and then for Dzerzhinsky in the Cheka. . . . His attitude to Mayakovsky was warm, one might even say rapturous." (Katanyan 1974.) For more details see the Introduction.

2 A reference to Mayakovsky's 'melomime' *Moscow is burning (Moskva gorit)*, on which Brik collaborated. Mayakovsky read it on the 20th of February at the Politico-Artistic Council of the Central State Circus Board.

3 On the 22nd of February Mayakovsky signed a contract with the Central State Circus Board for a 'politico-satiric review' Hold on! (*Derzhis!*).

4 The "20 Years of Work" (*"20 let raboty"*) exhibition opened in Moscow on the 1st of February, and closed on the 22nd. It opened in Leningrad on the 5th of March, and Mayakovsky went there on the 2nd or 3rd of March.

5 Lili Brik did note down in her diary "all the work she did and everything she saw".

6 See No. 332, note 3, and in Lili Brik's diary for the 25th of February: "Went to Malik".

398.	1	See No. 400, note 1.
399.	1	See No. 404.
	2	Schneidt was the dog of the owners of the Kufürstenhotel.
	3	Mayakovsky was accepted into RAPP on the 6th of February, but Osip and Lili remained in Ref.
	4	The servant.
	5	Snob was the name Mayakovsky gave to his friend Lev Elbert. See No. 67, note 2.
400.	1	The postcard is of the Kurfürstenhotel. See Lili Brik's diary for the 22nd of February: "The old Kurfürstenhotel turned out to be no longer there — we booked into its replacement. There was neither table nor chair, just a large bed! Floral blankets. Pink curtains at the windows. Not for Osya and me. And 20 marks a day. The next day we found out the new address of our old hotel and moved there."
403.	1	See No. 404.
404.	1	Included with the letter are a photograph of Lili Brik with the lion cub described in postcard No. 403 in her arms, and a photograph of the dog Schneidt. See below in this letter.
	2	In 1930 David Maryanov was the representative of Modpik in Berlin. The power of attorney for Maryanov for the edition of *The Bedbug* was sent from Moscow to Berlin on the 14th of January 1930. After receiving the power of attorney, Maryanov wrote to Mayakovsky on the 16th of February that the Malik Verlag publishing house, to which Mayakovsky had given rights for Germany, had transferred its rights to *The Bedbug* to the Ladyzhnikov publishing house, which, however, had not "so far" translated the play. Maryanov went on to say that the Max Pfeiffer publishing house in Vienna had translated the play and was now offering it to German theatres — ". . . as regards the new play [i.e. *The Bath-House*, B.J.], if you send me it in time, with authorisation only for me, I shall secure the rights to it and shall be able to act, otherwise it will be the same old story as with 'The Bedbug'".
		Lili Brik's diary has an entry for the 14th of January 1930: "Tomorrow's the première of 'The Bedbug' in Frankfurt", but the play was not in fact staged.
	3	As Lili Brik recalls: "I don't know why, but they'd got my period of service down wrongly on my union card. I asked Vladimir Vladimirovich to find out what was up."
	4	As Lili Brik recalls: "It was fine in Gendrikov Lane, but very cramped. The books wouldn't fit in, and we kept them padlocked in a cupboard on the landing of the common entrance staircase. If you wanted to get a book in winter you had to put your fur coat on. Mayakovsky dreamed of having more space and tried to get it through the co-operative housing development. On the 4th of April 1930 he paid a share for himself and for Osip Brik."
	5	Leonid Obolensky (b. 1900), film director who had brought a letter and presents from Lili Brik from Berlin. Lili Brik wrote in her diary for the 3rd of March: "Obolensky's off to Moscow — I took him round some trifles for Volodya."
	6	Elsa Triolet and Louis Aragon arrived in Berlin on the 22nd of March. See No. 409.
406.	1	The German writer Ludwig Turek (b. 1898), a member of the German Communist Party. His book *Ein Prolet erzählt* (1929) appeared in Russian in 1931.

2   At the bottom of the copy of the letter are the words: Maria Gresshöner in Lili Brik's handwriting. Maria Gresshöner worked for Malik Verlog.

407. 1   The Moscow première of *The Bath-House* took place on the 16th of March in the Meyerhold theatre. The Leningrad première took place on the 30th of January.

2   Maksim Shtraukh (1900-1974) played the part of Pobedonosikov.

3   Critical opinion, like that of the first night audience, was divided. Most reviews were negative. The review by Vladimir Yermilov was particularly influential since his position was supported by editorial comment in *Pravda* of the 9th of March.

4   In the wake of the introduction of the "uninterrupted working week" or "five day week" on the 26th of August 1929, "Saturdays" and "Sundays" were abolished and days off fell on various days of the five day week. On the 8th of September Mayakovsky read his poem "We vote for non-interrupton" (*"Golosuyem za nepreryvku"*) on the radio. Mayakovsky's friends came to visit him on their days off.

5   Vsevolod Meyerhold (1874-1940), actor and theatrical director. He directed the Theatre of the Revolution until 1924, and then created his own theatre, based on his 'bio-mechanical' system of acting. His theatre was closed in 1938. He was arrested, after a defiant public refusal to accept the doctrine of Socialist Realism in art, in 1939, and died in prison in 1940. The Meyerhold theatre left on tour for Berlin and Paris at the end of March 1930.

6   Part of the Meyerhold company was to visit Saratov on tour.

7   Klavdiya Kirsanova (1908-1937), wife of the poet Semyon Kirsanov.

8   A reference to a disagreement which had broken out between Aseyev and Kirsanov, on the one hand, and Mayakovsky on the other. The quarrel, which happened in January and February 1930, was caused by Mayakovsky's "Twenty Years of Work" exhibition, which opened on the 1st of February, and by Mayakovsky's joining RAPP a few days later. As Lev Grinkrug recalls: "In January 1930 Mayakovsky set about organising an exhibition which was to sum up all his literary, artistic and social activity over twenty years. He got very little help in setting up the exhibition, he had to do almost all the work himself. . . . He didn't even get any help in organising it . . . from his closest friends Aseyev and Kirsanov. . . . As is known, Mayakovsky alone of the entire Ref group had joined RAPP. This was the basis for a major quarrel between the friends. All contact between them ceased. . . . I particularly remember the last evening on the day the exhibition closed [the 22nd of February, B.J.]. . . . The people closest to him, the Briks, had gone away, his friends Aseyev and Kirsanov weren't there. He wandered solitarily through the rooms still hoping that they would at least turn up on this last evening. Once or twice he asked me: 'Have you seen Kolya and Syoma?' But they didn't come. . . . All three of them took the quarrel very badly, all of them equally wanted to make things up. I tried in all sorts of ways to reconcile them. The first one to make it up with him was Kirsanov. It happened very soon after the exhibition closed. One day when he was at my place, Kirsanov telephoned Mayakovsky, who without wasting words, quite simply, invited Kirsanov and his wife over that evening. They went, and not a word was said about the quarrel.

Things were more complicated with Aseyev. For a long time neither of them would make the first move, though they both wanted to be reconciled. . . . At the beginning of April I decided come what may to bring about the reconciliation between them. On the 11th of April I was on the telephone from morning till night, ringing the two of them in turn. . . . Mayakovsky would say: 'If Kolya phones me, I'll immediately make it up with him and invite him over.' When I told Aseyev he answered: 'Let Volodya be the one to phone' — if Volodya phoned he would go over immediately.

And this went on the whole day. In the end, just before seven in the evening, I told Mayakovsky I was sick of making phone calls: 'Rise above all this, phone Kolya and invite him over.' Aseyev came and that evening five of us (Polonskaya*, Yanshin**, Mayakovsky, Aseyev and I) had a game of poker. Mayakovsky played carelessly, he was nervous and said little, which was quite unlike him." (Grinkrug)

Aseyev and Kirsanov were indignant that Mayakovsky had joined RAPP. Aseyev called it "the action of a Hussar" (Katanyan, 1974). According to Aseyev, Mayakovsky had entered into RAPP "without prior agreement with the other members of his group. This struck us as undemocratic and wilful: to tell the truth, we felt that we had been abandoned in a forest of contradiction. Where should we go? What should we do next?"

*Veronika Polonskaya (b. 1908), Moscow Arts Theatre actress with whom Mayakovsky was having a love affair at the time (see the Introduction).

**Mikhail Yanshin, Moscow Arts Theatre actor, husband of Polonskaya.

409. 1 On Osip Brik's lecture, see the next letter. See also Lili Brik's diary entry for the 11th of March: 'Osya's been offered lectures in German in Berlin, Königsberg and Hamburg."

2 In 1930 Piscator staged the play by Vladimir Bill-Belotserkovsky (1884-1970), *The Moon from the Left* (*Luna sleva*) as *Mond von Links* in Berlin. There is no evidence of a Frankfurt production; perhaps it was a touring production by the Berlin Wallner-Theater.

410. 1 Lili Brik's mother (in English Helen Kagan).

2 On the audience reaction, see Lili Brik's diary entry for the 25th of March: "The orators had their say. In praise of long novels. In praise of real human beings, about art having the right to be anything it likes except boring. Only one young fellow said that Osya was right, that as long as there remained even one man out of work somewhere in the world, as long as the class war was not over, every man must fight for the proletariat — with literature as well as every other weapon." Brik's lecture was greeted with bewilderment in Moscow. As Vasily Katanyan recalls: "Various rumours from RAPP sources were going around Moscow about Osip Maksimovich's Berlin lecture. Had he said what he should have? I was phoned up and questioned by *Literaturnaya gazeta* (*The Literary Gazette*)." (Katanyan 1974)

3 The long poem "At the top of my voice" ("*Vo ves golos*"), the first introduction to which Mayakovsky had written in January 1930

4 Vera Georgiyevna was a poor woman to whom Lili Brik gave material help.

412. 1 The postcard is of Windsor Castle. See the entry in Lili Brik's diary for the 1st of April: ". . . we went by car to see Windsor Castle. We came back through Eton — boys in top hats — it's straight out of Dickens."

414. 1 The postcard is of the House of Commons in session. See Lili Brik's diary for the 4th of April: "In rain and fog, by car, we saw the Parliament, the Abbey, the War

Ministry", and also the entry for the 9th of April: "We had lunch at the Parliament. We looked round the building. We saw the speaker's procession. We listened. They laugh; they sprawl about on their seats."

2 Dmitry Bogomolov (1890-1937) was from 1929 until 1932 Counsellor of the Soviet Embassy in London. He and Mayakovsky met in Warsaw, where he was Soviet Ambassador from 1927 until 1929. Victim of the purges.

3 Richard Collingham Wallhead (1869-1934), Labour Member of Parliament, member of the Anglo-Russian Parliamentary Committee. He had visited Russia in 1920 and 1925.

4 William Peyton Coates, member of the Labour Party, secretary of the Anglo-Russian Parliamentary Committee. Author of more than fifteen books about the USSR, including *A History of Anglo-Soviet Relations*, I-II, London 1945-58.

416. 1 On the 13th of April, Lili and Osip Brik left London for Amsterdam. This postcard was sent on the day of Mayakovsky's suicide. In her diary for that day Lili Brik noted: "Sailors with pipes in front of the Stock Exchange — they've probably brought the fish. Countless numbers of cigar and pipe shops. We bought Volodya a cane and a box of cigars. Today we're off to Berlin." Osip Brik recalls: "We arrived in Berlin on the morning of the 15th of April. . . . The hall porter gave us letters and a telegram from Moscow. 'That'll be from Volodya,' I said, and put it in my pocket unopened. We went up in the lift to our room, unpacked, and only then did I open the telegram.

Our embassy already knew all about it. They immediately got us all the necessary visas, and that very same evening we left for Moscow." The Briks arrived in Moscow on the 17th of April.

2 The postcard is of fields of hyacinths in bloom, *Hollandsche Bloemenvelden*.

BIBLIOGRAPHY

Some of Mayakovsky's letters and telegrams to Lili and Osip Brik were first published, with cuts, in the USSR in *Literaturnoye nasledstvo*, volume 65 (*Novoye o Mayakovsom*), Moscow, 1958.

The major collection of Mayakovsky's works in Russian is *Polnoye sobraniye sochineniy*, thirteen volumes, Moscow 1955-1961. All quotations of Mayakovsky's work are based on this edition.

UNPUBLISHED MATERIALS

Brik, L.
1929 (?) [Memoirs 1905-1917] Manuscript. Lili Brik archive. Some of these memoirs appeared in L. Brik 1934.
1929-32 Diary. Manuscript. Lili Brik archive.
1951 ["Anti-Pertsov"] Typescript. Lili Brik archive. Commentaries to the first edition of Pertsov's three volume study of Mayakovsky.
1956. "From my memoirs". Typescript. Lili Brik archive. Intended for the second part of *Literaturnoye nasledstvo*, volume 65, which, however, never appeared.
[No date] "How it was". Manuscript. Lili Brik archive.
Bryukhanenko, N.
1940-52. "Memoirs". Typescript. Lili Brik archive.
Burlyuk, D.
1956. "Verbatim record of an evening dedicated to a meeting with D. D. Burlyuk, 10th of May 1956." Typescript. Bengt Jangfeldt archive.
Dorinskaya, A.
[No date] "My memoirs of meetings with V. V. Mayakovsky". Typescript. Lili Brik archive.
Grinkrug, L.
[No date] [Memoirs of Mayakovsky] Typescript. Lili Brik archive.
Jones, E.
1926-29 Letters to Mayakovsky. Lili Brik archive.
Katanyan, V.
1974 "Not only memoirs". Typescript. Vasily Katanyan archive.
Khvas, I.
1939 "About V. V. Mayakovsky". Typescript. Lili Brik archive.
Krasnoshchokov, A.
1934 "A short autobiography of A. M. Krasnoshchokov". Typescript. Llewella Varshavskaya archive.
Polonskaya, V.
1938 [Memoirs of Mayakovsky] Typescript. Lili Brik archive.
Punin, N.
1920 Diary. Humanities Research Centre. The University of Texas at Austin.
Shamardina, S.
[No date] [Memoirs of Mayakovsky] Typescript. Lili Brik archive.
Sokolova (Zhemchuzhnaya), Ye.
[No date] [Memoirs of Osip Brik] Manuscript. Lili Brik archive.
Varshavskaya (née Krasnoshchokova), L.
[No date] "What I remember . . .". Typescript. Lili Brik archive. Memoirs of Mayakovsky and the Briks.

PUBLISHED MATERIALS

Guide Books

Ves' Peterburg (Petrograd). *Adresnaya i spravochnaya kniga*, 1900-1917.
Vsya Moskva. *Adresnaya i spravochnaya kniga*, 1890-1917, 1924-1930.
Karl Baedecker, *Russland nebst Teheran, Port Arthur, Peking. Handbuch für Reisende*, Leipzig 1912.

Memoirs and Criticism: Russian

Annenkov, Yu.
1966 "Vladimir Mayakovsky", *Dnevnik moikh vstrech*, I, New York.
Aseyev, N.
1963 "Vospominaniya o Mayakovskom", *V. Mayakovsky v vospominaniyakh sovremennikov*, Moscow.
Bely, A.
1980; "Vospominaniya ob Aleksandre Aleksandroviche Bloke"*, Aleksandr Blok v vospominaniyakh sovremennikov*, I, Moscow.
Brik, L.
1921 "O noveyshey russkoy literature i poezii (Zametki)", in the newspaper *Novyy put'*, No. 225, 30th of October, Riga.
1934 "Iz vospominaniy", in the almanac *S Mayakovskim*, Moscow.
1940 "Chuzhiye stikhi", *Znamya*, 3.
1941 "Iz vospominaniy o stikhakh Mayakovskogo", *Znamya*, 4.
1942 *Shchen (Iz vospominaniy o Mayakovskom)*, Molotov.
1942a "O Mayakovskom", *Novyy mir*, 11/12.
1963 "Chuzhiye stikhi", *V. Mayakovsky v vospominaniyakh sovremennikov*, Moscow. (A variant of L. Brik 1940.)
1975 "Posledniye mesyatsy", *Vladimir Majakovskij. Memoirs and Essays*, Stockholm.
Brik, O.
1940 "IMO — Iskusstvo molodykh", in the collection *Mayakovskomu*, Leningrad.
Bryukhanenko, N.
1940 "Vstrechi s Mayakovskim", *Literaturnyy sovremennik*, 4.
1983 "Ya pomnyu", *Tallin*, 4.
Chertok, S.
1983 *Poslednyaya lyubov' Mayakovskogo*, Ann Arbor.
Cheryomin, G.
1975 *Put' Mayakovskogo k oktyabryu*, Moscow.
Fevral'sky, A.
1971 *Pervaya sovetskaya p'esa*, Moscow.
Fleishman, L.
[1981] *Boris Pasternak v dvadtsatiye gody*, München.
Jakobson, R.
1923 *O cheshskom stikhe, preimushchestvenno v sopostavlenii s russkim*, Prague.
1931 "O pokolenii, rastrativshem svoikh poetov", in *Smert' Vladimira Mayakovskogo*, Berlin.
1956 "Noviye stroki Mayakovskogo", *Russkiy literaturnyy arkhiv*, New York.
Kamensky, V.
1940 *Zhizn' s Mayakovskim*, Moscow.

Katanyan, V.
1961 *Mayakovsky. Literaturnaya khronika*, Moscow.
1963 "Iz vospominaniy o V. V. Mayakovskom", in *V. Mayakovsky v vospominaniyakh sovremennikov*, Moscow.
Kemrad, S.
1970 *Mayakovsky v Amerike*, Moscow.
Koloskov, A.
1968 "Tragediya poeta", *Ogonyok*, 23 and 26.
Lavinskaya, Ye.
1968 "Vospominaniya o vstrechakh s Mayakovskim", in *Mayakovsky v vospominaniyakh rodnykh i druzey*, Moscow.
Lavut, P.
1969 *Mayakovsky yedet po Soyuzu*, Moscow.
Mayakovsky, V.
1941 *Polnoye sobraniye sochineniy*, X, Moscow.
1973 Sobraniye sochineniy, I-VI, Moscow.
1978 Sobraniye sochineniy, I-XII, Moscow.
Neznamov, P.
1963 "Mayakovsky v dvadtsatykh godakh", in *Mayakovsky v vospominaniyakh sovremennikov*, Moscow.
Pertsov, V.
1972 *Mayakovsky. Zhizn' i tvorchestvo (1925-1930)*, Moscow.
Rakhmanova, L., Valerianov, V.
1964 *Shest' adresov Vladimira Mayakovskogo*, Moscow.
Rayt, R.
1963 "'Tol'ko vospominaniya'", in *V. Mayakovsky v vospominaniyakh sovremennikov*, Moscow.
1967 "Vse luchshiye vospominaniya . . .", *Oxford Slavonic Papers*, XIII.
Skhlovsky, V.
1964 "O kvartire Lefa", in his *Zhili-byli*, Moscow.
1965 *Za sorok let. Stat'i o kino*, Moscow.
1974 "O Mayakovskom", *Sobraniye sochineniy*, III, Moscow.
Spassky, S.
1940 *Mayakovsky i yego sputniki*, Leningrad.
Triolet, E.
1975 "Voinstvuyushchiy poet", in *Vladimir Majakovskij. Memoirs and Essays*, Stockholm
Volkov-Lannit, L.
1981 *Vizhu Mayakovskogo*, Moscow.
Vorontsov, V., Koloskov, A.
1968 "Lyubov' poeta", *Ogonyok*, 16.

Memoirs and Criticism: Other Languagues
Barooshian, V.
1978 *Brik and Mayakovsky*, The Hague/Paris/New York.
Blake, P.
1975 "The Two Deaths of Vladimir Mayakovsky", in *Vladimir Mayakovsky. The Bedbug and Selected Poetry*, Bloomington/London.

Brik, L.
1978 *Con Majakovskij*. Intervista di Carlo Benedetti, Roma.
Brown, E.
1973 *Mayakovsky. A Poet in the Revolution*, Princeton.
Charters, A. and S.
1979 *I Love. The Story of Vladimir Mayakovsky and Lili Brik*, New York.
Dreiser, T.
1928 *Dreiser looks at Russia*, New York.
Erlich, V.
1969 *Russian Formalism. History, Doctrine*, The Hague/Paris.
Ipatieff, V.
1946 *The Life of a Chemist*, Stanford.
Jakobson, R.
1964 "Postscript", in "O. M. Brik. Two Essays on Poetic Language", *Michigan Slavic Materials*, 5, Ann Arbor.
1973 "On a Generation that Squandered its Poets", in *Major Soviet Writers, Essays in Criticism*, ed. E. J. Brown, London/Oxford/New York.
Jangfeldt, B.
1975 "Notes on 'Manifest Letučej Federacii Futuristov' and the Revolution of the Spirit, in *Vladimir Majakovskij. Memoirs and Essays*, Stockholm.
1975a "Majakovskij and the Publication of '150,000,000'. New Materials", *Scandoslavica*, 21.
1976 *Majakovskij and Futurism 1917-1921*, Stockholm.
1979 "Russian Futurism 1917-1919", in *Art, Society, Revolution. Russia 1917-1921*, Stockholm.
1980 "Osip Brik: A Bibliography", *Russian Literature*, VIII.
Katanian, V.
1978 *Vita di Majakovskij*, Roma.
Markov, V.
1968 *Russian Futurism. A History*, Berkeley/Los Angeles.
Matthias, L.
1921 *Genie und Wahnsinn in Russland. Geistige Elemente des Aufbaus und Gefahrelemente des Zusammenbruchs*, Berlin.
Pomorska, K.
1968 *Russian Formalist Theory and its Poetic Ambiance*, The Hague/Paris.
Rosenfeldt, N. E.
1978 *Knowledge and Power. The Role of Stalin's Secret Chancellery in the Soviet System of Government*, Copenhagen.
Shklovsky, V.
1974 *Mayakovsky and his Circle*, London [New York, 1972].
Stahlberger, L.
1964 *The Symbolic System of Majakovskij*, The Hague/Paris.
Stepanova, V.
1981 "Occasional notes", in *From Painting to Design. Russian Constructivist Art of the Twenties*, Köln.
Terras, V.
1983 *Mayakovsky*, Boston.
Triolet, E.
1939 *Maïakovski. Poète russe. Souvenirs*, Paris.

282

INDEX OF NAMES

Numbers in italics refer to photographs.

288

289

290

INDEX OF MAYAKOVSKY'S WORKS

Numbers in italics refer to photographs.

294